THE IMPACTS OF
WELFARE CONDITIONALITY

Welfare Conditionality series

Series Editor: **Peter Dwyer**, University of York, UK

This series explores whether welfare conditionality works and asks how and why it might work differently for different people in diverse circumstances. It aims to develop an empirically and theoretically informed understanding of the role of welfare conditionality in promoting behaviour change among welfare recipients over time.

Also available

Dealing with Welfare Conditionality
Implementation and Effects
Edited by **Peter Dwyer**

Coming soon

Women and Welfare Conditionality
Lived Experiences of Benefit Sanctions, Work and Welfare
By **Sharon Wright**

Find out more
**policy.bristoluniversitypress.co.uk/
welfare-conditionality**

THE IMPACTS OF WELFARE CONDITIONALITY

Sanctions Support and Behaviour Change

Peter Dwyer, Lisa Scullion, Katy Jones, Jenny McNeill
and Alasdair B.R. Stewart

First published in Great Britain in 2023 by

Policy Press, an imprint of
Bristol University Press
University of Bristol
1–9 Old Park Hill
Bristol
BS2 8BB
UK
t: +44 (0)117 374 6645
e: bup-info@bristol.ac.uk

Details of international sales and distribution partners are available at
policy.bristoluniversitypress.co.uk

© Bristol University Press 2023

British Library Cataloguing in Publication Data
A catalogue record for this book is available from the British Library

ISBN 978-1-4473-2011-1 hardcover
ISBN 978-1-4473-4373-8 paperback
ISBN 978-1-4473-4374-5 ePub
ISBN 978-1-4473-4372-1 ePdf

The right of Peter Dwyer, Lisa Scullion, Katy Jones, Jenny McNeill and Alasdair B.R. Stewart to be identified as authors of this work has been asserted by them in accordance with the Copyright, Designs and Patents Act 1988.

All rights reserved: no part of this publication may be reproduced, stored in a retrieval system, or transmitted in any form or by any means, electronic, mechanical, photocopying, recording, or otherwise without the prior permission of Bristol University Press.

Every reasonable effort has been made to obtain permission to reproduce copyrighted material. If, however, anyone knows of an oversight, please contact the publisher.

The statements and opinions contained within this publication are solely those of the authors and not of the University of Bristol or Bristol University Press. The University of Bristol and Bristol University Press disclaim responsibility for any injury to persons or property resulting from any material published in this publication.

Bristol University Press and Policy Press work to counter discrimination on
grounds of gender, race, disability, age and sexuality.

Cover design: Andrew Corbett
Bristol University Press and Policy Press use environmentally responsible print partners.
Printed and bound in Great Britain by CMP, Poole

Contents

List of figures and tables	vi
List of abbreviations	vii
About the authors	viii
Acknowledgements	ix

one	Introduction	1
two	Conditionality in the UK welfare state	20
three	Welfare conditionality and behaviour change	48
four	From welfare to work? The effectiveness of welfare conditionality in moving people into paid employment	68
five	Welfare conditionality and problematic or antisocial behaviour	94
six	Unintended outcomes? The wider impacts of compulsion and benefit sanctions in social security	116
seven	Ethical debates	137
eight	Conclusions	155

Methods appendix	161
References	169
Index	202

List of figures and tables

Figures
4.1	Employment trajectories of 339 welfare service users interviewed two or three times over a two-year period	70
6.1	Estimated annual total number of benefit sanctions before challenges, all benefits	117

Tables
2.1	Conditionality groups and work-related requirements in Universal Credit	30
A.1	Policy stakeholders	163
A.2	Focus groups undertaken with practitioners	164
A.3	Overview of welfare service user sample characteristics at wave a	166
A.4	Number of welfare service users taking part in each of the three waves of repeat interviews	167

List of abbreviations

ABC	Acceptable Behaviour Contract
ALMPs	Active labour market policies
APAs	Alternative Payment Arrangements
ASB	antisocial behaviour
ASBO	Antisocial Behaviour Order
CAMHS	Child and adolescent mental health services
CSCS	Construction Skills Certification Scheme
DWP	Department for Work and Pensions
ESA	Employment and Support Allowance
FIP	family intervention project
FIT	Family Intervention Team
FTT	fixed-term tenancy
HB	Housing Benefit
IB	Incapacity Benefit
IS	Income Support
JCP	Jobcentre Plus
JSA	Jobseeker's Allowance
PLM	paid labour market
QLR	qualitative longitudinal research
SLB	street level bureaucrat
TANF	Temporary Assistance for Needy Families
TFP	Troubled Families Programme
UC	Universal Credit
WCA	Work Capability Assessment
WFI	work-focused interview
WHP	Work and Health Programme
WP	Work Programme
WRAG	Work Related Activity Group
WSU	welfare service user

About the authors

Peter Dwyer is Emeritus Professor of Social Policy at the University of York. His research and teaching focuses on social citizenship. He led the large Economic and Social Research Council funded Welfare Conditionality: Sanctions Support and Behaviour Change (2013–19) project.

Lisa Scullion is Professor of Social Policy and Co-Director in the Sustainable Housing and Urban Studies Unit at the University of Salford.

Katy Jones is Research Fellow in the Centre for Decent Work and Productivity at Manchester Metropolitan University.

Jenny McNeill is a project manager at Groundswell. She previously worked at the University of Sheffield and University of York on the Welfare Conditionality project.

Alasdair B.R. Stewart is Lecturer in Social and Public Policy in the School of Social and Political Sciences at the University of Glasgow.

Acknowledgements

We are extremely grateful to all those people, that are too numerous to name individually, who supported and enabled the production of this book and the research project that underpinned it. We are especially appreciative of all those individuals subject to various types of welfare conditionality who took part in the repeat interviews that inform the analysis presented in this book. Thanks must also go to the wider group of colleagues and students, outside of the authors of this book, who were involved in delivering the WelCond project and its myriad outputs throughout its duration. The support of the Economic and Social Research Council under grant number ES/K002163/2 in enabling this research is also gratefully acknowledged. Finally, we would like to offer our thanks to Laura Vickers-Rendall and the rest of the team at Policy Press for their patience and support in bringing this book to fruition.

ONE

Introduction

Welfare conditionality links eligibility to publicly funded welfare benefits and services to recipients' specified compulsory responsibilities or particular patterns of required behaviour. It has been a key component of welfare state reforms in many nations since the mid-1990s (Watts and Fitzpatrick, 2018a). Conditional welfare arrangements, which combine compulsory engagement with various interventions to move social welfare benefit recipients into work (for example, mandatory work activity, job search and training activities) and/or promote the cessation of problematic behaviour (for example, antisocial behaviour (ASB), substance abuse) with different types of sanction for non-compliance, are now an established part of policy within many social security, housing, homelessness, ASB and criminal justice and migration systems.

The UK has been at the forefront of this behavioural turn in policy. Over the last two decades welfare conditionality within the social security system has been extended to incorporate previously exempt groups including many disabled people, lone parents of young children, and since 2013 with the introduction of Universal Credit (UC), low-paid workers and their partners who are in receipt of in-work housing and low-wage supplements and various working tax credits (Dwyer, 2016). Simultaneously, the length and severity of benefit sanctions that can be applied has been intensified (DWP, 2012a; Adcock and Kennedy, 2015) with unprecedented numbers of people made subject to their application. In the period of the 'great sanctions drive' (Webster, 2016) between 2010 and 2015, approximately 25 per cent of Jobseeker's Allowance claimants experienced a benefit sanction (Butler, 2017) with numbers peaking in 2013 when 1,037,000 were imposed (Adler, 2016).

Advocates of welfare conditionality routinely assert that various combinations of sanction and support are both a fair and an effective way to move people off welfare benefits and into paid work and/or make people desist from antisocial or problematic behaviour (see, for example, Mead, 1982; Blair, 2006; Duncan Smith, 2014; Dunn, 2014). Conversely, those who oppose the use of welfare conditionality believe that it is unfair, intentionally punitive, ineffective in promoting paid employment and personal responsibility and likely to exacerbate the poverty and social exclusion of already disadvantaged populations (see, for example, Dwyer, 1998, 2018b; Etherington and Daguerre, 2015; Fletcher and Wright, 2018; Patrick, 2017; Adler, 2018).

Regardless of which side of the debate people are situated, many of the assertions about the acceptability and effectiveness of welfare conditionality in changing welfare recipients' behaviour remain open to challenge. Over 20 years ago it was noted that '[f]or more and more claimants, benefit entitlement is going to be dependent on satisfying work related conditions. Where that leaves the concept of a right to benefit is a matter for speculation. The impact on claimant attitude and behaviour is yet to become fully apparent' (Treolar, 2001: 3). A decade later, a review of international evidence highlighted that the gulf between the rhetoric used by policymakers to justify the extension of sanction-backed conditionality within ongoing welfare state reform, and evidence about its impacts remained (Griggs and Evans, 2010).

In March 2013, the Welfare Conditionality: Sanctions, Support and Behaviour Change project (WelCond) was established.[1] Funded by the Economic and Social Research Council (grant number ES/K002163/2), this was a major five-year collaborative research project involving researchers from six universities in England and Scotland;[2] many of whom had records of previously undertaking work on the operation and impacts of welfare conditionality across a range of policy areas. WelCond had two core aims. First, to develop an empirically and theoretically informed understanding of the role of welfare conditionality in promoting and sustaining behaviour change among a diversity of welfare recipients over time. Second, to consider the particular circumstances, if any, in which the use of conditionality may, or may not, be considered ethically justified. In essence, WelCond provided an understanding of a number of linked questions about the impacts and effects (intended or otherwise), and fairness of, welfare interventions underpinned by, and delivered according to, a principle of conditionality.

WelCond was a qualitative project that generated substantial new empirical data through three linked fieldwork elements. First, semi-structured interviews with 52 policy stakeholders were undertaken. Second, 27 focus groups were carried out with frontline welfare practitioners involved in supporting welfare service users (WSUs) subject to welfare conditionality across the range of policy fields under investigation. Third, and central to the project, was a large, repeat qualitative longitudinal panel study undertaken with a diversity of WSUs subject to varying types and degrees of conditionality. This qualitative longitudinal component was specifically chosen to allow for the development of a dynamic understanding of the impacts and effects of welfare conditionality that was firmly grounded in the experiences of those people directly subject to it. The aim was to enable comprehension of how and why, over time, welfare recipients' choices and actions may potentially be influenced by a range of personal factors and, importantly, the application of specific sanction or support initiatives. Nine different groups (panels) were purposively sampled according to criteria appropriate for each group under consideration. These groups were: recipients of working age social security benefits, (that is, jobseekers, lone parents, disabled people, UC recipients – both in and out of work claimants), homeless people, social tenants, individuals/families subject to ASB orders/family intervention projects, offenders and migrants. A total of 1,082 WSU interviews were undertaken with respondents interviewed up to three times between 2014 and 2017, at on average 12-month intervals across a two-year period. Due to attrition, of the 481 WSUs interviewed at wave a, 339 were interviewed again at wave b, with 262 subsequently completing a third and final interview at wave c. The interviews took place in 11 locations across England and Scotland with broadly equal numbers of men and women recruited (see methods appendix for fuller details on methods and sampling).

A key aim of this book is to provide an original, empirically informed understanding of the impacts, effectiveness and ethicality of welfare conditionality at it plays out over time within the lives of a diversity of welfare recipients. Utilising the qualitative, longitudinal dataset generated by the WelCond project (which is unique in both its size and scope), our objective is to offer analysis grounded in the understandings and experiences of WSUs subject to welfare conditionality to consider three core questions. First, how effective is conditionality in promoting and sustaining movements into paid work and/or the cessation of problematic behaviour? Second, how is welfare conditionality perceived and experienced over time by welfare recipients and what are its impacts on people's circumstances, behaviour and opportunities? Third, under what circumstances (if any), and why, might the use of welfare conditionality be justified? However, before embarking on this task, it is first important to consider how the notion of welfare conditionality fits within broader debates about the purpose and priorities of welfare states.

Welfare states and conditionality: questions of principle and priority

Welfare states are routinely in the business of deciding 'who ought to get what?' (Taylor-Gooby, 1998: 39). The resolution of this question depends on a number of interlinking considerations. These include the social, political and economic factors that have shaped the development of a particular nation and the competing philosophical and normative frameworks that set out often competing visions of the 'good society'. In turn, these inform a number of diverse principles that set out the eligibility criteria that individuals have to satisfy in order to access collectively provided welfare benefits and services. For example, the meeting of social need is one central concern of welfare institutions and social policy (Dean, 2010; Manning, 2016). However, the ways in which different governments may manage this task and the content and substance of any welfare rights that then ensue will vary greatly depending upon varying priorities and preferred approaches for delivering welfare. For example, social liberal/social democratic supporters of universalism believe that an extensive array of welfare state services should be accessible to all on the basis of either common citizenship status (for example, Marshall, 1949/1992), or universal human rights derived from shared human frailties/personhood (Dean, 2013). In contrast New Right thinkers who favour the market and are opposed to state welfare (for example, Nozick, 1974; Murray, 1984, 1999; Mead, 1986, 1997) often prefer the operation of selectivism (aka a social assistance principle), and, at best, a much smaller welfare state 'reserved' for poor people (Deacon and Bradshaw, 1983). Significantly, in both these approaches the meeting of need remains a primary focus, but the two differing principles take us in very different directions in respect of welfare provision. Underpinned by a broad definition of need, the universal vision favours the provision of extensive common rights to public welfare. In contrast, a narrower selectivist definition of needs leads us towards a smaller residual welfare state in which access to benefits and services is often subject to means tests, and eligibility is based not on extensive and asserted social rights, but more often on the discretionary judgements of welfare bureaucrats (Lister and Dwyer, 2012).

Beyond identified need, and disagreements about the role and generosity of welfare states in meeting such need, eligibility to collectivised systems of welfare has long been dependent on whether or not individuals are seen as 'deserving' of support. Deliberations about who deserves access to public welfare and, importantly, whose claims are seen as 'undeserving' and therefore illegitimate, have long been significant (Mann, 1992) and continue to inform welfare policy and practice (van Oorschot et al, 2017). Desert-based systems of welfare often foreground 'social contract' type requirements where claims to a share in a society's collective welfare benefits and services are linked to an individual's prior contribution to the wider community. Although, on occasions, contemporary welfare states tacitly recognise other forms of socially valued contribution to the common good (for example, informal familial care), engagement with paid work is regularly valorised as being *the* form of individual contribution most deserving of recognition and support. Consequently, welfare delivered according to a contributory/ social insurance principle may offer somewhat enhanced benefits. However, these are routinely only available to those who have made the required prior contribution to the common good and wider economy through their activities in the paid labour market alongside associated tax and National Insurance payments. Here an interesting and significant shift in emphasis occurs. The focus in resolving the 'who ought to get what' question shifts away from meeting needs, to fix on whether or not an individual deserves collective support based on their prior fulfilment of socially defined individual responsibilities or obligations. It is important to note that once communities enter into debates about the necessity for people to engage in some form of required, socially valued behaviour in order to be eligible for welfare, the central question is no longer whether an individual needs welfare but whether they are seen to have a deserving claim to a share in the collective welfare based on their prior conduct.

Welfare conditionality takes the reciprocity and the welfare contractualism inherent in the social insurance principle a stage further. A principle of welfare conditionality holds that access to certain basic, publicly provided, social welfare benefits and services should be made contingent on individuals first agreeing to meet particular compulsory duties or patterns of responsible behaviour (Deacon, 1994). If states meet their side of the bargain and provide certain welfare benefits and services as part of a recognised package of collective citizenship rights, then *quid pro quo* contractualism, for many, offers a powerful, 'common sense' rationale for requiring citizens to meet their reciprocal responsibilities/duties in return for their rights (Patrick and Fenney, 2015; Watts and Fitzpatrick, 2018a) and the linked assertion that it is 'reasonable to use welfare to enforce [*individual*[3]] obligations where it is part of a broader contract between government and the claimant' (Deacon, 2004: 915). A heightened focus on contractualism which emphasises that social rights must engender attendant individual responsibilities has structured much political debate and rhetoric about the substance and principles governing access to collective social provisions over the past 30 years. Some (for example, Mead, 1992) assert overtly paternalistic justifications for the imposition of welfare conditionality. Others, critical of its advance, look to promote more expansive human rights based frameworks (Dean, 2013; Dermine and Eleveld, 2021) and/or emphasise states having statutory duties to provide basic social rights to all individuals, regardless of their prior conduct or contribution (McKeever and Walsh, 2020). While welfare contractualism is not the only rationale used to justify the welfare conditionality that is now an established principle of the UK provision (and in many other welfare states around the world), it remains one of the most frequently used justifications (Dwyer, 2020). However, before exploring both the emergence and extent to which welfare conditionality is embedded with contemporary welfare states and the ethical debates it triggers (covered more fully in Chapter Seven), it is necessary to define the term more precisely.

Defining welfare conditionality

As already noted a number of competing principles set the eligibility criteria required for receipt of the myriad benefits and services that welfare states deliver with very few, if any, being wholly unconditional. For example, Clasen and Clegg (2007) offer a consideration of welfare conditionality in its broadest sense and identify three 'levels', or types, of conditions operating within welfare states that work to govern an individual's access to social security benefits. First, a recipient must meet certain 'conditions of category', linked to membership (for example, recognised national citizenship status). Second, 'conditions of circumstance', that is, the specific eligibility and entitlement criteria that define who shall have access to a benefit depending on the particular rules in operation for a specific benefit; rules that commonly operate according to one or more of the principles highlighted in the introductory discussion in this chapter, are also applied. Third, Clasen and Clegg identify what they call 'conditions of conduct', that is, the 'behavioural requirements and constraints imposed upon different kinds of benefit recipients' (Clasen and Clegg, 2007: 174). To be clear, when using the term welfare conditionality in this book, we are referring specifically to this third element of Clasen and Clegg's typology, which others have labelled 'behavioural conditionality' (see, for example, Curchin, 2019; Stinson, 2019a). As Watts and Fitzpatrick note:

> Conditional forms of welfare with a conduct component differ from other forms of welfare provision in three key aspects they specify behavioural requirements which determine initial access to and/or continued receipt of benefits, goods and services: they employ monitoring and surveillance processes that verify compliance with those requirements and they impose sanctions in the event of non-compliance or in some cases offer incentives for compliance. (2018a: 31)

Welfare conditionality has increasingly become a defining feature of many welfare states across the globe, especially, but not exclusively, in relation to the reform of social welfare benefits. Within social security systems, welfare conditionality makes continued access to benefits routinely contingent on an individual claimant's engagement with mandatory work focused interviews, training/support schemes and/or job search requirements; with failure to undertake such specified activities potentially leading to benefit sanctions (Dwyer, 2016). That said, the reach of welfare conditionality now extends beyond social security and the use of conditional welfare arrangements that combine elements of sanction and mandatory engagement with specified support is now an established feature across many diverse fields of welfare policy relating to, for example: ASB and family intervention projects (Rodger, 2006; Flint, 2014; Ball et al, 2015; Crossley and Lambert, 2017; Hoggett and Frost, 2018; Ball, 2019); homelessness interventions (Johnsen et al, 2018a; Watts et al, 2018); social housing (Dwyer, 2000; Flint, 2006; Fitzpatrick and Pawson, 2014; McNeill, 2016; Nethercote, 2017; Jones, 2019); immigration and asylum policy (O'Brien, 2013; Shutes, 2016; Scullion, 2018; Dwyer et al, 2019; Morris, 2019; Serpa, 2019); criminal justice (Povey, 2017, 2019; Fletcher and Wright, 2018; Flint, 2019; McNeill, 2020); and aspects of healthcare provision (Dwyer, 2004; Curchin, 2019).

On a basic level, welfare conditionality is unambiguously about linking eligibility to publicly financed, collectivised welfare rights to individual behavioural responsibilities of recipients of benefits and services. However, a further distinction can be identified beyond this broad, 'amorphous' requirement to behave responsibly; a more 'concrete', tightly specified and increasingly personalised conditionality, such as requiring unemployed benefit recipients to apply for a specific number of jobs and/or accept any job offer (Paz-Fuchs, 2008). Flint (2009a) similarly highlights a distinction between 'earned' and 'conditional' citizenship when considering how welfare conditionality is implemented. In the former, various sanctions are applied to those who fail to behave as required with 'pre-existing entitlements being rescinded as a result of inappropriate conduct' (Flint, 2009a: 89), such as failing to undertake work-related training and job search activities or engaging in ASB. On the other hand, an 'earned citizenship' rationale also operates under the rubric of welfare conditionality. This seeks to reward individuals' proactive endeavours and positive behaviour with access to collectivised social provisions. Here rights are secured in the first instance through positive contribution and/or meeting communally defined duties. Examples include the cultural conditionality that links citizenship and settlement rights for migrants to language or financial self-sufficiency requirements (Dwyer and Scullion, 2014) or making social housing tenancies dependent on acceptance of wider communal engagement through methods such as a Mutual Aid Clauses and Good Neighbour Agreements (see Young and Lemos, 1997; Croucher et al, 2007).

Welfare conditionality and the reconfiguration of social citizenship

Social liberal/social democratic theorists were prominent in setting out the scope and vision of social citizenship in the post-Second World War period. In his influential essay on citizenship, T.H. Marshall (1949/1992) stressed that it was the addition of social rights (welfare entitlements delivered through the varied institutional frameworks of a particular society), alongside civil and political rights, that gave the concept of citizenship substantive meaning and made a measure of autonomy possible for large numbers of individuals within a national community, especially those most economically disadvantaged. Despite many subsequent and valid critiques (for example, Lister, 2003; Dwyer, 2010), Marshall clearly intended that social citizenship entailed, at the very least, entitlement to a minimum level of decommodified social security benefits 'granted on the basis of citizenship rather than [labour market] performance' (Esping-Andersen, 1990: 21). Beveridge (1942) likewise famously envisaged a system of 'cradle to grave' provision of state welfare to tackle the five giants of want, disease, ignorance, squalor and idleness. In a retort to the early critics of the expansive social democratic welfare state, Titmuss (1958) was also keen to show that welfare states provided a host of benefits and services (through three linked systems of social, fiscal and occupational welfare[4]), which redistributed income and resources to meet the multitude needs of different individuals and groups rather than simply providing social welfare benefits for those experiencing poverty. Critical of explanations of poverty based on individual failings or inappropriate individual behaviour, these architects and advocates of the post-Second World War welfare settlement envisaged that publicly provided welfare would lessen material inequalities and foster a sense of social solidarity between individuals who, based on their common status as citizens, could call upon their entitlements to welfare as citizens in times of need (Deacon, 2002).

Although focused primarily on the development and delivery of substantive welfare rights, embedded within a social democratic/social liberal approach there was, nonetheless, an attendant underpinning expectation that citizens would willingly accept the 'corresponding duties of citizenship' (Marshall, 1949/1992: 46) and, by engaging in paid work and paying taxes and National Insurance, contribute to both their own individual wellbeing and the collective welfare rights available to all citizens. A similar reciprocity between their welfare rights and the responsibilities of citizens was also central to Beveridge's social insurance-based vision for future welfare. 'Social security must be achieved by co-operation between the State and individual. The State should, offer security for service and contribution' (Beveridge, 1942: 6). However, in subsequently stating that 'for the limited number of cases of need not covered by social insurance, national assistance subject to a uniform means test will be available' (Beveridge, 1942: 11), he was also clear that a right to social welfare delivered according to a social assistance principle, based on need, should, and would, be available to those individuals who were unable to make the required contributions.

Such conceptualisations of social citizenship and their attendant envisioning of status based entitlement to welfare have long been contentious for many, with those on the right of the political spectrum mounting a comprehensive (and arguably successful challenge) to the social-democratic orthodoxies of the post-Second World War welfare settlement from 1970s onwards. Two New Right thinkers from the US, Murray (1984, 1999) and Mead (1982, 1986, 1997), have been highly influential in critiquing the notion of entitlement to public welfare benefits and services. Both authors share common ground in forcefully asserting that, rather than helping to prevent poverty, access to out of work benefits are likely to promote 'idleness' and entrench 'welfare dependency' among a section of the wider population. Arguing that largely unconditional social rights help to foster and reproduce a welfare-dependent 'underclass' (distinguishable by their dysfunctional behaviour rather than economic inequality and cut off from the work norms of wider society), both believe that the answer to the problem of the 'underclass' lies in fundamental reform of the welfare state. However, they offer somewhat different solutions. Murray's (1994) preferred option is essentially to do away with all working age, state social welfare benefits, except for short-term unemployment insurance payments. As the option of reliance on publicly provided cash welfare benefits will no longer be available, he believes this will enforce the personal responsibility by making individuals take any paid job and work for their living. In contrast, rather than removing the welfare state, Mead's (1982, 1986), solution is to urge governments to look 'beyond entitlement' and make welfare conditionality the central organising tenet of reformed welfare state provision. Mead believes that those reliant on social welfare can be re-socialised away from unemployment and 'irresponsibility' by the enforcement of paid work through a combination of mandatory engagement with work search activity training programmes backed up by the application of benefit sanctions. 'Government must now obligate [welfare] program recipients to work rather than just entice them ... it has to be enforced by sanctions, in this case the loss of welfare grant' (Mead, 1982: 28).

The subsequent emergence of New Communitarianism in the 1990s, which highlighted the role of expansive liberal, rights based philosophies in triggering a crisis in Western democracy, while simultaneously emphasising the primary importance of citizens recognising their individual responsibilities to the communities they inhabit, further challenged the notion of welfare entitlement. The leading protagonist of this approach, Etzioni, viewed extensive state welfare provision as undermining the establishment of a 'good' society primarily because it removes duties of welfare and care from the realm of individuals, families and voluntary associations where he believes such responsibilities should lie (Etzioni, 1995, 1997). Selbourne (1994) offers greater clarity on New Communitarians' inherent hostility to the idea of entitlement to welfare as a legitimate core component of citizenship. Echoing the distinction between negative and positive rights favoured by those on the right, Selbourne is clear that so-called 'social rights' do not possess, and should not be afforded, the same legal status as civil and political rights. Rather, they should be more properly seen as potential privileges that a society may choose to bestow on those dutiful members who meet their personal responsibilities and behave in a manner deemed appropriate by the wider community. As Plant notes, among new communitarians, welfare conditionality is seen as a common sense, non-negotiable, foundational principle for the delivery of collective welfare:

> The ideas of reciprocity and contribution are at the heart of this [communitarian] concept of citizenship: individuals do not and cannot

have a right to the resources of society unless they contribute to the development of that society through work or other socially valued activities, if they are in a position to do so. (Plant, 1998: 30)

New Right and New Communitarian commentators such as those discussed draw on very different traditions of political thought. Nonetheless, the critiques emerging from these two different positions have been highly influential in proclaiming a shared view that passive and unconditional entitlement to social benefits and services has promoted a corrosive rights based culture of irresponsible 'welfare dependency' (see, for example, Heron and Dwyer, 1999; Deacon, 2003). Today many nations' governments, drawn from across the political spectrum, endorse welfare conditionality as a panacea for individual irresponsibility. Some commentators have, erroneously, emphasised the social contractual obligations of individual citizens as set out within the Beveridge Report (1942), and implied in Marshall's *Citizenship and Social Class* (1949/1992), when looking to justify the reconfiguration of social citizenship and the emergence of new, more highly conditional welfare state regimes. For example, in pointing to the perceived moral hazards of unconditional, permissive welfare regimes, Mead directly invokes Marshall by calling for 'a return to a citizenship rationale, but this time with the emphasis on obligations rather than rights' (1997: 220). Others have made strong justifications for 'welfare contractualism' (White, 2000) as part of a modernised conceptualisation of social democracy 'where rights come with responsibilities' (Giddens, 1994, 1998).

Although some at the forefront of advocating and extending welfare conditionality (see, for example, Blair, 1998; Freud, 2007; DWP, 2008a) have been keen to emphasise its long-standing provenance, it is clear that a new form of 'instrumental behaviourism' has become more prominent in social policy in the UK and other nations since the 1990s (for example, Halpern et al, 2004; Commonwealth of Australia, 2007; Darnton, 2008a, 2008b; Mulgan, 2010; Southerton et al, 2011; Harrison and Saunders, 2016; Taylor et al, 2016). There has been an intensification of welfare conditionality in many welfare states, characterised by realigned relationships between entitlement, conduct and support and the enhanced use of sanctions for non-compliance (Cox, 1998; Handler, 2004, 2009; Betzelt and Bothfeld, 2011). A new, more constrained and qualitatively different welfare state than that envisaged by its post-Second World War architects (Dwyer, 2004; Wright, 2011a, 2011b) has been constructed. Using Hall's (1993) terminology, second and third order change in respect of the techniques and ideas that underpin policy has occurred. Welfare conditionality is routinely now the prism through which many politicians and members of the public view the state's 21st century welfare role (Dwyer, 2008). Although various eligibility conditions have long defined citizens' access to welfare benefits and services, the focus is now squarely on the behavioural requirements that states demand of their citizens.

> The result has been a profound change in what is understood to be the contract between claimant and state, from rights based on social citizenship and the claimant's insurance contributions when in work, to the idea that the claimant must first earn their right to benefits by complying with the state's demands about their behaviour. (Dwyer and Webster, 2017: 2)

Today many governments endorse welfare systems that prioritise individual responsibility and the management of citizens' behaviour, over and above status based entitlement to social rights as an integral part of the citizenship package. This shift is significant, not least because when states demand that citizens must conform to specific behavioural requirements in order to qualify for social rights, the exclusive capacity of citizenship is heightened and its potential to deliver even a limited measure of equality is undermined. Using the notion of decommodification, Esping-Andersen (1990) highlights why social citizenship may offer something of substance. However, he also notes how welfare states, depending on the eligibility conditions that govern access to the benefits and services they provide, structure the societies in which they operate.

> [Decommodification] occurs when a service is rendered as matter of right and when a person can maintain a livelihood without reliance on the market. ... A minimal definition must entail that citizens can freely, and without potential loss of job, income or general welfare, opt out of work when they themselves consider it necessary. ... If social rights are granted on the basis of citizenship rather than performance, they will entail a de-commodification of the status of individuals vis a vis the market. ... It is not the mere presence of a social right, but the corresponding rules and preconditions, which dictate the extent to which welfare programmes offer genuine alternatives to market dependence. ... The welfare state is not just a mechanism that intervenes in, and possibly corrects the structure of inequality; it is, in its own right, a system of stratification. It is an active force in the ordering of social relations. (Esping-Andersen, 1990: 22–3)

Although a right to social security is embedded in international human rights law and treaties, including Article 9 of the International Covenant on Economic, Social and Cultural Rights (UN, 1966), the combination of significant ongoing economic change and sustained welfare reform agendas has seen the emergence of a 'new politics of welfare' (Pierson,

2001; Bonoli and Natali, 2012) for the 21st century; a politics in which the affirmation of welfare conditionality has become a prominent feature in many varied settings.

Welfare conditionality: towards an active world of welfare?

In different settings, various terms (welfare-to-work, insertion, activation, workfare, active labour market policies [ALMPs]), are used to describe and analyse the policies that are at the heart of the reconfiguration of welfare states towards greater welfare conditionality (Dean et al, 2005). It lies beyond the scope of this book to systematically map and detail the extent to which welfare conditionality has become a central, embedded component of many welfare states across the globe. However, it is important to note that the behavioural turn in social policy is now very much an international phenomenon. At the supranational level, welfare conditionality, under the guise of activation, has found expression in European Union policy, particularly in the European Employment Strategy (Peck and Theodore, 2000; Wincott, 2003; Dean et al, 2005; van Berkel and van der Aa, 2005). Likewise, the Organisation for Economic Co-operation and Development (OECD, 2015) endorses welfare conditionality as a valuable tool for increasing labour market participation with ALMPs of one sort or another; an accepted part of contemporary unemployment policy among the majority of OECD governments (Raffass, 2017). Intensified and extended welfare conditionality increasingly frames welfare policy and practice in many nations. Analysis of welfare conditionality regimes in 21 OECD countries highlights that recipients of unemployment benefits face stricter benefit conditions and sanctions and are 'clearly under greater pressure to actively seek work and to be willing to change occupations than they used to be three decades ago' (Knotz, 2018: 102). Numerous nations now require unemployed jobseekers and many working aged disabled people in receipt of long-term sickness and incapacity benefits to actively prepare for, or seek work, to retain benefit eligibility (Lindsay and Houston, 2013; Grover and Piggott, 2015; Baumberg Geiger, 2017; Dwyer et al, 2020; Williams, 2021), and lone parents in a host of national settings are increasingly subject to similar requirements (for example, Knijn et al, 2007; Betzelt and Bothfeld, 2011; Wright, 2011a; Whitworth and Griggs, 2013; McLaren et al, 2018; Millar, 2019; Murphy, 2020).

Welfare conditionality is often closely associated with high-income Anglophone nations characterised as 'liberal' welfare states by comparative theorists such as Esping-Andersen (1990), and certainly such nations have been at the forefront of embracing it. In the mid-1990s, ending the right to welfare was central to US welfare reforms that saw the adoption of workfare policies (Deacon, 2002) and it remains an established principle within contemporary social assistance schemes such as the Temporary Assistance for Needy Families (TANF) programme (Davis, 2019; Haskins and Weidinger, 2019). The pivotal assertions of US advocates about the need for, and effectiveness of welfare conditionality, have been influential in the UK (Deacon, 2000, 2002; Daguerre and Taylor-Gooby, 2004; Dwyer and Ellison, 2009) and among other policymakers further afield. Australian governments have enthusiastically embraced welfare conditionality within their Job Network/jobactive and ParentsNext programmes for unemployed people and lone parents (McDonald and Marston, 2005; DSS, 2015: Taylor et al, 2016; Brady, 2018; McLaren et al, 2018). It is also central to the controversial Income Management Policy[5] that has been criticised as both racist (Bielefeld, 2015) (because it has been overwhelmingly applied within remote indigenous Australian communities in the Northern Territory) and largely ineffective (Bray et al, 2014). Additionally, as Curchin (2019) notes, following the example of several states in the US, a 'no jab no pay' policy makes receipt of a number of child welfare benefits and tax reliefs conditional on parents having their children immunised. Conditionality practices are also evident in the allocation of social housing to people experiencing homelessness (Clarke et al, 2020). Elsewhere, in Ireland (Boland and Griffin, 2017; Murphy, 2017, 2020), New Zealand (Lunt and Horsfall, 2013; Humpage, 2014, 2016; Pierson and Humpage, 2016) and Canada welfare conditionality has advanced and 'workfare type policies combine coercive paternalism and conditional entitlement effectively to reduce the rights of more vulnerable citizens' (Deeming, 2017: 413).

That said, welfare conditionality has become rooted in nations beyond those categorised as liberal welfare regimes. There is an extensive established literature that documents and discusses the advance of welfare conditionality within continental European welfare states (see, for example, Lødemel and Trickey, 2001; Van Berkel and Hornemann Møller, 2002; Barbier and Ludwig-Mayerhofer, 2004; Wright et al, 2004; Palier, 2010; Betzelt and Bothfeld, 2011; van Berkel et al, 2011; Ervik et al, 2015; Eleveld, 2017); a body of work that highlights 'repeated examples of moves towards a more active labour market policy' (Esping-Andersen, 2010: 14) across Europe. The 'conditional benefits and behavioural incentives' now inherent in many European welfare states, reach beyond employment into child benefit and truancy policies (Cantillon and van Lanker, 2012) and outreach work with people experiencing homelessness (Grymonprez et al, 2020). Regardless of how welfare state regimes might be classified for comparative purposes (for example, liberal, conservative-corporatist social democratic (Esping-Andersen, 1990), southern European (Ferrera, 1996), and so on), welfare conditionality and activation are now significant components, and to a certain degree, almost accepted by a majority of governments, as essential and required characteristics of a properly functioning 21st century welfare state. Enthusiastic uptake of conditionality is not limited to more mature welfare systems. Many of the relatively new welfare states in the Global South (for example, many Latin American countries, Bangladesh, Brazil, Chile, India, Mexico and South Africa), operate conditional cash transfer systems that attach behavioural conditions to the continued receipt of social assistance benefits in anti-poverty programmes (see, for example, Bastagli, 2009; Barrientos, 2011, Lund, 2011; Standing, 2011; Papadopoulos and Velázquez Leyer, 2016a, 2016b).

Substantive differences in how welfare conditionality is implemented clearly exist both within and beyond Europe and it is over-simplistic to understand its operation in different settings as uniform. Levy (2004), for example, distinguishes between 'thin' and 'thick' forms of activation. 'Thin' activation policies, such as those pursued in the US and UK, attribute labour market inactivity to the personal failings of benefit recipients and the existence of overgenerous, 'passive' welfare benefits. They are typically characterised by a 'work first' stance (Peck and Theodore, 2000), which places the onus on individuals to take up any offers of employment, irrespective of wage levels or their personal circumstances, or face losing their right to benefit through sanction. In contrast, Levy characterises activation policy in certain European countries, Sweden, for example, as enacting a 'thick' or 'human capital' approach when applying welfare conditionality. Here an enabling state is portrayed as being primarily concerned with enhancing the skills of marginalised individuals and providing them with high-quality training and employment opportunities, rather than merely enforcing work norms. He argues that such 'thick' activation 'demands much more of the state as well as the individual' (Levy, 2004: 190) in that substantial financial commitment is required on the part of governments to fund extensive educational/training and employment opportunities.

A similar analysis that differentiates between 'liberal' and 'universalistic' activation policies in European welfare states has been offered by Barbier and Ludwig-Mayerhofer (2004), while Lødemel (2001) has suggested that two very different welfare experiments are taking place on either side of Atlantic. In Europe he contends that welfare reform is primarily about a move away from unconditional welfare, whereas policy in the US combines an end to welfare entitlement with 'an accompanying emphasis on hassle rather than help' (2001: 335) alongside an unremitting preoccupation with enforcing individuals' responsibility to meet their welfare needs by undertaking any paid work in preference to reliance on public benefits and services.

Although institutional arrangements and the types and combinations of sanction and support vary across, and sometimes within, nations (Maas, 2013), welfare conditionality is now integral to a reconfigured notion of social citizenship in which 'universality and solidarity are giving way to selectivity and individual responsibility' (Cox, 1998: 1) and a 'new politics of welfare ... intent on converting the welfare benefits system into a lever for changing behaviour' (Rodger, 2008a: 87) prevails. This is certainly the case in the UK, where in recent decades governments from across the mainstream political spectrum have endorsed and advanced a more Liberal 'work first' (Taylor, 2017) approach to the implementation of welfare conditionality within and beyond the social security system.

Outline of chapters

Having defined welfare conditionality and located it within broader discussions about the social rights and responsibilities of individual citizens and the role of the state in delivering welfare, several key points should be apparent. First, welfare conditionality, where eligibility to collective welfare is built around reciprocity, individual behavioural responsibility and prior contribution to the common good, has become an increasingly common feature of many welfare states internationally. Second, that through the extension and intensification of welfare conditionality, successive UK governments have enthusiastically embraced the behavioural turn that is a significant feature of much global welfare reform. Third, the acceptance of welfare conditionality as an underpinning principle of welfare delivery significantly impacts on how societies resolve the key question of 'who ought to get what' when making decisions about access to collectively funded social welfare. Fourth, and linked to the previous point, the affirmation, acceptance and elevation of welfare conditionality within public welfare systems triggers significant consequences. Its implementation routinely relegates many claims to collective social provisions asserted on grounds of basic human need or entitlement through common citizenship status to secondary importance. Publicly provided welfare is effectively reserved for 'deserving' citizens. Only those identified as having made some prior form of individual contribution to the common good are afforded a 'right' to welfare (Dwyer, 2005). To paraphrase Flint (2009a), welfare conditionality works to reward 'good' citizens with access to collective welfare and punish irresponsible ones by making them ineligible.

As previously noted, this book is centrally concerned with questions about the efficacy and ethics of welfare conditionality. The book is broadly divided into two parts. In the first part, Chapters Two and Three provide relevant contextual information and further discussion about the development of the UK's highly conditional welfare state and locate this change in wider international discussions and debates about the fairness and effectiveness of using various combinations of sanction and support to change the behaviour of social welfare recipients. More specifically, Chapter Two outlines the expansion of welfare conditionality within the UK welfare state since the late 1980s. Discussions focus on in three core policy areas, namely social security, social housing and homelessness and ASB policy (including family intervention programmes), all of which have seen significant advances of welfare conditionality in recent decades. The last section of this chapter also locates welfare conditionality within the wider reforms of the UK welfare state post-2010; a period of significant welfare reform played out against the backdrop of both austerity policies (Taylor-Gooby, 2012; Edmiston, 2016, 2018; Portes and Reed, 2018) and increasing devolution of welfare powers within the UK (Kennedy et al, 2019).

Chapter Three explores a key rationale that is routinely cited in defence of the implementation of welfare conditionality, that is, that various combinations of sanction and mandatory engagement with support can be used instrumentally to trigger and sustain positive behaviour change among recipients of social welfare benefits and services. Initial discussions consider how behaviour change within welfare policy has been theorised and how certain approaches to understanding how policy might be used to influence the behaviour of citizens have come to be accepted by policymakers and politicians attracted to the idea of behavioural conditionality. In response to this dominant approach, the empirically grounded understanding of behaviour change that is central to this book and the analysis it presents is then set out. This approach makes use of qualitative longitudinal methods to provide a dynamic and empirically informed understanding of how welfare conditionality works and the kinds of behavioural changes, intended or otherwise, it engenders in people's everyday lives. The second part of the chapter considers the arguments put forward by both advocates and adversaries of conditionality before moving on to consider competing evidence about its effectiveness in bringing about positive changes in behaviour.

Having outlined the contested character of much debate and evidence on the effectiveness of welfare conditionality, the second substantive part of the book consists of three chapters (Chapters Four, Five and Six) that present analysis of the qualitative data derived from the fieldwork central to the WelCond project. These chapters draw on analysis of the repeat semi-structured interviews undertaken with WSUs who were subject to welfare conditionality across various aspects of their lives. The extensive repeat panel study at the heart of the WelCond project constructed a new kind of hybrid approach for undertaking qualitative longitudinal work with WSUs; one that was large scale in terms of ambition, scope of enquiry and sample size, but which simultaneously retained the rationale and explanatory potential of smaller-scale qualitative longitudinal studies for exploring behaviour change, or the lack of it, over time. Using a film metaphor, Neale (2021) has subsequently labelled this as an attempt to construct an 'intimate epic' and in many ways the analysis presented in Chapters Four–Six is just that. Each chapter explores how the grand narratives and processes of welfare conditionality, constructed by policymakers, practitioners and academics, actually play out over time in the everyday lives of ordinary people. To present a temporal analysis of the impacts of welfare conditionality and explore how the macro-level visions of governments often clash with the micro-level experiences of individual welfare recipients, we present a series of extended qualitative longitudinal case studies in Chapters Four, Five and Six. These enable the development of 'detailed new insights into the (often perverse) consequences of the application of welfare conditionality' (Dwyer and Patrick, 2021: 63). In Chapter Seven, where longitudinal analysis is not required, discrete pieces of standalone data derived from within the three waves of interviews is used to consider WSUs' views on the ethicality of welfare conditionality

In Chapter Four the effectiveness of welfare conditionality in moving people off social security benefits and into paid work is considered. The differing welfare/work trajectories of WSUs who took part in the study are mapped. The impact of differences in individual circumstances and capabilities (for example, family care responsibilities, impairment, and so on) in triggering specific outcomes are then explored. The second part of the chapter then moves on to discuss the effectiveness of the core components of welfare conditionality (that is, benefit sanction and mandatory engagement with support and training activities), in moving people into, or nearer to, the PLM. The exercise of discretionary powers by the Department for Work and Pensions (DWP) and Work Programme staff, and the importance of this in triggering both positive and negative outcomes for benefit claimants is then addressed. The final section of this chapter explores how the extension of welfare conditionality to low-paid workers, brought about by the introduction of UC in 2013, has impacted on the lives and work opportunities of 'in-work' UC claimants.

One objective of the WelCond project was to look beyond social security benefit regimes to consider the machinations of welfare conditionality in other policy areas. Consequently, we sampled WSUs who experienced mandatory support and sanction mechanisms in relation to other aspects of public welfare delivery; for example, social housing, homelessness support services, ASB initiatives and family intervention projects. Discussions in Chapter Five begin by focusing on the tensions between care and control that are inherent within highly conditional welfare interventions. We then move on to assess the effectiveness of 'coercive welfare' (Phoenix, 2008) strategies in triggering and maintaining engagement with support services among those facing complex and sometimes multiple issues in their lives, such as impairment, substance addiction and homelessness. In the second part of the chapter the notion of 'compound conditionality' is introduced and defined. Here discussions focus on how welfare conditionality, when implemented separately within distinct policy areas, often then intersects to impact negatively on individuals who are simultaneously subject to behavioural requirements in more than one aspect of their lives.

Chapter Six focuses on the consequences engendered by the implementation of highly conditional social security systems built around the twin elements of compulsion and benefit sanctions. The chapter first sets out the scope of benefit sanctions within the UK context before moving on to consider how the use of sanctions impact on the lives of those subject to them. Analysis presented in the second part of the chapter documents how and why the threat and/or implementation of benefit sanctions routinely trigger profoundly negative outcomes in relation to people's financial situation and physical and mental wellbeing. The third and final part then moves on to consider the diverse ways in which people respond to benefit sanctions and how this varies dependent upon their personal circumstances.

Ethical questions about the underpinning principles and the practical implementation of welfare conditionality are the focus of analysis in Chapter Seven. Initial discussions set out four important and differing normative positions (that is, contractualism, paternalism, mutualism and unconditional entitlement) that are often used to support or oppose the use of welfare conditionality. In the second part of the chapter discussions then explore the extent to which citizens deem a general principle of welfare conditionality (which broadly asserts that access to collective welfare provisions should be made contingent on citizens accepting specified individual responsibilities), to be fair. The chapter then moves on to consider more practical questions about the appropriateness and issues of fairness related to extending welfare conditionality within social security to previously exempt groups, namely lone parents, disabled people and low-paid workers. However, before making an assessment of the ethicality or effectiveness of welfare conditionality in bringing about behavioural change it is necessary to outline its development and significance within the contemporary UK welfare system.

Notes
[1] www.welfareconditionality.ac.uk
[2] The University of Glasgow, Heriot-Watt University, University of Salford, University of Sheffield, Sheffield Hallam University and the University of York which acted as the WelCond project's central hub.
[3] Our insertion in italics.
[4] See Titmuss' (1958) thesis, 'The social division of welfare', for fuller discussions. 'Social welfare' consists of the publicly provided funds and services (social security benefits, local authority housing, the National Health Service, personal social services, and so on) that are often the single focus of dispute when the welfare state is discussed. In addition Titmuss emphasised the importance of 'fiscal welfare' (tax allowances and reliefs), and also 'occupational welfare', that is, the perks derived

from advantageous employment in the labour market (for example, pensions and fringe benefits such as cars, meals, private health schemes, and so on).
5   This 'limits the amount of income support paid to people as an unconditional cash transfer and imposes restrictions on how the remaining – sometimes termed "quarantined" – funds can be spent. Income management was designed to ensure that these funds are spent on essential "basic" items and to limit the amount of income that can be spent on tobacco, alcohol, pornography, and gambling' (Bray et al, 2014: xix).

TWO

Conditionality in the UK welfare state

Attaching behavioural requirements and conditions to receipt of social welfare benefits in the UK is not a new phenomenon. In 1911 the establishment of unemployment benefit saw claimants required to regularly attend the Labour Exchange office and sign a declaration that they were 'available for employment' to maintain their claim (see Harris, 2008, for fuller discussion of historical developments in unemployment benefit policy). In the early 20th century workfare type requirements, including non-negotiable attendance at labour camps by young unemployed men in the 1920s and 1930s, were also periodically introduced, particularly during times of economic crisis (Fletcher, 2014a; Cooper, 2021). However, since the late 1980s successive UK governments have embraced, extended and intensified welfare conditionality to an unprecedented extent with more stringent behavioural requirements applied to greater numbers of people in receipt of welfare benefits and services, and penalties (that is, benefit sanctions) for non-compliance have increased significantly in recent years. Concentrating on key policies initiated since the mid-1990s, discussions in this chapter outline developments in relation to the implementation of welfare conditionality in three substantive areas of the UK welfare state, namely: social security; social housing; and the management of antisocial behaviour (ASB) among groups of citizens variously labelled as problematic or vulnerable in different contexts (Brown, 2017; Brown et al, 2017).

The social security system

As noted in Chapter One, prominent American New Right thinkers were at the forefront of propagating the view that unconditional entitlement-based rights to social benefits were instrumental in establishing and sustaining a welfare dependent 'underclass' (see, for example, Murray, 1984; Mead, 1986). Despite the loss of much UK manufacturing industry and significant periods of economic downturn, much government rhetoric since the late 1970s drew on this narrowly defined narrative of welfare dependency to emphasise the individual failings of benefit claimants rather than wider structural changes as a key cause of unemployment (Jordan, 2014). In line with their general antipathy towards the idea of social rights and an extensive welfare state, the Conservative administrations of the Thatcher and Major governments (1979–97) instigated significant reductions in both the numbers able to claim unemployment benefits and the generosity of payments while simultaneously increasing the behavioural requirements attached to continued receipt of unemployment benefits. For example, new rules introduced in September 1988 ended the automatic right of 16- and 17-year-old school leavers to out of work benefits, and participation on the government's Youth Training Scheme (which was originally a voluntary programme), became compulsory with refusal to accept a place leading to loss of benefit (Mizen, 1990). Throughout the 1980s more stringent eligibility tests for unemployment benefit were introduced and recipients were required to attend regular 'restart' interviews (Deacon, 1994). The Social Security Act 1989 underlined the UK's governments preference for a 'work first' (see Chapter One) approach to welfare conditionality. Sections 10–12 of the Act detailed that unemployment benefit recipients would be required to 'actively seek work' and accept any job once an initial short period of benefit receipt had expired. Claimants were no longer allowed to refuse a job on the grounds that it was not suitable to their prior skills and experience, nor because the pay was inadequate (Harris, 2008). The Jobseeker's Act (1995) saw further significant developments introduced. Perhaps the most important change being the introduction of the 'Jobseekers Agreement'. Beyond any general declaration to actively seek work, this required claimants to 'indicate the number of employers they will write to, telephone and visit every week; the number of times they will visit the Jobcentre, the newspapers they will consult for vacancies and the employment agencies they will register with' (Novak, 1997: 104).

The Act also increased the powers of 'Client Advisors' (the new name given to Department for Work and Pensions [DWP] frontline workers in benefits offices), who could subsequently issue Jobseeker Directives, that is, mandate individuals to attend training or employment programmes. Additionally, Client Advisors were also given powers to instruct claimants to improve their appearance and/or behaviour if they believed it was likely to impact on their client's chances of securing work. Failure to sign the Jobseekers Agreement, deliver on its specified work search activities or refuse to comply with an advisers' directive could lead to an initial two-week suspension of benefit; doubled to four weeks for any subsequent offence (Novak, 1997). As its 18 years of government drew to an end, the Conservative Party signalled its willingness to further advance behavioural conditionality by endorsing the expansion of its pilot Project Work scheme in its general election manifesto. This workfare type scheme required those who had been unemployed for two years or more to 'work for a specific period on a community project' (Conservative Party, 1997: na) in return for benefit.

Having rebranded and repositioned itself while in opposition around a Third Way 'no rights without responsibilities' mantra that explicitly emphasised a reworking of the welfare contract between the citizen and the state (see, for example, Giddens, 1994, 1998; Blair, 1996, 1998; DSS, 1998; Dwyer, 1998; Powell, 1999), the New Labour governments of Blair and Brown (1997–2010) also enthusiastically advanced welfare conditionality in social security policy throughout their time in government. Accepting in principle many core elements of the critiques advanced by their New Right influenced Conservative predecessors, in particular the potential for unconditional welfare rights to promote dependency and a subsequent need to further promote individual responsibility among the citizenry (Clarke, 2005; Lister, 2011), successive New Labour administrations overtly used welfare conditionality in an attempt to change the expectations and behaviour of those in receipt of social welfare benefits. Promoting paid work as the best form of welfare, passive reliance on benefits was actively challenged by extending claimant requirements for engagement with mandatory work search and training accompanied by the application of benefit sanctions for non-compliance.

The wholehearted endorsement of what had been previously been denounced 'as the blunt Tory strategy of compulsion' (Labour Party, 1994: 28) was clearly signalled with the advent of New Labour's flagship training policy, the New Deal for Young People, announced in 1997. Under this scheme, 18–24-year-olds who had been unemployed for over six months were required to take up one of four options: on job training with the private sector; work with the voluntary sector; placement on an environment task force; or full-time education and training, with refusal leading to reduction or loss of benefit. Across their period in office further New Deals, for disabled people, lone mothers and long-term unemployed people and their partners, became a central element of Labour's welfare-to-work reforms in an attempt to tackle wider labour market inactivity beyond registered unemployed jobseekers. In contrast to their predecessors, the New Labour government also initiated a range of important support measures and incentives to 'make work pay' and encourage people to enter the paid labour market (PLM). These included Employment Zones in areas of high unemployment, the Pathways to Work scheme for disabled people (see Finn, 2011), a national minimum wage, the introduction of various tax credit schemes to support low-paid workers through the tax system, and an extended system of publicly funded childcare (Hirsch and Millar, 2004).

However, this enhanced support was accompanied by extended compulsion as engagement with work-focused activities and training backed up by attendant sanctions for non-compliance was slowly but surely introduced to include the majority of working aged social welfare benefit recipients including working age lone parents and disabled people (Treolar, 2001). For example, those claiming Income Support (IS) or Incapacity Benefit (IB) were initially exempted from the requirements placed on Jobseeker's Allowance (JSA) claimants and, likewise, their participation in the New

Deals was initially voluntary. However, as New Labour was re-elected, conditionality within the social security system was intensified and its reach expanded. From 2001 attendance at a work-focused interview (WFI) to discuss future opportunities to return to work became compulsory for lone parents on IS with children aged 13 plus; by 2003 this condition applied to all lone parents on IS (Dwyer, 2004). Additionally, incremental reductions in the age thresholds at which lone parents' continued receipt of benefit became conditional on active job search activities, further indicating that they too were increasingly to be subject to conditionality moving forwards (Davidson, 2012; Johnsen, 2014).

Emboldened by two independent, DWP-commissioned reviews (Freud, 2007; Gregg, 2008) that recommended the application of stronger JSA type conditionality for the majority of working age benefit recipients, New Labour introduced Employment and Support Allowance (ESA) in the 2007 Welfare Reform Act. ESA replaced IB and IS paid on grounds of impairment and brought many working age recipients of incapacity related benefits under the remit of welfare conditionality and sanctions for the first time. From October 2008, new claimants unable to work because of illness or disability had to undergo a Work Capability Assessment (WCA), a much criticised points based assessment that attempts to measure a person's functional capabilities (see, for example, Patrick, 2011; Garthwaite, 2014; Shakespeare et al, 2017), which determined both the level of benefit they received and the degree to which individuals would be subject to conditionality. Following the application of a WCA individuals were allocated to one of three groups. Those deemed 'fit for work' were transferred directly on to the JSA regime with its stricter conditionality rules and lower benefit payments. Others who scored enough WCA points and whose impairments were recognised as inhibiting their capacity to undertake paid work at the time of their WCA were assigned to the Work Related Activity Group (WRAG). These claimants received a slightly higher benefit payment (above that paid to JSA recipients), but were also required to attend WFIs and engage in job search and other work-related activities/training as instructed by their Jobcentre adviser and could have benefit sanctions applied. Those with such severe impairments that were deemed unlikely to work in the future were placed in the Support Group, where an enhanced level of ESA is paid and claimants were not subject to work-related conditionality or sanctions. Whereas New Labour's approach initially stressed supporting disabled people into paid work through voluntary participation in the New Deal, over time this morphed into a policy underpinned by compulsion and sanction (Dwyer, 2017).

The New Labour governments' unambiguous acceptance of welfare conditionality is further illustrated by its use in two schemes that provided means-tested support for low-income new parents to help with the additional costs of the birth of a child and milk/healthy food for mothers and young children, that is, the Sure Start Maternity Grant and Welfare Food Scheme. Significant rises in the monetary value and scope of the schemes were accompanied by the imposition of conditionality in the form of compulsory engagement with appropriate healthcare professionals. Those who did not comply with these requirements were refused access to the support (see Dwyer, 2010: box 5.2 for details). Although, unlike their Conservative predecessors, New Labour were concerned to use aspects of welfare policy to alleviate poverty, they nonetheless also viewed the use of both compulsion and sanction as legitimate and appropriate tools for managing the behaviour of social welfare recipients. As Deacon (2003) notes, New Labour's attempt to level the playing field was accompanied by a conscious decision to use the twin tools of welfare conditionality – sanction and mandatory engagement with support – to activate the players.

Universal Credit: ubiquitous conditionality in social security?

In 2010, in the midst of an ongoing global economic crisis and an inconclusive general election, a Conservative/Liberal Coalition government was formed as New Labour's years in government ended. The Coalition subsequently introduced a series of austerity policies and instigated a period of unprecedented cuts in public spending, especially in relation to the welfare state. This 'systematic restructuring' (Taylor-Gooby, 2012) of public welfare financing was accompanied by an unequivocal endorsement of behavioural conditionality as an appropriate tool to reduce reliance on welfare benefits and enforce responsible behaviour. In Opposition, ideas emerging from the centre-right think tank the Centre for Social Justice (founded by Iain Duncan Smith[1] in 2004), Conservative Party documents painted a bleak picture of the UK's 'dark side'; sink estates, populated by workless people from broken homes living in areas with high levels of benefit dependency and addiction (Cameron, 2009). Analysis once again placed the individual behaviour of a dysfunctional 'underclass' and the inadequacies of a complex social security system (Duncan Smith, 2007), rather than structural inequalities, as a key cause of poverty. Unsurprisingly, the Coalition pledged to 'further transform the welfare system by making work pay, implementing stricter WCAs [and] … reinforcing the conditional nature of jobseeker benefits' (Finn, 2011: 139). Ultimately, the Coalition more than delivered on these promises and throughout its time in office enhanced, extended and personalised welfare conditionality became a central feature of social security reform. For example, the advent of the Jobseeker's Allowance (Mandatory Work Activity Scheme) Regulations (2011) gave Jobcentre Plus (JCP) advisers (subsequently renamed Work Coaches) the power to compel individual benefit claimants, who they believed would benefit from engagement with the discipline of a working environment, to undertake up to 30 hours per week unpaid work with a specified employer for a maximum of four weeks. Refusal to participate triggered a 13-week loss of benefit (SSAC, 2011).

Using language reminiscent of New Labour's ambition to reform the welfare state around a rejuvenated work ethic two decades earlier (see DSS, 1998) the Coalition introduced Universal Credit (UC) as a core component of the Welfare Reform Act 2012. Writing in the forward to the Coalition's 2010 White Paper, Iain Duncan Smith, the then Secretary of State for Work and Pensions, stated:

> A life on benefits is a poor substitute for a working life but too much of our current system is geared toward maintaining people on benefits rather than helping them to flourish in work; we need reform that tackles the underlying problem of welfare dependency. That is why we are embarking on the most far-reaching programme of change that the welfare system has witnessed in generations. Universal Credit: welfare that works marks the beginning of a new contract between people who have and people who have not. At its heart, Universal Credit is very simple and will ensure that work always pays and is seen to pay. (DWP, 2010: 1)

UC is a single monthly variable benefit payment that combines and replaces four existing means tested social welfare benefits and two tax credits (IS, JSA, ESA, Housing Benefit [HB], Working Tax Credits [WTC] and Child Tax Credits [CTC]).[2] Its phased introduction built on earlier pilot and pathfinder projects and national rollout was originally planned to occur between October 2013 and 2017. However, the implementation of UC has triggered a number of problems and controversies and completion of full rollout (at time of writing) with all those claiming legacy benefits and tax credits moved over to UC is now scheduled for September 2024 (Harker, 2022). The three key aims underpinning UC, that is, simplifying working age benefits, making work pay and increasing benefit take up while simultaneously reducing fraud and error (DWP, 2010), are in many ways highly commendable. UC was initially conceived and designed with the twin intentions of removing barriers to paid work/smoothing transitions off benefits and into employment and also eradicating disincentives built into the benefits it replaces that prevented people from taking on extra hours of paid work without significant negative financial impacts (Pennycook and Whittaker, 2012). It was envisaged that UC would achieve these outcomes in three main ways. First by lowering participation tax rates of many people (that is, the percentage of gross earnings lost in tax and withdrawn benefit when a person enters work [see Adam et al, 2006 for a fuller explanation]), thus leading to an attendant increase in the earnings that individuals would retain. Second, by lowering marginal deduction rates, that is, 'the rate of deductions that occurs through increased Income Tax and National Insurance, and reduced means tested benefit payments incurred on earning an additional £1' (Family Action, 2012: 1). Third, by simplifying movements from periods of labour market inactivity into paid work, or taking up additional work, by clarifying the financial gains of moving off benefits in to paid employment and/or increased hours for benefit claimants. The key idea here is that UC should have the agility to adjust to people's changing circumstances. Consequently, as an individual's earnings from paid work increase, due to entering the PLM, or taking on more hours or an additional job(s), the amount of UC they receive is reduced and vice versa. Monthly adjustments to the level of UC benefit paid, both upwards and downwards, can then be made depending on any variations in the amount of income an individual earns from paid employment in any given month.

However, despite the political rhetoric surrounding UC asserting that 'people will be consistently and transparently better off for each hour they work and every pound they earn' (DWP, 2010: 1), the reality of its implementation to date has been somewhat different. Indeed, the government acknowledged that some people were always going to be worse off following the introduction of UC (Royston, 2012) and the DWP's own in-house equality assessment calculated that although around 3.1 million households would likely see their monthly income rise by an average of £168, approximately 2.8 million households' entitlements would fall by an average of £137 monthly (DWP, 2012b). Additionally, in the period since the equality assessment was published, subsequent benefit freezes and cuts to payment rates, work allowances and the taper rate (the rate at which UC is withdrawn in relation to earnings), announced in the 2015 Budget, have further undermined the potential financial rewards that were anticipated for 'in-work' UC claimants. Such measures have diminished the potential of UC to boost poor people's incomes since its initial introduction (Finch, 2016; CPAG, 2017).

UC further heightened the use of welfare conditionality within the UK social security system in two important ways. First, to prepare for UC's introduction, the Coalition announced an enhanced benefit sanction regime in October 2012. Claimants who failed to undertake job search activities or punctually attend WFIs or training activities as specified by their JCP Work Coach faced sanctions ranging from loss of full benefit for four weeks, for an initial low level transgression such as being late for a WFI, through to up to three years loss of benefit for a repeat third, high level offence such as failure to apply for a job as instructed (DWP, 2012c; see Table 1 in Dwyer, 2018b for more details). Second, the incorporation of 'in-work' rent and wage supplements (that is, HB, CTC and WTC paid to low-paid workers) within UC, extended behavioural conditionality and its associated sanctions regime, beyond 'inactive' benefit recipients, to include people in low-paid, insecure and part-time work for the first time. In doing so, UC effectively broadened the definition of problematic welfare dependant behaviour to encompass low-paid workers who 'are now held to be solely responsible, not only for a lack of paid employment, but also partial engagement with the paid labour market and the levels of remuneration they may receive' (Dwyer and Wright, 2014: 33). What this means on a practical level is that low-paid workers in receipt of the in-work components of UC and whose earnings are below the 'conditionality earnings threshold' (routinely set at a level equivalent to a 35-hour working week paid at the UK National Living Wage rates), are routinely expected to engage with a Work Coach and actively look to increase their employment hours and/or seek further job(s) until the earnings threshold is reached, again under threat of benefit sanctions for non-compliance (WPC, 2016).

The argument that increasingly stringent benefit sanctions are now a 'core component of the highly conditional "work first" 21st Century UK welfare state' (Dwyer, 2018b: 148) should not be dismissed lightly. In 2002, a first sanction for non-compliance under New Labour's 'New Deal for Young People' led to partial loss of benefit for a 14-day period (TUC, 2002). As previously noted, by 2012 sanctions had been extended beyond young and long-term unemployment benefit recipients to cover the majority of working age social security benefit claimants, including many disabled people, lone parents and low-paid workers in receipt of in-work components of UC. Following changes instigated in 2012 any initial 'low level' benefit sanction involves routine loss of all benefit for a month rather than a fortnight. Also, at the other end of the spectrum, as previously noted, repeat offences could ultimately trigger loss of the right to benefit for up to a maximum of three years. However, this maximum sanction period was reduced to six months in May 2019 when Amber Rudd, then Secretary of State for Work and Pensions in the Conservative government (that succeeded the Coalition) announced that from 2020, the maximum length of sanction would be six months; acknowledging that three-year benefit sanctions undermined the stated policy objective to move people into work (Rudd, 2019).

Mandatory support for social security benefit claimants

Benefit sanctions are only one side of the conditionality coin, however, with compulsory engagement with mandated work search and training being the other. Within the UK benefit system there are two broad elements to the compulsory support that those claiming benefits are routinely required to engage with. First, there are the online and face-to-face interactions with DWP staff that are required in order to establish and retain eligibility to benefits. Second, is engagement, as variously required, with WCAs, job search activity and/or employment focused training, much of which is delivered by subcontracted private companies (the majority) and non-governmental organisations within a quasi-market system (see Bennett, 2017 for fuller discussions).

UC introduced a number of significant changes in the administration and delivery of social welfare benefits. These include: the establishment of a 'digital by default' system, in which application and delivery is routinely online; a switch from fortnightly to monthly benefit payment with variations in the level of UC benefit paid, in arrears, depending on the amount of income (if any) earned from employment in the previous month; and an assessment period between initial claim and first payment (often described as the 'five-week wait'). Although simplification and transparency have been promoted as central foundational principles of UC, some of the changes instigated have been criticised for placing unreasonable demands on claimants, exacerbating poverty and hardship, promoting confusion and undermining the ability of benefit recipients to manage the day-to-day realities of life on a low income (for example, Millar and Bennett, 2016; Wright et al, 2016, 2018a, 2018b; APPG-UC, 2019; Summers and Young, 2020).

Given the level of administrative change initiated and the work-related responsibilities that the majority of UC claimants are expected to meet, DWP guidance highlights the importance of Work Coaches (that is, frontline DWP staff in JCP) who 'will be able to guide and support you [the claimant] and, where appropriate, help you into work by providing personalised advice using their knowledge of local work opportunities' (DWP, 2020a: np). In order to access this support and retain eligibility, a UC claimant is routinely expected to accept certain individual responsibilities. This includes managing their UC claim and payments by notifying the DWP of any variations in their circumstances and effectively organising their monthly budget including rent and other housing costs. At the outset of any claim, both in-work and out-of-work UC applicants are required to complete a personalised Claimant Commitment with their Work Coach that specifies any support available to them and the work search/preparation activities they are required to undertake. Partnered couples are expected to make a joint UC claim, but agree separate individual Claimant Commitments. Requirements ordinarily include work preparation tasks such as writing a CV, undertaking work experience or training and recording job search activities and applications, 'in most cases' up to a maximum of 35 hours a week. Failure to meet the requirements set out in the Claimant Commitment can lead to a benefit sanction for both in-work and out-of-work claimants (SSAC, 2019). The level of conditionality that an individual is subject to in their Claimant Commitment varies dependent upon claimants' individual or household circumstances, individual characteristics and earnings. Taking these factors into account, each claimant is assigned to one of four conditionality groups set out in Table 2.1 that then determines the level and types of requirement attached to each person's benefit claim (APPG-UC, 2019; DWP, 2020a). Readers should note, however, that in-work UC claimants who meet the specific requirements of the 'light touch regime' within the 'All Work Related Requirements' group are, somewhat paradoxically, not subject to work-related requirements.

As Stinson (2019a, 2019b) notes, other mechanisms of support are available for Work Coaches administering UC in their interactions with individual claimants. The first is a system of discretionary loans and alternative payment arrangements (APAs) that can be made available to vulnerable clients in specific situations. These include an Advance Payment for those without the money to support themselves during the assessment period before an initial UC payment is made, Hardship Payments for qualifying individuals who are subject to a benefit sanction and Budgeting Advances granted in response to emergency household costs (for example, replacing a cooker, funeral fees), or to enable an individual to enter or remain in employment. The important point to note here is that all of these payments, if granted, are, recoverable loans deducted in monthly instalments from any future UC payments. Work Coaches may also consider claimant requests for APAs to be implemented. Regulations allow for those individuals who are struggling to budget on a monthly basis to apply for fortnightly, and in exceptional circumstances, weekly payments. Claimants can also apply to have their rent costs deducted at source and paid directly to their landlord each month. Finally, individuals in a joint UC claim can apply for any UC money to be split and paid into two different bank accounts in situations where domestic violence has occurred or if partners have differing responsibilities (DWP, 2020a).

Second, alongside these financial mechanisms that have been introduced to offset the poverty and at times extreme financial hardship that the design and ongoing delivery of UC can produce (see, for example, Wright et al, 2016, 2018a; Fitzpatrick et al, 2018; Fitzpatrick, McKeever and Simpson, 2019; Barnard, 2019), 'easements' can also be applied by Work Coaches to support UC recipients. Easements allow for the reduction or removal of the work-related conditions attached to an individual's claim for a specific period of time in response to a number of adverse personal circumstances. These include, following the death of a partner or child, being the victim of domestic violence, drug/alcohol dependency if engaging in structured treatment, various specified unfitness to work/limited capability for work/ limited capability for work and work-related requirements (including being terminally ill) linked to WCA and sickness criteria, carrying out public duties (for example, jury service) and those in witness protection schemes. DWP guidance states that easements, for various detailed periods, are compulsory in such circumstances and that claimants must inform their Work Coach so that the Claimant Commitment can be amended. Additionally, Work

Table 2.1: Conditionality groups and work-related requirements in Universal Credit

Conditionality group	Universal Credit claimants to whom it applies	Expectations of work preparation/work-related requirements
1. All Work Related Requirement Group This group consists of two labour market regimes, that is, *(1a) Those under the 'Intensive Work Search Regime'*	(i) Unemployed claimants who are not working (ii) In work claimants on very low earnings expected to take action to increase their earnings from paid work (iii) Those with an impairment or health condition where a Work Capability Assessment is ongoing (iv) Some self-employed claimants and lead carers whose youngest child is aged three or four	Do all you can to find a job Undertake up to 35 hours' job search per week Searching for a specified number of jobs each week Creating a CV and online job profiles and obtaining references Attending WFIs and job interviews
and *(1b) Those under the 'Light Touch Regime'*	(i) Claimants on very low earnings, between two DWP set thresholds – that is, those with individual or household earnings above the Administrative Earnings Threshold (AET) but below the corresponding individual/household conditionality earnings threshold (CET)*	No work-related requirements
2. Work Preparation Group	(i) Claimants deemed to have limited capability for work (LCW) following a WCA (ii) Lead carers where youngest child is aged two	Expected to work in the future but currently not required to actively seek work Required work preparation activities may include, for example: • Attending a skills assessment • Taking part in training • Creating and maintaining job profiles • Developing a business plan • Investigating childcare provision and costs
3. Work-Focused Interview	(i) Claimants who are lead carers and foster carers of children under one year of age	Expected to work in the future but currently not required to actively seek work due to informal caring responsibilities.

Table 2.1: Conditionality groups and work-related requirements in Universal Credit (continued)

Conditionality group	Universal Credit claimants to whom it applies	Expectations of work preparation/work-related requirements
	(ii) Claimants that have assumed responsibility for a friend/relative in the previous year and certain foster carers of children aged over one in certain special circumstances	Required work preparation activities may include, for example: • Regular WFIs or phone contact with Work Coach • Identify potential training opportunities • Assessing prospects for remaining in or finding future paid work
4. No work-related requirements	(i) In work claimants who are earning enough – that is, employees earning above the CET and self-employed claimants earning above the Minimum Income Floor** (ii) Claimants not required to undertake any work-related activity including those deemed to have 'limited capability for work and work related activity' (LCWRA) due to impairments, individuals over State Pension age or with significant caring responsibilities	No work search or related requirements

Note:* As noted in previous discussions, this is set at a level equivalent to a 35-hour working week paid at the UK National Living Wage. ** The Minimum Income Floor applies to 'gainfully self-employed' claimants who have been in business for a minimum of one year. Specifically, 'the MIF is an assumed level of earnings. This is based on what we would expect an employed person to receive in similar circumstances' (DWP, 2020b: np).
Source: Developed from APPG-UC (2019) and DWP (2020a)

Coaches may exercise discretion in applying easements to conditionality in response to domestic emergencies, homelessness and temporary childcare requirements (see DWP, 2020a: section 1.4 for details).

Aside from these various financial support mechanisms and discretionary easements that may be available via JCP, UC recipients also have to mandatorily engage with employment focused training/work search activities delivered by organisations external to the DWP, as instructed by their Work Coach. In 2011 the Conservative/Liberal Democrat Coalition government replaced New Labour's New Deals with the Work Programme (WP). The WP delivered back to work and work search training to young and long-term unemployed people and disabled recipients of ESA required to undertake work-related activities. With training supplied by 18 'prime contractors' (16 private companies and two charities), which subcontracted to approximately 900 smaller organisations, the WP heralded an expanded and largely privatised welfare-to-work industry in the UK. WP providers received an initial payment for each person they supported, but the majority of their fees were linked to successful work placement and job sustainment outcomes. This payment by results approach was an attempt to overcome 'creaming' and 'parking' practices associated with previous quasi-marketised schemes (Finn, 2013; Carter and Whitworth, 2015[3]). Additionally, the WP operated on a so-called 'black box' approach to frontline implementation. This allowed WP providers a large degree of discretion in the particular mix of personalised compulsion and/or voluntary support they applied to individuals referred to them. Nonetheless, failure or refusal by a claimant to do as instructed by a WP provider routinely led to the individual being referred back to the DWP and the benefit sanction process initiated (see Finn, 2011, 2013; Newton et al, 2013; WPC, 2013; Jordan, 2018 for fuller discussions of the WP).

It should be apparent from the preceding discussions that, for a benefit reform that promised to deliver simplicity, the administration of UC remains a complex process. This is due in no small part to successive UK governments' stated wish to deliver individually tailored support and personalised conditionality within social security provision (DWP, 2008b, 2020a; Gregg, 2008). Moving forward the ongoing retention of contribution based unemployment and incapacity benefits in the form of 'New Style JSA' and 'New Style ESA' for those who have sufficient National Insurance contribution records further complicates the contemporary UK social welfare benefits landscape. Receipt of these two 'new style' benefits is restricted to a maximum of six and 12 months respectively and, importantly, claimants of both will routinely also be subject to varying levels of welfare conditionality depending on their particular situation (DWP, 2018a, 2020a). However, a commitment to the principle and practice of conditionality extends beyond social security into other policy areas. The next section considers its advance in relation to UK social housing.

Social housing

Welfare conditionality has become a key feature of social housing policy in recent decades. Although discussions here focus on UK developments, behavioural requirements in relation to accessing and retaining social housing have also become significant elsewhere, for example, in Australia, Canada, the US and several European welfare states (Fitzpatrick and Pawson, 2014; Watts and Fitzpatrick, 2018a; Clarke et al, 2020; Costarelli et al, 2020). Within the UK, successive governments have long sought to utilise enhanced conditionality within social housing tenancies and housing-related benefits to influence tenants' behaviour (Dwyer, 2004; Flint and Nixon, 2006; Morgan, 2010) and to achieve four linked aims: activate people into work; facilitate moves out of social housing; moderate harmful or inappropriate behaviour; and encourage individuals to positively participate in their local community (McNeill, 2016). In England especially, the increased acceptance of welfare conditionality has been seen as undermining the principle of a right to a secure tenancy that grants indefinite occupation of an allocated home unless a tenant is in breach of their tenancy agreement. Simultaneously, the priority needs based approach to the allocation of scarce social housing resources has been eroded by shifts in policy that encourage providers to offer preference on their housing waiting lists to more responsible, 'deserving' groups of citizens who have made some form of wider contribution to society, for example, those in paid work or Armed Forces veterans (Watts and Fitzpatrick, 2018a).

The Housing Act 1996, instigated by a Conservative government, initiated a series of significant changes that linked social housing to tenants' behavioural responsibilities. The Act also made it easier for landlords to evict secure and assured tenants on the grounds of ASB. A new form of tenure, introductory tenancies, of initially 12 months' duration (sometime also referred to as starter/probationary tenancies), were introduced for new social housing tenants. Tenants behaving in an 'antisocial'[4] manner within the introductory period became liable to eviction and faced potential revocation of any future right to a secure tenancy. Additionally, the Act permitted the power of arrest to be attached to court injunctions taken out by social landlords to address ASB if violence was threatened or occurred (Dwyer, 2000). Tenants also became responsible for the behaviour of household members and visitors, both within and around the immediate location of their homes (Burney, 2005).

Post-1997, successive New Labour governments enacted a host of further measures in an attempt to manage the behaviour of social housing tenants and within specific local communities. The Crime and Disorder Act 1998 saw the creation of antisocial behaviour orders (ASBOs), that is, new civil court orders that gave a local authority or the police the powers to prohibit an individual from acting in an antisocial manner and/or to exclude them from their home or other specified locality. Breaching the conditions attached to an ASBO is a criminal offence that may potentially lead to imprisonment. Across New Labour's time in office, tenancy conditions were further strengthened with the introduction of demoted tenancies and family intervention tenancies that reduced tenants' rights to occupancy if they engaged in ASB or accrued rent arrears (see Flint, 2006; Flint and Pawson, 2009; Flint and Hunter, 2010; Morgan, 2010 for further details). Indeed, Hunter (2006: 151) argues that 'by lessening the security of their tenants, primarily through the use of introductory and starter tenancies', New Labour gave social landlords greater legal instruments to control the behaviour of tenants. She notes how, over time, the welfare conditionality that was initially introduced to govern the behaviour of individual social tenants was further extended to incorporate policymakers' concerns about wider ASB and the management of the conduct of specific marginalised groups:

> The law has been changed to widen the role from one that is concerned primarily with the relationship between the landlord and tenant, to one where the landlord is concerned with the behaviour of those who are not tenants, and encompasses behaviour not just towards immediate neighbours, but also all those in the 'locality' or 'neighbourhood'. (Hunter, 2006: 151)

Alongside a desire to curb ASB (see the section on the management of antisocial behaviour for further discussions), New Labour's then Minister for Employment and Welfare Reform, Caroline Flint, argued that social tenancy agreements should also require new tenants to proactively seek paid employment as part of their housing contract (BBC, 2008). Ultimately, this call did not lead to legislation; however, it is indicative of a wider shift in the function of social landlords away from dealing solely with housing issues, towards a wider role that entails managing ASB and also supporting tenants to move into paid employment (McNeill, 2016; Wilding et al, 2019).

The Conservative/Liberal Coalition and subsequent Conservative governments continued to drive forward policy reform in social housing. The Localism Act 2011 introduced new flexibilities for social landlords, which empowered them to initially offer renewable fixed-term tenancies to new tenants; routinely of five years' duration but also for a minimum of two years in certain specified exceptional circumstances. Although this move raised concerns about potential increases in homelessness and the undermining of local communities, it reflects the commitment of recent UK governments to challenge the idea of a social tenancy as providing a lifelong home and promotes a short-term, residualised vision for public housing (McNeill, 2016; Fitzpatrick and Watts, 2017). The Housing and Planning Act 2016 progressed policy further by making use of fixed-term tenancies (between two and ten years in duration) mandatory for most local authorities. On completion of a fixed-term tenancy, landlords are required to undertake a review before reaching a decision about offering a new tenancy, and aside from situations where an existing secure tenancy passes on to a spouse/civil partner following bereavement, any secure tenancies will be replaced by a fixed-term one (CIH, 2016). Although housing associations were exempt, they could continue to use assured or fixed-term assured short hold tenancies (see Shelter Legal, 2020 for details), signalling that 'security of tenure [would] end for almost all new council tenants in

England' (Fitzpatrick and Watts, 2017: 1023). In the Bill that preceded the Act, under what are known as 'Pay to Stay' plans, the government stated its original intention of making it mandatory for local authorities to charge increased rents from higher-earning tenants. The rationale here was that it is unfair for the public purse to subsidise the rents of 'better off' social tenants who, in line with the ideological preferences of the government could, and indeed should, be looking at private rental or home ownership to meet their needs. However, in light of extensive criticism as the Bill passed through Parliament, including the view that 'Pay to Stay' would undermine work incentives, the government dropped this plan (CIH, 2016).

Fitzpatrick and Pawson (2014) argue that the advance of behavioural conditionality, and the accompanying loss of security of tenure that it promotes, are important as they challenge the principles and practices that have long held sway within UK social housing. Drawing on the work of Stephens (2008), they note that in previous decades social housing allocation in the UK operated on a 'safety net' basis, offering a legally enforceable right to housing for certain specified people experiencing homelessness who met particular priority need based categorisations. Additionally, once such criteria had been met, any social tenancies granted were typically regarded as offering a secure and long-term/permanent right to a home regardless of any subsequent (positive) changes in the prosperity of a household. However, the replacement of secure tenancies with fixed-term tenancies that the 2011 and 2016 Acts brought about in England, marked a transition towards social housing becoming more of a 'ambulance' type service that offers temporary and time-limited access to social housing, reserved for the poorest and most vulnerable people who face a housing crisis. Significantly, once the period of crisis has passed and/or a household achieves a certain level of economic success they may no longer meet the eligibility criteria required to remain in social housing and should accordingly be expected to find alternative provision themselves, most likely in the private rental sector, or as owner-occupiers rather than relying on subsidised public housing (see Fitzpatrick and Pawson, 2014 for fuller discussions).

The management of antisocial behaviour

Welfare conditionality has become an important element of many governments' policies that focus on the reduction of antisocial and harmful behaviour and the wider management of public spaces (see, for example, Tosi, 2007; Watts and Fitzpatrick, 2018a). In the UK, the introduction of ASBOs in the Crime and Disorder Act 1998 signalled New Labour's early intent to tackle ASB and further legislation (that is, the Anti-Social Behaviour Act and the Criminal Justice Act, both 2003) subsequently brought about the introduction of a host of new powers including dispersal orders, parenting contracts, demoted tenancies, individual support orders and acceptable behaviour contracts, to promote and enforce responsible behaviour (see, for example, Squires, 2006; Milne, 2007; Flint, 2014). Over time policy rhetoric in relation to ASB has evolved to acknowledge that many people routinely associated with problematic and harmful behaviour face a range of significant and often overlapping issues (including homelessness, substance misuse and addiction, histories of offending, mental and/or physical impairments, lack of basic literacy and numeracy skills, debt and entrenched poverty), that require additional, personalised support if individuals are to successfully turn their lives around (see Bauld et al, 2012; Batty, 2020). For example, New Labour's 'Respect Action Plan' promised enhanced tailored support for 'problem' families and socially excluded individuals (RTF, 2006). However, such support remained highly conditional and the government made it apparent that where individuals failed to engage with the support offered and continued to participate in irresponsible, antisocial or criminal activities, or provide inadequate parenting, the use of severe sanctions such as imprisonment, loss of tenancy and potential removal of children into public care remained justifiable and necessary. Furthermore, the Welfare Reform Act 2007 enabled English local authorities to reduce or withdraw the right to HB from social tenants evicted due to ASB or criminal behaviour with those who persisted in ASB facing loss of the right to HB for up to five years.

Although keen to differentiate itself from New Labour, the Conservative/Liberal Democrat Coalition's approach to the management of ASB retained many core elements of its predecessors. The Coalition's flagship 'Strategy for Social Justice' policy expressly focused on 'breaking the cycle' of multiple disadvantages faced by a 'dysfunctional' minority whose lives, the government argues, were routinely blighted by six interlinked issues: worklessness; the collapse of the traditional family unit; drug and alcohol dependency; poor educational attainment (often accompanied by high levels of school exclusion); debt; and involvement in crime. Promise of a 'second chance' society, and support for vulnerable individuals who are committed to transforming their lives for the better, was to be based on five key principles:

1. A focus on *prevention and early intervention*;
2. Where problems arise, concentrating interventions on *recovery and independence*, not maintenance;
3. Promoting work for those who can as the most sustainable route out of poverty, while offering *unconditional support* to those who are severely disabled and cannot work;
4. Recognising that the most effective solutions will often be designed and delivered at a *local level*;
5. Ensuring that interventions provide *a fair deal for the taxpayer*. (HMG, 2012: 10, emphasis in original)

These principles further informed the changes in ASB policy for England and Wales instigated by the Conservative/Liberal Democrat Coalition. The Anti-social Behaviour, Crime and Policing Act 2014 broadened the definition of ASB[5] while simultaneously streamlining and replacing 19 pre-existing powers that New Labour had introduced (including ASBOs, with the exception of Scotland where they are still in use), with six new instruments. Three of these focus on people, that is, ASB Civil Injunctions, Criminal Behaviour Orders and Community Protection Orders while the other three relate to spaces and buildings, namely, Public Space Protection Orders, Dispersal Powers and Closure Powers. In line with the localism favoured by the Conservative/Liberal Democrat Coalition and the subsequent Conservative governments, social landlords, the police and local authorities are variously jointly responsible for tackling ASB within local communities. A 'community trigger' requires that the relevant public authorities take action when multiple complaints about a particular issue or household are received. Similarly, a new 'community remedy' requirement obliges the police and local crime commissioners to consult with local communities about the range of appropriate sanctions to be used in tackling ASB. Local authorities, the police and social landlords share responsibility for tackling ASB at a local level. These public bodies have a variety of powers ranging from fixed penalty notices (fines) to five years' imprisonment for breach of a Criminal Behaviour Order (Brown and Sturge, 2020).

Conditional welfare interventions and vulnerable people

Utilisation of the mechanisms of welfare conditionality to manage the 'perceived irresponsibility and problematic conduct of the poor' (Flint, 2019: 250) has become an established component of contemporary policies attempting to increase PLM engagement and reform the behaviour of a host of marginalised populations within the UK (Reeves and Loopstra, 2017; Fletcher and Flint, 2018; McNeill and Bowpitt, 2021). Targeted interventions have focused on groups such as people experiencing homelessness, offenders, drug users and 'problem'/'troubled' families, with many individuals in these discrete groupings often facing common, multiple and intersecting issues that negatively impact on their lives (MOJ, 2013; Bacon and Seddon, 2019; Cromarty, 2019).

With reference to homelessness, for example, as Johnsen et al note (2018a: 1108), 'eligibility for support from homelessness service providers has become more explicitly tied to compliance with conduct-related conditions and "engagement" with the help on offer'. Since New Labour's period in power, UK governments have promoted policy frameworks in which homelessness support agencies have been asked to demand more from their clients in return for the opportunities and support they provide

(Whiteford, 2008; Dobson, 2011). In England especially, rough sleepers and others engaged in 'street culture' activities such as begging and/or drinking in public places, have faced an increase in interventionist strategies by certain service providers. These range from 'hard' interventions, for example, Controlled Drinking Zones, Dispersal Orders, arrest under the Vagrancy Act 1824, and the various mechanisms initially introduced in the Crime and Disorder Act 1998 and developed in subsequent legislation, to 'softer' assertive outreach approaches which attempt to persuade people off the streets and into accommodation (Johnsen et al, 2014, 2018a; Watts et al, 2018). Homeless benefit claimants are also subject to welfare conditionality in much the same way as other claimants within the social security system. However, under UC rules, Work Coaches may vary or temporarily suspend any work-related benefit eligibility requirements for homeless claimants while they search for accommodation or deal with other crises. Although welcome, such 'easements' of conditionality are, as noted previously, available at the discretion of the Work Coach and may not consistently be granted (Cromarty, 2019).

As Fletcher (2014b) notes, for those who have left the criminal justice system, ensuring opportunities for paid work among ex-offenders has long been highlighted by UK policymakers as key to reducing recidivism rates. Indeed, inculcating the work ethic by ensuring access to training alongside the routines and discipline associated with steady employment are seen as key to tackling the problematic behaviour of the prison population. 'Prison should be a place where work itself is central to the regime, where offenders learn vocational skills in environments organised to replicate as far as practical and appropriate, real working conditions' (MOJ, 2010: 15).

Perhaps not unsurprisingly, welfare conditionality is considered as an appropriate mechanism by which to rehabilitate prisoners and promote paid work on their release from incarceration. The Coalition government, recognising early intervention as crucial in preventing reoffending, and that many prison leavers who claim unemployment and other welfare benefits continue to experience significant barriers to work, determined that entry to the WP from 'day one' of their release would be mandatory for those leaving prison. Any ex-offender claiming JSA within 13 weeks of release also had to compulsorily engage with the WP (Fletcher, 2014b). However, limitations in the mandatory support on offer to offenders, the increasing surveillance now associated with the benefits system and the negative impacts of the more punitive side of welfare conditionality (that is, benefit sanctions) have been found to push offenders (many of whom may already be hostile towards, or wary of, authority) away from both the UK social security system and the paid labour market (Povey, 2019; Batty, 2020). Although acknowledging differences in the conception and operationalisation of conditionality within penal and welfare systems, McNeill (2020: 306) argues that conditionality serves to simultaneously both discipline and degrade delinquent citizens by 'producing symbolic, political, and material effects ... to push away those that it has made vulnerable and whose vulnerabilities it has itself magnified through conditionality'.

Family based intervention programmes, many of which, rhetorically at least, demand the 'non-negotiable' engagement of families facing multiple challenges, are another arena in which welfare conditionality has become a significant part of the policy landscape (Flint and Hunter, 2010; Flint et al, 2011; NAO, 2013). Emerging from concerns identified in the Respect Action Plan (RTF, 2006), family intervention project (FIPs) became New Labour's 'flagship mechanism for tackling the problematic conduct of the most vulnerable families' (Ball et al, 2015: 264). In England, over 250 projects were variously delivered by local authorities, social landlords and charities with similar projects set up by the Scottish and Welsh governments. Designed to tackle the antisocial and criminal behaviour of 120,000 'problem families', interventions varied in intensity and adopted a range of approaches but were routinely centred around a key worker working with family members and local agencies to address their behavioural issues (Batty and Flint, 2012; Ball et al, 2015; Bate, 2016). Built on public facing political rhetoric that emphasised 'tough love', accompanied by sanctions for families that failed to engage, New Labour went on to make great claims about the effectiveness of FIPs in 'turning round' the lives of the families they targeted. However, these claims have been disputed and FIPs have been roundly criticised for demonising the families that they were supposed to help and failing to deliver the 'sustained reductions in ASB' asserted by their architects (Gregg, 2010).

The Conservative/Liberal Democrat successors subsequently developed further FIPs, announcing the launch of the 'Troubled Families Programme' (TFP) in 2012. By this time the discourse underpinning policy had arguably shifted from targeting 'people who have problems to people who cause problems' (Wenham et al, 2015: 5). The 'troubled families' to be included were identified as meeting three out of four specific criteria, namely, they are 'involved in youth crime or antisocial behaviour, have children who are regularly truanting or not in school, have an adult on out of work benefits, cause high costs to the taxpayer' (DCLG, 2012: 9).

The TFP retained the multi-agency approach of its predecessor, but with a greater emphasis on localised autonomy of delivery centred around common key elements set out by central government. A dedicated key worker assigned to each family to offer practical hands-on support in a persistent, assertive and challenging manner was again central to the programme. This key worker was tasked with working with the family as a whole to identify problematic behaviour within families and coordinate a multi-agency response and action plan to address it (DCLG, 2012; Wenham et al, 2015; Wenham, 2017). Additionally, the DWP simultaneously, but separately, also established the

'Families with Multiple Problems programme' (2011–15) alongside the TFP to intervene in the lives of families with long histories of inactivity in the PLM. The Public Accounts Committee (see NAO, 2013) was critical of this uncoordinated twin track approach, highlighting a lack of integration between the two programmes, and concerns around the targeting of the same families for intervention under separate schemes (Bate, 2016).

The current UK government clearly remains committed to the TFP as an effective way to 'provide earlier support to families experiencing difficulties and improve outcomes for children' (MHCLG, 2020: 19). A second phase running from 2015 to 2020 was initiated following on from its previous implementation and a further £165 million in funding was announced in November 2020 to extend its operation into 2022 (Loft, 2020). In its current and enlarged iteration, in order to be included in the TFP, families must include dependent children and exhibit two or more of an expanded list of factors including: having a child involved in crime or ASB; regular non-attendance at school by a child; having a child(ren) identified as in need of additional support; a family member aged 16–18 not in education employment or training; being affected by domestic abuse; parents or children living with a range of physical or mental health needs; and, families experiencing or at risk of worklessness and/or financial hardship (MHCLG, 2020). It is interesting here that guidance defines the last 'family problem' specifically as 'if an adult is in receipt of out of work benefits; or an adult is claiming Universal Credit and subject to work related conditions' (MHCLG, 2020: 20). Under UC rules this could potentially include low-paid, working parents in receipt of 'in-work' housing and wage supplements. Evidence perhaps to support the assertion that the conditionality built into UC has expanded the definition of problematic welfare dependency to include not just unemployed benefit recipients but also low-paid workers (Wright and Dwyer, 2022).

Aside from debates about the effectiveness or otherwise of the TFP (see Chapter Three) a number of commentators have criticised the ideological and conceptual foundations underpinning the TFP and intensive family intervention policies more widely, noting the influence and acceptance of a stigmatising 'underclass' narrative focused on individual failings and parental irresponsibility while failing to adequately acknowledge and respond to the structural inequalities faced by those targeted by these programmes (Macnicol, 2017; Nunn and Tepe-Belfrage, 2017; Parr, 2017; Sayer, 2017; Wenham, 2017).

Conditionality in context: UK welfare reform since 2010, austerity, retrenchment and devolution

Following an indecisive general election result in May 2010 a Conservative/ Liberal Democrat Coalition government was formed with the Conservative

Party very much the dominant partner. Prior to forming the Coalition, the Conservative Party had been keen to disassociate itself from the New Right influenced policy of the Thatcher and Major governments of the 1980s and 1990s. Initially, much was made of a 'Big Society' vision that reduced the welfare role of the state, while enabling individuals, local communities and the voluntary sector to take a greater role in the delivery of services wherever possible. This would be done by the government devolving power to local government, opening up public services and encouraging more philanthropic giving. Faced with managing the outcomes of the 2008 global financial crisis, Cameron defended this approach against claims that it was merely a smoke screen for Coalition-instigated cuts in public expenditure:

> [The Big Society] is not a cover for anything. ... But I would make this argument: whoever was standing here right now as Prime Minister would be having to make cuts in public spending, and isn't it better if we are having to make cuts in public spending, to try and encourage a bigger and stronger society at the same time? If there are facilities that the state can't afford to keep open, shouldn't we be trying to encourage communities who want to come forward and help them and run them? (Cameron, 2011: np)

As previously discussed, welfare conditionality has become a central pillar of the Coalition and its Conservative successors' welfare reform programme; a programme that was instigated against a backdrop of unprecedented welfare state retrenchment and austerity. The Coalition government's commitment to austerity soon marginalised the compassionate 'one nation Conservativism' rhetoric about the need to mend a broken Britain. Presenting austerity as the inevitable policy response to the 2008 global fiscal crisis, the Coalition attempted to ignite a collective imagery of one nation united in the face of adversity:

> We are all in this together, and we will get through this together. We will carry out Britain's unavoidable deficit reduction plan in a way that strengthens and unites the country. We are not doing this because we want to, driven by theory or ideology. We are doing this because we have to, driven by the urgent truth that unless we do, people will suffer and our national interest will suffer. But this government will not cut this deficit in a way that hurts those we most need to help ... that divides the country ... or that undermines the spirit and ethos of our public services. Freedom, fairness, responsibility: those are the values that drive this government and they are the values that will drive our efforts to deal with our debts and turn this economy around. So yes, it will be tough. But we will get through this together – and Britain

will come out stronger on the other side. (Cameron, 2010: np, cited by Clarke and Newman, 2012: 5)

However, a more critical alternative view sees austerity as a deliberate rather than inevitable act of policymaking. Clarke and Newman (2012), for example, regard austerity as political 'shape-shifting'; an ideologically informed project that provided the tools for neoliberal policymakers to deflect attention away from the irresponsibility of the financial sector and the markets that caused the 2008 global financial crisis. They argue that austerity, as a policy, simultaneously enabled the identification of 'the unwieldy and expensive welfare state and public sector' (Clarke and Newman, 2012: 300) and the irresponsibility of 'welfare dependent' citizens as necessitating cuts to public expenditure; thus, ushering in an era of unparalleled welfare state retrenchment to restore the economic and moral order. In many ways the justification for austerity was made possible by the punitive welfare policies and narratives of 'welfare dependency' adopted by preceding Conservative and New Labour governments to legitimate increased welfare conditionality (Levitas, 2012; Edmiston, 2016). As funding was withdrawn and public sector pay frozen, austerity thus triggered unprecedented cuts to national and local authority welfare budgets with long-term ramifications for future public spending (Taylor-Gooby, 2012). Initial cuts to the welfare budget in 2010 amounted to £11 billion, with a further £12 billion reduction announced in the Summer Budget of 2015. It is estimated that, overall, welfare reforms introduced since 2010 reduced social security spending by £27 billion per year to 2021 (Beatty and Fothergill, 2016).

This systematic reduction in welfare spending was accompanied by substantial welfare state reforms. Aside from the overt conditionality central to previously discussed initiatives (for example, the introduction of UC, the TFP, and so on), a series of fundamental changes tightened up eligibility criteria and reduced the generosity of social security provisions. For example, changes to HB in 2011 saw the removal of the Spare Room Subsidy (aka the 'Bedroom Tax') and those deemed to be 'under occupying' accommodation in the social rental sector (that is, living in houses with excess bedrooms) subsequently faced reductions in the amount of HB they received. Individuals are now required to fund any shortfall themselves, either from other benefits they receive, or preferably through earnings from taking up employment. Alternatively, they are expected to relocate to smaller accommodation. Defended on grounds of fairness, the government argued that the social security system should not be subsidising benefit recipients to live in properties beyond their means at taxpayers' expense. Reductions in the amount of Local Housing Allowance, paid to assist low-income households living in private sector accommodation with their rental costs, were also introduced. Additionally, a three-year freeze on the value of Child

Benefit was introduced in 2010, alongside the initiation of a means test that ended any entitlement for households with a higher earner. Reductions in the payment rates and eligibility for CTC and WTC paid to lower- and middle-income households, including increase in working hours requirement for WTC, were also introduced (see Lowe and Meers, 2015; Batty, 2017; Beatty and Fothergill, 2018).

In 2012 the Coalition announced the phasing out of Disability Living Allowance. Its replacement, the Personal Independence Payment, featured stringent eligibility criteria and the reassessment process saw the many recipients' accounts of impairment discredited and dismissed, with numerous individuals placed on lower bands of entitlement and reduced benefit (Roulestone, 2015; Pybus et al, 2019). The following year, a new £500 per week maximum ceiling on the total benefit payments a household could receive was instigated (aka the 'Benefit Cap'). The year 2013 also saw rules introduced limiting the up-rating in value of most working age benefits to 1 per cent for the next three years. In the same year the Discretionary Social Fund was abolished with its nationally funded components of Community Care Grants and Crisis Loans supplanted by a funding scheme devolved to local authority level (CPAG, 2013). Furthermore, Council Tax Benefit was replaced by the localised Council Tax Reduction Scheme accompanied by a 10 per cent reduction in payments from central government to local authorities. This led to decreases in the benefit received by many working age claimants (Adam et al, 2019). The reforms continued with the election of a Conservative government in 2015, when it was announced that Tax Credits and family benefits payable within UC would be limited for families with more than two dependent children (unless born before 6 April 2017 or where special circumstances apply), to the first two children (aka the 'two-child limit') and that unemployed 18–21-year-olds would no longer automatically be entitled to claim HB. Additionally a new, more stringent Benefit Cap further reduced the maximum a family could receive each year in benefits from £26,000 to £23,000 in London and £20,000 elsewhere and a further four-year freeze on most working age benefits from 2016 to 2020 was introduced (see Batty, 2017; Beatty and Fothergill, 2018).

A further policy development, devolution, is also relevant to any discussion of the wider context in which the conditional UK welfare state now operates. Following referenda in favour of devolution in the late 1990s certain powers have been transferred from the UK government in Westminster and devolved to the Scottish government, the Northern Ireland executive and to a much lesser extent the Welsh government. The most substantive changes have occurred in relation to Scotland and 'the period between 2012 and 2016 saw Scotland and Northern Ireland take steps towards greater regional autonomy in social security' (Simpson, 2017: 647), with Wales remaining the 'poor relation' in terms of powers devolved from Westminster. In some respects the devolved administrations' desire for further powers to be transferred to them from Westminster reflect a dissatisfaction with the highly conditional vision of social citizenship endorsed by consecutive UK governments (see Simpson, 2017, 2022 for fuller discussions).

Indeed, the choice of fieldwork sites for generating the qualitative data that informs this book was in part motivated by a desire to explore the application of conditionality in both England and Scotland, where, at the time the study was conceived in 2011, shared social security law sat alongside different legislative frameworks for housing, homelessness and criminal justice. Since then, however, further change has occurred with certain (limited) powers in relation to social security subsequently transferred to the devolved administrations.

However, in respect of welfare conditionality it is important to note that although some powers to deliver training and support for social welfare benefit claimants have been gradually devolved, the UK government retains reserved powers on benefit sanctions and a single unified system continues to operate. Conditionality, mandatory engagement with JCP and compliance with any work-related requirements and so on, set out within a personalised Claimant Commitment and the application of benefit sanctions for non-compliance, therefore, remain part of the social security system across the four nations of the UK. Given these reserved powers it is perhaps not too surprising to note that our subsequent analysis revealed limited differences between England and Scotland in relation to the use and application of benefit sanctions. Indeed, the judgements and decisions of individual 'street level bureaucrats' (Lipsky, (2010 [1980]) in their face-to-face interactions with benefit claimants appeared to be far more significant in structuring different outcomes for individuals than issues of national geography (see Chapter Three for a fuller discussion of discretion). That said, the Scottish government has been keen to distance itself from the welfare reforms and austerity instigated by the UK government. Under powers devolved in the Scotland Act 2016, the Social Security (Scotland) Act 2018 established the principles of 'dignity, fairness and respect' as fundamental to the policy and practice of any new social security legislation delivered by the Scottish government moving forwards.

Leaving aside issues of principle and approach, devolution has been significant for the provision of employment support programmes for benefit recipients. The Scotland Act 2016 transferred the employment support budget to the Scottish government who now deliver the Fair Start Scotland Scheme. Importantly, engagement with this scheme is entirely voluntary and free from the threat of benefit sanctions (Wright et al, 2018b). In late 2017, the WP in England and Wales was replaced by the smaller Work and Health Programme (WHP). In six regions the WHP is delivered by four nationally contracted providers working with partner organisations to deliver locally relevant programmes of employment-related skills support. Additionally, in certain areas, including Greater Manchester and London, funding has been devolved and the relevant regional authorities can select their own providers. Primarily aimed at supporting disabled people and those who have been unemployed for over two years, individuals belonging to a number of other specified groups who regularly face additional barriers to accessing paid employment (for example, public care leavers, people experiencing homelessness, ex-offenders, refugees, victims of domestic violence, and so on) can also be referred to the WHP by JCP Work Coaches. Significantly, in England and Wales engagement with the programme is now also largely voluntary, with compulsion and sanctions only retained for those unemployed benefit recipients who have been out of work for more than two years (Powell, 2020). Readers should note that that the interviews that inform this book were conducted prior to the establishment of the WHP so any analysis and findings presented in later chapters relate to its predecessor the WP.

Beyond the social security system, devolution is also factor in housing and ASB policy across the UK. For example, there appears to be limited appetite among policymakers in Scotland to follow the direction of travel of their English counterparts and extend the use of behavioural conditionality through specific types of tenancy agreement and/or allocation criteria (Fitzpatrick et al, 2014). In England and Wales, ASB remains a reserved issue with the UK government setting the legislative framework. However, in practice (as previously discussed), the police and local authorities have a range of powers they can implement within local communities as appropriate, so some variation of approach does occur (Brown and Sturge, 2020). ASB powers in Scotland fall under the remit of the Scottish government (that is, the Antisocial Behaviour etc (Scotland) Act 2004, with the Housing Act (Scotland) 2014 introducing new regulations for the management of ASB), but in many ways the Scottish government takes a similar approach to the other nations of the UK by placing local authorities and the police at the forefront of ASB policy implementation (see Legislation.gov.uk, 2020).

Conclusions

As the preceding discussions show, mandatory engagement with specified work search and training requirements is now an established feature of the UK social security system. Since 1997, and New Labour's avowed commitment to rewriting the welfare contract between citizen and state, greater numbers of benefit recipients who are not active in the paid labour market, including unemployed people, disabled people and lone parents, have been required to meet increasingly extensive and demanding work-related requirements to retain eligibility to benefit. The introduction of UC by the Conservative/Liberal Democrat Coalition further broadened the reach of conditionality to encompass low-paid workers and simultaneously heralded a unique period of intensification in the severity and use of benefit sanctions for non-compliance. In other settings, most notably social housing and the management of antisocial behaviour, the instrumental use of welfare conditionality continues to be seen as an appropriate tool to control the irresponsible conduct of a host of vulnerable groups. Indeed, as welfare conditionality within the UK has expanded, its amorphous character is perhaps best illustrated by the various programmes and initiatives designed to tackle the ill-defined concept of antisocial behaviour. These straddle aspects of social security, housing, criminal justice and family policy in an attempt to manage and change the problematic behaviour of certain citizens.

In the past decade welfare conditionality has been advanced in tandem with policies that have delivered austerity and significant welfare state retrenchment and reform, accompanied to some extent by a limited increase in the devolution of powers away from the UK government to the Scottish and Welsh governments, and the Northern Ireland executive. The discussions and analysis presented within this book are focused upon welfare conditionality, and to be clear welfare conditionality, austerity and the wider welfare reforms of the past decade cannot, and should not, be conflated and seen as one and the same. Welfare conditionality advanced significantly in UK during the New Labour years prior to the onset of the global financial crisis of 2008, it was not a by-product of austerity, nor invented by the Coalition or more recent Conservative governments. In many ways, welfare conditionality and austerity are key components of a contemporary 'neoliberal orthodoxy' that has 'emerged, reinvigorated and with a strengthened mission to shrink the state' (Farnsworth and Irving, 2017: 192). This was the context in which the research presented in this book was undertaken.

The powerful narratives of conditionality and austerity have undoubtedly combined to deliver welfare reform policies that undermine the content and scope of social citizenship (Edmiston, 2016). There is plenty of evidence to suggest that the burdens of welfare state reform and austerity policies in the past decade have been distributed unevenly in terms of geography, gender, ethnicity and class (for example, Beatty and Fothergill, 2018; Hudson-Sharp et al, 2018; Portes and Reed, 2018; Cheetham et al, 2019). However, although conceptual clarity is valuable and differentiation of the core elements of recent UK welfare reform processes is useful, it is important to state that those at the sharp end of such policies, that is, the people whose voices and experiences inform the empirical analysis subsequently presented in this book, do not routinely and neatly differentiate between these varied components. They experience the realities of welfare reform and behavioural interventions simultaneously rather than in isolation, and react to, and make sense of, their implementation and allied impacts as best they can. In Chapters Four, Five and Six we identify and explore the specific role of welfare conditionality on the lives of those subject to its implementation in the UK. Before undertaking that task Chapter Three considers differing theories, assertions, debates and evidence about the effectiveness and ethicality of welfare conditionality in triggering and sustaining behaviour change.

Notes

[1] Duncan Smith was subsequently Secretary of State for the Department of Work and Pensions 2010–16.

[2] ESA will not disappear entirely. Disabled people with the required level of previous National Insurance contributions and placed in the WRAG will be able to claim the so-called 'new style ESA' for up to a year. There is no time limit for those allocated to the ESA Support Group (DWP, 2018a).

[3] Carter and Whitworth (2015: 279) note that '"creaming" refers to provider behaviour that prioritises attention for unemployed claimants with fewer barriers to work and who are therefore felt to be easier, cheaper and also more likely to move into paid work and release outcome payments. In contrast, "parking" refers to provider behaviour that deliberately neglects giving time, energy or resources to unemployed claimants with more substantial barriers to work, given that such claimants are considered to be relatively unlikely to move into paid work and/or to require considerable, and usually expensive, employment support to make a move into paid work likely (and hence an outcome payment)'.

[4] ASB was defined in the Act as 'conduct causing or likely to cause a nuisance or annoyance to a person residing in, visiting or otherwise engaging in lawful activity in residential premises' (Housing Act, 1996: 92).

[5] The Anti-social Behaviour, Crime and Policing Act 2014 section 2(1) (a)–(c) defines ASB as (a) conduct that has caused, or is likely to cause, harassment, alarm or distress to any person; (b) conduct capable of causing nuisance or annoyance to a person in relation to that person's occupation of residential premises; (c) conduct capable of causing housing-related nuisance or annoyance to any person. We are grateful to Kirsty Cameron for pointing this out.

THREE

Welfare conditionality and behaviour change

Powerful actors and institutions have long sought to make people behave in specific ways. Within feudal societies, nascent forms of the state were designed to deliver a monarch's bidding and the threat or use of violence was a key tool in getting subjects to obey the sovereign power. Although retaining a monopoly on the legitimate use of force remains a defining element of the modern state, today, democratically elected governments tend to look beyond brute force and employ a range of techniques and tools to persuade citizens to act in particular ways (Kelly, 2016). Questions about how to make individual citizens behave more responsibly, particularly in relation to public health and environmental concerns, have become a more prominent concern within public policy in recent decades (Collins et al, 2003: 6 et al, 2010; Spotswood, 2016). As Kelly (2016: 11) describes: 'Behaviour change is usually about making people different from how they are now.' Policymakers use a range of tools to variously incentivise, persuade, cajole and compel people to behave in prescribed ways regarded as beneficial for the individual concerned and wider society.

This chapter explores how highly conditional welfare interventions are now regarded as important instruments of behaviour change by many governments. The first part of the chapter offers an initial brief overview of broader economic and psychological theories on behaviour change that have held sway within social science and continue to heavily influence the thinking of contemporary policymakers. In the second part, a consideration of how agency and behaviour have been conceptualised within the welfare conditionality literature and the relevance of different policy tools (that is, sanction, support, sermons and nudges) that policymakers have at their disposal when attempting to change the behaviour of those reliant on social welfare benefits and services is then offered. The third part reviews existing evidence on the effectiveness of welfare conditionality, in either moving those reliant on social welfare benefits into paid work or promoting the cessation of problematic behaviour among sections of the population.

Theorising behaviour change

The literature theorising human behaviour and the various models for understanding and generating behaviour change is vast. An in-depth discussion of these debates lies beyond the focus of this chapter (see, for example, Halpern et al, 2004; Darnton, 2008a, 2008b for further insights). However, it is widely recognised that the approaches developed within economics and psychology have dominated social scientific understandings of behaviour and decision-making since the early 1970s and that the insights and methodologies of these disciplines remain highly influential within policymaking circles. When seeking explanations of how people behave, much of the thinking that prevails has its roots in classic economic theory, which offers 'an analytical approach based on "atomistic" or socially-isolated individuals acting in pursuit of their own interests' (Darnton, 2008b: 5). As such this model proposes an idealised understanding of behaviour built around self-interested, well-informed, rational individuals. Actors weigh up the options available to them and then act in ways which they believe will best serve their personal economic interests. This is a simplified, abstracted understanding of behaviour, which in many ways fails to take on board the complexities of the social reality, with many economists now open to recognising limitations of this 'utility maximiser model' (Leggett, 2014). Nonetheless, its common-sense logic continues to appeal to many in positions of power and, as Chatterton (2016) notes, the assumptions central to economic theory were influential as social psychologists looked to further extend understandings of the factors that motivate human behaviour.

For example, social psychologists Fishbein and Ajzen (1975) built on the goal-orientated thinking at the heart of classic economics to develop their 'expectancy-value' theory. Retaining a rational decision-maker approach, they moved beyond a focus solely on economic outcomes to argue that people's behavioural decisions may be driven by a wider set of goals that reflect the values and beliefs that different individuals hold. Significantly, this grounds an individual's goals and their motivations for choosing to behave in a particular way (that is, to pursue a particular end goal), within a person's subjective social reality rather than the idealised objective setting of 'homo economicus'. Subsequently, they moved on to consider other issues (such as why people may not always act in accordance with their stated intentions and the role of people's perceptions of social norms and/or behavioural controls), to set out a more developed theory of planned behaviour (Ajzen and Fishbein, 1980; Ajzen, 1991). However, this remains an essentially individualised understanding of behaviour which places 'responsibility for behavioural control firmly on the individual's state of mind and motivations with no clear process for assessing the impact on behaviour of external conditions other than as they are perceived by the individual' (Chatterton, 2016: 35).

Triandis' (1989) 'theory of interpersonal behaviour' attempts to address this shortcoming by situating the individual, their sense of self and the decision-making processes that influence behaviour within people's wider social contexts. Moving beyond a focus on intention, he highlights the importance of habits, mundane behaviours routinely performed without recourse to conscious, intention-informed processes. Arguing that people engage in habitual behaviours almost automatically through frequent repetition, Triandis identifies 'facilitating conditions' that include not only subjective factors, such as an individual's personal skills, abilities and emotions, but also wider environmental or social factors as important in enabling or inhibiting particular types of behaviour, including habitual ones. This acceptance of extrinsic factors in shaping and changing individual behaviour helped pave the way for others to subsequently develop multi-layered models that, although placing the individual at the centre, encompass personal lifestyle, local networks and wider social and environmental factors as significant in influencing people's behavioural decisions (Chatterton, 2016).

More recently, these psychological theories that attempt to explain why people do not always behave rationally, or in line with their stated intentions, have found further expression via the emergence of 'behavioural economics' and the associated 'nudge' techniques it proposes (Thaler and Sunstein, 2008; Gandy et al, 2016). This approach asserts that, in making decisions, human beings are capable of rationally reflecting upon what is in their best interests but that ultimately 'people make repeated mistakes in pursuit of their objectives' (Leggett, 2014: 5). A number of factors are highlighted to explain this fallibility. People may not possess all the relevant information, nor have the time and/or inclination to process it, and social norms can also be influential in subverting the decision-making process. Ultimately, however, Thaler and Sustein (two key proponents) believe that impulsive, 'automatic' decisions driven by the emotions that are part and parcel of the human condition may routinely prevail over what is rationally the 'right' choice (Leggett, 2014; Wright, 2016). This is where two components of Thaler and Sunstein's theory of behaviour change, that is, 'nudges' and 'choice architecture', assume importance. In simple terms, choice architecture is the 'context in which people make decisions' (2008: 5). A 'nudge':

> [i]s any aspect of the choice architecture that alters people's behavior in a predictable way without forbidding any options or significantly changing their economic incentives. To count as a mere nudge, the intervention must be easy and cheap to avoid. Nudges are not mandates. … A good system of choice architecture helps people to improve their ability to map and hence to select options that will make them better off. (Thaler and Sunstein, 2008: 6)

Nudge economics, as it is sometimes known, has been particularly successful in catching the attention of policymakers across the globe, with Thaler and Sunstein assuming high-profile roles advising the UK and US governments respectively on how the behavioural sciences might assist them in steering citizens to make better choices (Leggett, 2014; Hallsworth and Sanders, 2016; Curchin, 2019; John and Stoker, 2019). At the heart of their approach is a recognition that humans are social beings powerfully influenced by those who surround them and that, consequently, 'human behaviour is often complicated, messy and flawed' (Silva, 2017: 27). Consequently, advocates argue that policymakers should make use of behavioural economics' insights and techniques to nudge citizens into making choices in their own best interests (Gandy et al, 2016; Sanders et al, 2021).

Models of behaviour change informed by the theoretical insights of economics and psychology command contemporary policymakers' attention and dominate many governments' understandings of how policy might be used to change people's behaviour. Influenced by a preference towards methodological individualism, such theories exhibit a predilection for seeing behaviour as derived from the internal psychological processes of individual actors. Behavioural science has also been criticised for identifying the causes of irresponsible behaviour, the barriers that prevent behaviour change and the pathways to more positive behavioural outcomes firmly at the individual level, without due regard for the range of wider social conditions and contexts that are themselves subject to ongoing processes of change (Chatterton, 2016). The 'nudge' school of behavioural economics has also been roundly criticised on ethical grounds for being paternalistic, manipulative and disempowering. It has routinely been associated with neoliberalism by critics who argue that it has proved a useful tool for right-wing policymakers looking to advance individual responsibility and highly conditional, minimal welfare regimes (Leggett, 2014; Deeming, 2016; Hallsworth and Sanders, 2016; Curchin, 2017). However, as Curchin (2017) argues, this outcome is not inevitable and the insights from behavioural science into decision-making may also open up more 'progressive possibilities'. That said, as our subsequent discussion of 'carrots, sticks and sermons' makes clear, the applicability of the 'nudge' approach for making sense of behaviour change among those subject to welfare conditionality may be limited.

Understanding the agency and behaviour of social welfare recipients

Welfare conditionality is unequivocally about behaviour change. More specifically, it is consistently about changing the behaviour of those people who are reliant on means tested or targeted social welfare benefits and services. Behaviour change often becomes a priority for policymakers once particular identified behaviours are deemed to be morally reprehensible and/or a particularly significant drain on state resources (Chatterton, 2016). Unsurprisingly, given its apparent promise to tackle both 'moral' (behavioural) and 'money' (financial) issues (Dwyer, 2000), welfare conditionality has great appeal for policymakers looking for 'common sense' policy solutions to change the attitudes, choices and actions of a poor, irresponsible 'underclass' (for example, Mead, 1982). Such behavioural explanations that identify inactivity in the paid labour market (PLM), individual irresponsibility and personal failure as root causes of a poverty have a long history. These narratives are regularly recycled and reinvented by policymakers to fit particular and ideological preferences and policy ends (Bagguley and Mann, 1992; Fletcher, 2014a; Macnicol, 2017). For example, the UK Conservative/Liberal Democratic Coalition government constructed its poverty rhetoric around dysfunctional behaviour with special emphasis placed on some people making a conscious decision to 'choose' a life dependent on social welfare benefits in preference to paid employment (Pemberton et al, 2016). Such individualist and behavioural approaches enable governments to promote a populist 'politics of resentment' that presents the withdrawal of basic social rights from 'feckless' poor people and systemic welfare retrenchment as necessary, reasonable and fair (Hoggett et al, 2013).

Competing assumptions about the choices, actions and behaviour of poor people who rely on social welfare benefits and services have informed policymakers' decisions to implement highly conditional welfare interventions. Discussions on the extent to which the architects of the UK's post-Second World War welfare settlement preferred non-judgementalism and focused on the structural determinants of poverty while avoiding issues of individual behaviour remain unresolved (see Rees, 1995; Welshman, 2004). However, the absence of a full consideration of individual behaviour as a causal factor in propagating poverty among social policy scholars who identify with the social democratic tradition associated with Titmuss (1958) and T.H. Marshall (1949/1992), arguably created the space for the overtly behavioural thinking of New Right and New Communitarian critics (see Chapter One) to capture the hearts and minds of policymakers (Deacon, 2002). Consequently, welfare conditionality, 'the principle that aspects of state support, usually financial or practical, are dependent on citizens meeting certain conditions which are invariably behavioural' (DWP, 2008a: 1), has increasingly been lauded by many as an appropriate and effective way to challenge and change the behaviour of citizens within social security, social housing, homelessness and antisocial behaviour policy settings.

Literature on the decision-making and conduct of those who are subject to welfare conditionality has tended towards identifying polarised conceptualisations of social welfare benefit recipients' agency. Fletcher et al (2016) highlight how political and popular narratives often present benefit claimants as 'cynical manipulators' who work the welfare system for personal gain, either to make fraudulent applications or avoid the mandatory work search or other behavioural conditions required to retain eligibility.

Reflecting the self-interested rationales underpinning the dominant theories of behaviour discussed previously, welfare recipients are characterised as utilising their capacity for rational action to maximise personal benefit. Equipped with enough understanding of the benefit system, they weigh up potential risks and rewards in order to 'play' the system to their best advantage. In direct contrast to this, others have constructed a narrative of confusion and incompetence around individuals who often face multiple forms of structural disadvantage subsequently further compounded by sanction-backed systems of welfare conditionality. Here people are depicted as socially excluded 'vulnerable victims' who lack the capacity and resources necessary to rationally identify the actions most likely to improve their conditions.

The wider salience of this dichotomy is best illustrated by the different solutions to the welfare-dependent 'underclass' proposed by its main protagonists. Murray's (1984) solution to the 'cynical manipulators' who, he argues, rationally choose a life of benefit dependency over the independence of paid work is simple; essentially get rid of the welfare state. Removing the option of reliance on social welfare will require people to have to choose paid work to survive. Conversely, Mead's (1982) view is that many social welfare recipients are 'dutiful but defeated' by their situations, and thus likely to make certain decisions that are not in their own, or society's, best interest. To some extent, this second orientation reflects a view that some poorer citizens people may be 'vulnerable' victims of circumstance. Subsequently, Mead argues that the state is fully justified in using the paternalistic authority of welfare conditionality to compel individuals to return to the PLM. This latter perspective is especially relevant to any discussion of welfare conditionality. As Fletcher et al's (2016) analysis highlights, the hegemonic logic of welfare conditionality (as a necessary remedy to counter the cynical manipulations of a welfare dependent 'underclass' who wilfully choose irresponsibility and reliance on benefits over paid work and civility), becomes internalised, and often dominates both welfare practitioners' and welfare recipients' perspectives on the causes and solutions to poverty.

Wright (2012, 2016) and Djuve and Kavli (2015) provide further discussions on how rational economic models of human behaviour continue to dominate conceptualisations of the 'active welfare subject' (Wright, 2016) that is a central component of contemporary conditional welfare regimes. Beyond its influence among right-wing 'underclass' theorists (as already noted) these authors highlight the economic paradigm's wider significance, discussing, for example, the prominence of Le Grand's (1997, 2003) work within welfare state settings, noting that 'Le Grand arrives at a model of motivation and agency in public policy where altruistic Knights and selfish Knaves in the social services meet service users who are either autonomous Queens or passive Pawns' (Djuve and Kavli, 2015: 238).

Originally Le Grand (1997) portrayed welfare service users/benefit recipients as submissive 'Pawns' open to manipulation by the bureaucrats who implement state-provided services. Given the shift away from the provisory state to a more regulatory one, Le Grand (2003) subsequently developed his analysis and recognised the opportunities for service users to become 'Queens', that is, active consumers, exercising greater choice within the quasi-market place of public welfare provision. He characterised the actions of service providers, however, as being motivated by either the ethos of 'Knights' (public-spirited actors motivated to help others regardless of the outcome for themselves), or 'Knaves', actors interested only in furthering their own interests and gains. Both of these later ideal types can, of course, also be used to understand the various actions of welfare recipients. For example, Titmuss's (1970) study on the altruism of blood donation in the UK might lead to the characterisation of ordinary citizens who freely give blood as public spirited 'Knights'. Conversely, the 'cynical manipulators' who feature in much contemporary political and public discourse (see Fletcher et al, 2016) are often regarded as self-interested 'Knaves.

Wright's (2012) review of the conceptualisation of individual agency within social policy also highlights that another body of work has developed a more nuanced approach. This emphasises agency and behaviour as 'context specific, negotiated and differentiated in relation to identities' (Wright, 2012: 313). For example, she cites Duncan and Edwards' (1999) discussion of 'gendered moral rationalities' which contextualises decisions about the motivations underpinning women's behavioural choices in relation to prioritising and balancing informal and paid work within the context of the gendered identity of motherhood alongside the increasing pressure on lone parents to actively seek paid employment. Likewise, Harrison and Davis' (2001) discussion of 'difference within difference' emphasises how, within unequal societies, the myriad interactions of social structure and individual agency differentially play out to mediate and limit the behavioural choices and actions available to different people. Lister similarly notes that people

> [a]re actors in their own lives, but within the bounds of frequently formidable and oppressive structural and cultural constraints, which are themselves the products of others' agency. This relationship between agency and structure is pivotal to the contemporary conceptualisation of poverty as a dynamic process rather than a fixed state. (2004: 157)

Recognising that agency is neither intrinsically positive or negative, Lister (2004) develops a four way typology for understanding the actions of those living in poverty. First, 'getting by' involves people adopting complex coping strategies, which may include juggling resources, going without basic necessities, and dealing with personal trauma and/or the stigma that poverty often brings. A lack of resources and support mean that many are constrained in their capability to exercise such agency. Nonetheless, in even the most straitened circumstances, people are not mere 'pawns' but actively try to cope and manage their available resources; often looking to familial or social networks (when available) for material and emotional support. Second, for Lister, 'getting back' involves poor people engaging in practices of everyday resistance, typically through individualistic rather than collective action. Here she offers the example of those who manipulate the benefit system to maximum advantage. A third option may be 'getting out', prioritising access to a good education or paid employment as a route out of poverty; choices which may be inaccessible to individuals with multiple vulnerabilities and complex needs. Finally, 'getting organised' recognises that, in spite of the obstacles they face, some people are able to establish and maintain collective forms of self-help and also more overt political action to assert their common needs and fight for social change to address wider inequalities.

The conceptualisation of agency and subsequent discussions about how to change the behaviour of social welfare benefit recipients are, simultaneously, locations in which governments have sought to advance the regulation and disciplinary control of welfare conditionality and also a site for wider contestation about understanding and interpreting the intentions and actions of those experiencing poverty (Morris, 2020). Wright (2016) neatly encapsulates the logics underpinning the dominant prevailing model and contrasts this with a more realistic one that recognises the lived realities of people whose agency is routinely curtailed by their specific circumstances and 'oppressive policy design':

> The dominant model views the welfare subject in isolation as a unitary rational individual, personally responsible for their adverse circumstances (and for taking action to resolve them), with self-interested or moral failings that need correction via conditional, residual, punitive or quasi-market welfare reforms. On the other hand, the counter model is based on a view of the welfare subject as connected to others and influenced by shared expectations and the needs of significant others, situated within dynamic politicised power relations, with capacities for reflection and action, but subjected to 'Othering' and in need of empowerment. (Wright, 2016: 249)

The significance of discretion

Although welfare policy design and the principles that underpin it are significant (see Chapter One), how policy is interpreted and implemented by frontline 'street level bureaucrats' (SLBs) is now widely recognised as a further important dimension. Lipsky (2010 [1980]) defined SLBs as relatively low level public servants who interact directly with the public and in doing so are able to exercise substantial discretionary powers that impact directly on the lives of welfare service users. 'The ways in which street level bureaucrats deliver benefits and sanctions structure and delimit people's lives and opportunities. ... In short they hold the keys to a dimension of citizenship. ... The poorer people are, the greater the influence street level bureaucrats tend to have over them' (Lipsky, 2010 [1980]: 4, 6).

An extensive literature has developed Lipsky's (2010 [1980]) initial work to explore the processes and impacts of SLBs' discretionary judgements when administering conditional welfare-to-work interventions for unemployment benefit recipients (for example, Wright, 2003; McDonald and Marston, 2005; Brodkin and Marsden, 2013; Molander, 2016; Jordan, 2018; Kaufman, 2020). As the gatekeepers to social rights, SLBs' discretionary powers are increasingly significant in decisions to allocate or deny benefits and services to a range of groups (Fitzpatrick et al, 2019), including: people experiencing homelessness (Dobson, 2011, 2015; Bretherton et al, 2013; Alden, 2015; Dwyer et al, 2015; Bowpitt, 2020), disabled people (Meershoek, 2012; Freidli and Stearn, 2015) and migrants (Dwyer et al, 2019; Ratzmann, 2021). Discretionary judgements where a benefit adviser, Work Coach, housing officer or social worker make decisions about the most appropriate response to a particular client's situation are a crucial aspect of conditional welfare states. Many SLBs make essentially moral judgements about the 'good' or 'bad' character or behaviour of their clients when deciding on what they deem to be an appropriate response to a specific claimant's circumstances (Wright, 2003; Jordan, 2018; Kaufman, 2020). Utilising Goodin (1986), who describes discretion as the space within the policy process created by imprecisely defined rules that affords SLBs the power to exercise various options in response to clients' actions, Watts and Fitzpatrick (2018a) make the important distinction between eligibility and entitlement:

> Being eligible for benefit means that you may receive it, whereas being entitled to means you must receive it ... discretionary forms of welfare ... are not a matter of right or entitlement but are instead distributed according to bureaucratically defined standards or norms and/or the decision making of individual officials. (Watts and Fitzpatrick, 2018a: 25)

The exercise of bureaucratic discretion is not an inherently good or bad thing. Nor should it be seen simply as the indiscriminate exercise of personal bias. Discretion can be defended on the grounds that it ensures the flexibility required to adapt policies to best meet the different needs and circumstances of diverse welfare service users (WSUs). Conversely, critics highlight how its arbitrary application may result in negative and counterproductive outcomes.

Regardless of its pros and cons, precisely because welfare conditionality is about linking people's eligibility to social welfare to compulsory patterns of behaviour and involves SLBs monitoring the actions of individual claimants and responding to non-compliance by recommending various sanctions, the consolidation and expansion of conditionality is likely to promote the more extensive use of discretion within welfare systems (Molander, 2016). Evidence from the UK (see, for example, Chapter Two discussions on Work Coaches' enhanced role in respect of 'easements' and the 'black box' approach within the Work Programme [WP]), supports this view. Welfare conditionality is very much concerned with curbing irresponsible behaviour or 'bad agency' of passive reliance on social welfare benefits, while also promoting 'good agency' such as actively searching for, and engaging in, paid work (Dean, 2007). Developing Dean's analysis, Djuve and Kalvi (2015) note the power imbalance in the relationship between the welfare bureaucrat and the service user central to conditional welfare interventions. It is the service provider (SLB) who routinely judges the actions of the WSU as good, bad or indifferent, and responds accordingly. In doing so they draw on the structured policy environment they are operating within, that is, the prevailing broad, ideological and financial milieu. Within contemporary welfare states this is a setting in which behavioural governance and the responsibilisation of individual claimants combine with austerity measures (Peeters, 2013). Additionally, SLBs must work within the specific rules and regulations of a particular policy that govern the discretionary options available to them. Guided by these structures they are, nonetheless, able to also exercise varying levels of judgement about the most appropriate response to a client's behaviour. How they choose to exercise their discretionary powers often depends on how they define their role. Do they see themselves as '*Clerks*', system orientated bureaucrats 'who maintain a professional distance and relies on rules and regulations to guide them in their interactions with users', or '*Carers*', SLBs orientated more towards support rather than sanction, 'whose loyalty lies with the service user ... and the need to adapt services to each individual participant' (Djuve and Kalvi, 2015: 240–1)? Either way, SLBs are at least afforded some measure of autonomy and choice when reaching the discretionary decisions that affect the lives of their clients; a privilege that is commonly denied to WSUs who are the focus of highly conditional welfare interventions. The inbuilt compulsion of welfare conditionality routinely negates rather than enhances the agency of poor people.

The tools of behaviour change: carrots, sticks, sermons and nudges?

Governments draw on a range of policy techniques and instruments to garner support for their policies and/or achieve social change. Bemelmans-Videc et al (1998) offer a framework for understanding the various tools available to governments. Defining policy instruments as 'concrete and specified operational forms of intervention by public authorities' (Bemelmans-Videc, 1998: 3) they note that successful policy programmes often utilise a mix of tools with policymakers influenced in their choices by several factors. These include prevailing political values, ideas and administrative cultures, available evidence on effectiveness and efficiency, and differing stances on an instrument's legitimacy in respect of the accepted laws and norms that govern the state–citizen relationship within different nations. Operating along a continuum ranging from 'freedom to control' (Vedung, 1998), governments may opt for cautious/minimal intervention in some settings, with more assertive/intrusive options preferred elsewhere. Interventions are regularly introduced by governments with the aim of reducing, reforming or eradicating undesirable, irresponsible behaviour or, conversely, promoting and rewarding preferred forms of conduct (Bemelmans-Videc, 1998). Arguably, policymakers generally prefer to use instruments that are least likely to interfere in the autonomy of citizens if possible (Linder and Peters, 1989). However, that is certainly not the case within highly conditional welfare systems where mandatory citizen engagement, backed up by the coercive threat of sanction for non-compliance, are well established tools (Whitworth, 2016).

Bemelmans-Videc et al (1998) propose a tripartite typology of stick–carrot–sermon as the policy tools used by governments to achieve behaviour change. The first, the 'stick', has the longest history and is associated with governments' authoritative regulation of citizens' behaviour, 'meaning that the controlled persons or groups are obligated to act in the way stated by the controller' (Bemelmans-Videc, 1998: 10). The second, the 'carrot', is about incentivising (motivating or encouraging a person to act in a specified way), by offering or withdrawing a '[c]onditional transfer of funds [an economic subsidy] by government to (or for the benefit of) another party for the purpose of influencing that party's behavior with a view to achieving some level of activity or provision' (Leeuw, 1998: 77).

Finally, 'the sermon' refers to governments seeking to influence people's behaviour through the delivery of information, widely defined to include: multimedia public communication campaigns, education, counselling, training programmes and personalised advice, in order to tell people how they should behave and also what they can and cannot do (Vedung and van der Doelen, 1998).

The relevance of this stick–carrot–sermon typology for understanding governments' attempts to instrumentally intervene in social welfare recipients' lives and change their behaviour is clear, but where does behavioural economics and its associated 'nudge' techniques fit in with the discussion of welfare conditionality and behaviour change? Some authors have understood the advance of welfare conditionality and the behaviour change mechanisms that underpin it in terms of 'nudging' people towards making the 'right' decisions (see, for example, Standing, 2011; Peeters, 2013; Johnson-Schlee, 2019). These authors are right to argue that behavioural economics is premised on the paternalistic belief that people need to be steered towards making 'good' choices because they are seen to be incapable of making decisions in their own best interests. However, it is erroneous to equate this directly with welfare interventions implemented via the more blunt and brutal twin policy instruments of mandatory engagement and sanction that are the central components of welfare conditionality regimes. First, as noted previously, Thaler and Sunstein (2008) are unequivocal that 'nudges are not mandates' and clearly state that 'to count as a mere nudge, the intervention must be easy and cheap to avoid' (2008: 6) and cannot prohibit or substantially change an individual's economic incentives or options. Removing the income required to meet a claimant's basic needs through the application of a benefit sanction, for example, undoubtedly contravenes these requirements. On a more mundane level it is absurd to argue that you are 'gently persuading' someone towards making the 'right' decision to mandatorily search for work by threatening them with 100 per cent loss of income for four weeks for relatively minor acts of non-compliance, as is the case in the UK. Not so much a 'nudge', more an unambiguous whack with a big stick!

Nudging aside, behavioural economics is compatible with the contemporary political culture that has generated and sustains welfare conditionality; one that asserts strong moral and financial grounds for increasing individual rather than collective responsibility for welfare. Advocates believe that the insights and tools of behavioural science can be used to enhance personal responsibility, change public behaviour, boost the efficacy of government policy and help alleviate poverty in cost-effective ways (Halpern et al, 2004; Gandy et al, 2016). Others remain more sceptical about the potential of behavioural science, built largely around economic and psychological models, to adequately theorise, understand and engender positive behaviour change. Critics point to an over-reliance on randomised control trials, an inadequate evidence base to support its claims, and argue that contemporary behavioural science entrenches a mechanistic and inadequate view of behaviour change within policy (Hallsworth and Sanders, 2016; Spotswood and Marsh, 2016). To support this last point, we refer readers to the diagram, 'Theory of change underpinning improved labour market outcomes' (DWP, 2016: 11). Here Stern's (2000) psychologically informed 'ABC' approach for theorising environmentally significant behaviour has been used to construct a theory of (behaviour) change model to evaluate the effectiveness of Universal Credit (UC). This model is mechanistic, linear and unidirectional and, as such, fails to capture many of the behavioural and other outcomes that are a significant part of the lived reality for those subject to highly conditional welfare interventions such as UC. Empirical analysis of the qualitative data generated by the WelCond study that informs Chapters Four to Eight of this book highlights a number of impacts that these more mechanistic models of behaviour change miss. Before presenting our own analysis, the next task is to offer an overview of existing evidence on the effectiveness of welfare conditionality in triggering and sustaining behaviour change.

The effectiveness of welfare conditionality?

The assertion that highly conditional social security systems, backed by benefit sanctions for non-compliance, are effective in triggering movements off social welfare benefits into sustained employment is open to challenge. Research in the Netherlands (Abbring et al, 2005) found that those who had experienced a benefit sanction were more likely to enter paid work. In a similar vein, two studies, one in Switzerland (Lalive et al, 2005), and one in Germany (Boockmann et al, 2014), also reported that when sanctions are applied more strictly, re-employment rates are likely to be higher than in locations with more lenient regimes. However, other international evidence points to sanction-backed systems of welfare conditionality having limited positive effects in relation to moving people off welfare benefits and into paid employment. For example, a study found that the introduction of sanctions had little impact on individuals exiting from the TANF social assistance scheme in Wisconsin, US (Wu et al, 2014). Others have found the application of a benefit sanction is likely to result in individuals being out of work for longer periods and more likely to enter more insecure, less well-paid work moving forward (Arni et al, 2013; Fording et al, 2013). Two international evidence reviews funded by the Joseph Rowntree Foundation point to similar outcomes. Griggs and Evans (2010) highlighted some evidence that sanctions applied to recipients of unemployment benefits were likely to raise unemployment benefit exit rates and job entry levels in the short term, but also noted a 'gulf' between policymakers' rhetoric and actual evidence on the effectiveness of sanctions in leading to sustained employment and behaviour change. A more recent review reiterated these findings and also argued that overall, the international evidence pointed to unfavourable longer-term impacts for individuals' 'earnings, job quality and employment retention' prospects when benefit sanctions were applied (Watts et al, 2014).

A body of UK evidence questions the effectiveness welfare conditionality in moving social welfare benefit recipients into employment. Loopstra et al's (2015) analysis of data from 375 local authorities between 2005 and 2014 concluded that although the enhanced use of benefit sanctions led to a corresponding 'substantial increase' in exit from Jobseeker's Allowance (JSA), the majority of those who left unemployment benefit did not enter paid work. Rather the threat and use of sanctions served to distance people, especially those dealing with multiple vulnerabilities, from collective social security provision (see also, Crisp and Fletcher, 2008; Dwyer and Bright, 2016). A National Audit Office (NAO, 2016) report similarly challenges the behaviour change logic asserted in support of conditionality within social security systems. First, it noted that although JSA sanctions had a large effect on in moving claimants off benefit, such individuals were just as likely to remain unemployed as they were to find paid work. Additionally, when sanctions were applied to Employment and Support Allowance (ESA) recipients they actually reduced claimants' likelihood of finding future employment. Second, it stated that the application of benefit sanctions had no positive effect on subsequent earnings. Third, those WP providers who referred the most people for a benefit sanction for non-compliance also had the worst employment outcome results. The key conclusion drawn was that the Department for Work and Pensions' (DWP) endorsement and increased use of sanctions-backed conditionality was linked 'as much to management priorities and local staff discretion as it is to [changing] claimants' behaviour' (NAO, 2016: 9). A Public Accounts Committee (PAC, 2017) report was less critical in its tone and more ambiguous in its findings, stating that although members accepted that benefit sanctions often triggered very negative outcomes for many people (see Chapter Six for full discussions) and may push some further away from work, they also believed others would be prompted to seek paid employment as a consequence of their application.

As welfare conditionality has been extended to cover a wider range of benefit claimants beyond those in receipt of unemployment benefit, studies have consistently highlighted that its use within long-term incapacity benefit systems is both inappropriate and ineffective (for example, Hale, 2014; Oakley, 2016; Dwyer et al, 2020). Over a decade ago, a review of the (now closed) Pathways to Work programme found that the use of sanctions for non-attendance at a work-focused interview (WFI) was deeply resented by disabled people and did little to change individuals' perceptions about their readiness and ability to work (Weston, 2012). The Work and Pensions Committee also stated that ESA was failing in its primary purpose of helping those disabled people who could work in the short/medium term back into employment and called for a fundamental redesign of the system (WPC, 2014). Subsequently, the same committee concluded there was limited evidence that benefit sanctions were effective in moving ESA claimants closer to paid work (WPC, 2015). Analysis of aggregate data suggests that the evidence that sanctioning disabled people may lead to increased employment rates is weak and that conversely there is strong evidence to suggest that it increases economic inactivity among disabled benefit claimants and pushes them further way from employment (Reeves, 2017).

Although the UK government has committed to halving the disability employment gap (DWP and DoH, 2016), further evidence suggests that the use of welfare conditionality to help achieve this aim is both extremely unpopular among disabled people and fails to deliver. Benefit off flow rates are reported to be 'incredibly low' with only 8 per cent of 'workless' people with a work-limiting health condition or disability moving into work annually (Oakley, 2016: 44). Additionally, over a two-year period the WP moved only 5 per cent of disabled people from the Work Related Activity Group (WRAG) into paid employment (against a performance target of 16.5 per cent) and a survey of 500 WRAG members concluded: 'The experience of participation into the WRAG is neither personalised nor supportive. … The regime of conditionality has left participants in the WRAG fearful, demoralised and further away from achieving their work related goals or participating in society than when they started' (Hale, 2014: 5).

Hale further notes that a DWP-funded evaluation of the WP concluded that the use of conditionality and sanctions within ESA do not work to move people into employment (see Newton et al, 2013). Similarly, the evaluation of a mandatory 'More Intensive Support' trial for WRAG members who had previously completed the WP but not found employment, triggered only a very 'marginal improvement' in benefit outcomes (that is, an additional 3.2 days off benefit in the subsequent year) (Moran, 2017). Other evidence on ESA is similarly damming. Barr et al (2016a) found that the Work Capability Assessment (WCA), integral to ESA, is independently associated within increased suicides, self-reported mental health problems and anti-depressant prescribing. Further they found no evidence that the reassessment of ESA claimants' capacities within WCAs helped increase disabled peoples' entry into paid employment. Conversely, it may have prompted adverse outcomes by moving those with mental health impairments onto the JSA regime, where they 'receive insufficient support and are subject to a punitive sanctioning policy which has severe consequences for their health and risk of poverty' (Barr et al, 2016b: 457).

UK lone parents are also increasingly subject to welfare conditionality. Across the last three decades, single parents of ever younger children have become subject to mandatory WFIs, work search and training requirements (Dwyer, 2004; Wright, 2011a; Whitworth and Griggs, 2013; Johnsen, 2014; Millar, 2019). An international review (conducted for the DWP) reported that although increasing work-related requirements for lone parents may promote short-term job entry, significant numbers return to the benefit system quite quickly (Finn and Gloster, 2010). Haux (2011) further suggests that UK governments' attempts to activate lone parents into paid work are unlikely to succeed due to the additional barriers and multiple disadvantages many lone parents face. Conditionality, and the overtly individualistic and behavioural drivers underpinning it, that prioritise forcing lone parents into employment rather than assisting them to address the personal and structural barriers that prevent them from working, is identified as a key reason why compulsory welfare-to-work measures are likely to be ineffective for this group (Whitworth and Griggs, 2013).

Despite evidence to the contrary, the DWP has long asserted that a host of international and UK based research offers clear, consistent data that conditionality and sanctions in welfare-to-work programmes have a positive effect on benefit exit rates (Griggs and Bennett, 2009). It is, therefore, perhaps not too surprising to see welfare conditionality fully embedded into UC. Originally designed with the intentions of smoothing out transitions between paid work and welfare and 'making work pay', research on the effectiveness of UC and whether or not it enhances claimants' entry into and, progression within, the PLM is still relatively scarce. A DWP-commissioned study reports broadly positive changes to UC claimants' behaviour with conditionality highlighted as the 'strongest driver of behaviour change'. Changes included people spending more time on job search activities, taking up jobs that claimants would have previously dismissed and increases in 'hours and earning' progression (that is, seeking and, on occasion, taking on extra hours or jobs) among part-time employed, in-work UC claimants. However, these positive effects were reduced among claimants with disabilities and others facing personal issues and/or lacking knowledge of how UC operates. Significantly, further emphasising the importance of how SLBs interpret and implement policy in their face-to-face interactions with clients, the report states that '[c]laimants were motivated by a supportive and encouraging approach from Work Coaches compared to a policing or monitoring role, which fostered less productive job search' (Rahim et al, 2017: 15).

The DWP also commissioned a randomised control trial to test the effectiveness of how varying combinations of support and conditionality might impact on in-work UC claimants' progression in the PLM over a 15-month period. Claimants were assigned to one of three groups with differing levels of compulsion and/or support attached. Interestingly, across the two waves of the survey, the overall employment rate of the respondents decreased by 6 per cent to 82 per cent and, regardless of assigned group, the report failed to find any statistically significant impact on self-reported earnings (Langdon et al, 2018).

Furthermore, initial analysis of data that informs this book found that the behaviour change logic underpinning UC conditionality was seriously undermined in cases where sanctions were applied because of administrative errors and IT system inadequacies, when claimants had good cause (for example, for being late or missing appointments) and when heavy penalties were incurred for very minor infringements by compliant claimants who were keen to work or already engaged in poorly paid employment. This last point is significant because UC introduced in-work conditionality for the first time, with full sanctions for non-compliance applicable to low-paid workers in receipt of in-work supplements such as tax credits and Housing Benefit (Wright et al, 2016). More critically it has been argued that in-work conditionality within UC has broadened the definition of dysfunctional welfare dependency to include low-paid workers and cemented a 'coerced worker claimant' model at the heart of UK benefit policy; a model that fails to meet the social security needs of claimants, the requirements of employers or deliver the ill-defined notion of 'in-work progression' (Wright and Dwyer, 2022).

The effectiveness of welfare conditionality in tackling antisocial behaviour

Beyond its use as a tool for moving people off welfare and into work, welfare conditionality is also seen as a potential solution for controlling and curbing the problematic and antisocial behaviour (ASB) of social housing tenants and marginalised citizens such as people experiencing homelessness, individuals with a history of interacting with the criminal justice system and 'problem' families (see Chapter Two). Qualitative research into the impacts of conditionality on these groups has regularly highlighted how the use of compulsion and sanctions are often ineffective in reducing ASB and push vulnerable people further away from the PLM and collectivised support systems, leading instead to increased alienation and engagement in counterproductive outcomes such as destitution and survival crime (Fletcher and Flint, 2018; Veasey and Parker, 2021). For example, the significance of providing long-term support, rather than sanction, has been highlighted as vital in helping ex-offenders change their behaviour and desist from criminal activity (Batty, 2020). However, although it is widely recognised that sanction-backed conditionality may lead to profoundly negative consequences (see Chapter Six), the potential for conditional interventions, when they include appropriate support, to promote more inclusive outcomes among marginalised populations has been noted (Flint, 2009b; Watts et al, 2014). Allied to this is a firm recognition that structural inequalities will have to be addressed, by the provision of enhanced economic and practical support for marginalised populations and communities, if problematic behaviour is to be effectively tackled (Rodger, 2008b; Flint, 2009b).

Variations in the 'modes of social control' available to homelessness service providers remain within UK policy (Johnsen et al, 2018a). Evidence suggests that benefit sanctions can act to trigger homelessness and push people away from the PLM. Additionally, much of the mandatory support on offer appears to be of limited use in helping many people experiencing homelessness to overcome the substantial barriers they face when looking for paid work (Batty et al, 2015; Reeve, 2017). However, some research suggests that, again, when accompanied by appropriate support, enforcement type measures may lead to beneficial outcomes for some homeless individuals living in desperate, and sometimes life-threatening, circumstances (Fitzpatrick and Johnsen, 2009; Johnsen and Fitzpatrick, 2010). Conversely, welfare conditionality potentially enables a disciplinarian turn in contemporary homelessness policy that seeks to 'punish perceived irresponsibility either by abandoning homeless people to the fate they "deserve", or by demanding they "get with the programme"' (Dwyer et al, 2015: 17) in order to access services. Welfare conditionality in turn may also stimulate a shift in the role of outreach workers who become increasingly involved in 'exclusion management' and controlling access to support services rather than ensuring entry to them (Grymonprez et al, 2020). This may hinder rather than facilitate positive change among some members of highly marginalised populations (Johnsen and Fitzpatrick, 2007; Bowpitt et al, 2014).

In two further policy areas the efficacy of welfare conditionality as a behaviour change tool remains contested. First, research on fixed-term tenancies (FTTs) in England reveals divergent views among social landlords about their value as a tool for encouraging responsible behaviour among tenants and notes that non-renewals of FTTs rarely occur. Tenants also have varying degrees of knowledge about their tenancy agreement with many either unaware or unconcerned about being housed under an FTT. For others, the onset of a FTT can trigger a palpable sense of anxiety about their future housing security (Fitzpatrick and Watts, 2017; Watts and Fitzpatrick, 2018b). Second, within the sphere of family intervention policy, the UK Coalition government initially trumpeted spectacular success for their Troubled Families Programme (TFP) claiming to have 'turned around' the lives of 99 per cent of the targeted families (DCLG, 2015). Later iterations of the programme also reported highly positive outcomes, alongside substantial savings to the public purse. However, others have been more sceptical of the government's highly optimistic, overstated claims about the effectiveness of the TFP (Crossley, 2015; Portes, 2015; PAC, 2016; Hoggett and Frost, 2018; see Loft, 2020 for further details). A more recent official evaluation of the TFP (2015–20) somewhat modestly points to only 'encouraging' evidence on improved outcomes and cites relatively small scale, 'realistic', improvements in the numbers of children in public care and reductions in convictions, imprisonment and claims for JSA as indicative of the effectiveness of its flagship family intervention policy (MHCLG, 2019). It is often very difficult to identify and measure the effectiveness of interventions such as family intervention policies due to the myriad outcomes that may ensue, some of which fail to match the headline indicators of transformative positive behaviour change (for example, entry into the PLM and/or the cessation of ASB) that policymakers highlight as evidence of successful policy outcomes. Nonetheless, research has noted the potential for frontline family intervention workers to positively engage with marginalised families to improve the quality of their lives and those around them (Batty and Flint, 2012; Parr, 2017).

Despite talk of 'evidence-based policy' and ongoing debate about the effectiveness, or otherwise, of welfare conditionality in changing behaviour, evidence is not the only factor influencing policymakers' decisions to introduce conduct-related eligibility criteria within the provision of welfare. Short-term political expediency, as policymakers cater to public opinion or compete to avoid negative media headlines, may trump evidence and the dominant ideological principles and normative preferences of politicians are also often powerful drivers in decisions to implement more intrusive interventions into citizens' lives (Linder and Peters, 1989; Deeming, 2016; Hallsworth and Sanders, 2016; Maryon-Davis, 2016). Interventions by the state operate on a continuum ranging from doing nothing (that is, endorsing a libertarian, laissez faire approach that does not interfere with individual autonomy), to behavioural regulation and ultimately direct compulsion (Maryon-Davis, 2016). Tellingly, a review of international evidence on welfare conditionality within social security systems noted that '[p]olicymakers continue to justify the extension of sanctions (and sanction-backed conditionality), on moral philosophy grounds whilst taking an ambivalent attitude to evidence' (Griggs and Evans, 2010: 4).

Conclusions

Much thinking on behaviour change within public and social policy has drawn on the insights of the disciplines of economics and psychology. Subsequently, policymakers have tended to endorse essentially individualised models of behaviour change built on the assumptions that people will rationally respond to the various carrots, sticks, sermons or nudges applied to them and alter their behaviour in prescribed and particular ways. The use and extension of welfare conditionality has been defended by its advocates on the grounds that through the implementation of various combinations of 'carrots' (mandatory support) and 'sticks' (sanctions) people living in poverty will be variously encouraged, cajoled or compelled into moving off welfare and into paid work and/or change their errant behaviour. More recent insights from those working within social and public policy have highlighted the ways in which social factors and inequalities limit and structure the agency and behaviour of disadvantaged people as they respond to, and live with, increasingly conditional welfare systems. Scholarship within social policy has also been at the forefront of highlighting the importance of the discretionary judgements of SLBs in shaping the agency of WSUs in frontline interactions with claimants. Due to the DWP's refusal to enable the WelCond research team access to those involved in the face-to-face implementation of welfare conditionality within Jobcentre Plus and WP settings, we are unable to offer insights from the perspective of SLBs themselves in this book. Nonetheless, reflections are possible on how discretion impacted on the behaviour of WSUs and this informs the empirical discussions in subsequent chapters.

The evidence review on the effectiveness of welfare conditionality offered in this chapter highlights contrasting opinions on the efficacy of welfare conditionality in triggering and sustaining the types of behaviour change claimed by its advocates. However, as previously discussed, evidence is not the only factor relevant to the introduction and expansion of a particular policy approach. Policies often 'survive and thrive not because of their intrinsic merits but because they "fit" with existing priorities and interests' (Spotswood and Marsh, 2016: 293). This has certainly been the case with welfare conditionality where many policymakers and advocates have been keen to assert a range of justifications, which draw on competing ethical frameworks (see Chapter Seven), when arguing for the continuation, expansion and intensification of conduct-based welfare conditionality, despite a growing body of evidence from adversaries of its limitations and harms. As Curchin (2017) notes, affording a central role to behavioural scientists for providing the scientific expertise for understanding poverty and the behavioural decisions that poor citizens make has certain consequences in respect of the methods used and types of evidence generated to support claims about how welfare conditionality works (compare Spotswood and Marsh, 2016). On one level this book, and the qualitative longitudinal methods, case studies and data it draws upon to build its arguments in forthcoming chapters, attempts to offer an alternative, dynamic and empirically informed understanding of how welfare conditionality actually works and the kinds of behavioural changes it engenders; an understanding that gives voice to the experience and expertise of those who are routinely subject to highly conditional welfare interventions. That said, it is interesting that even those fully committed in asserting the positive potential of behavioural science for informing welfare policy interventions have found that the 'cognitive load' that welfare conditionality places on people living in poverty is highly likely to be a factor in, to use their language, the 'sub-optimal decision-making' of benefit claimants (Gandy et al, 2016). This is in many ways recognition that the core structural components (or 'choice architecture' if you like) underpinning welfare conditionality (that is, compulsion, mandatory engagement and sanctions for non-compliance) can get in the way of people making the 'right' behavioural choices and may make things worse, not better.

FOUR

From welfare to work? The effectiveness of welfare conditionality in moving people into paid employment

A regularly repeated justification of welfare conditionality within social security systems is the claim that it is effective in moving people off social welfare benefits and into paid employment. Within the UK, the advent of 'in-work' conditionality within Universal Credit (UC), has further seen mandatory work search activity and benefit sanctions identified as appropriate tools for enhancing 'progression' within the paid labour market (PLM) and simultaneously reducing low-paid workers' reliance on rent and wage subsidies via paid welfare and taxation systems (see Chapters Two and Three; Jones et al, 2019; Wright and Dwyer, 2022). Drawing on analysis of the qualitative longitudinal data generated by WelCond this chapter explores these claims. The first part of the chapter maps and highlights the differing work and welfare related trajectories and outcomes that ensued for the welfare service users (WSUs) who took part in repeat longitudinal interviews. However, the numerical mapping and typology offered facilitates only a partial and incomplete view of the ways that highly conditional social security systems impact on peoples' pathways into, and out of, paid work. As Millar (2007: 537) notes, 'quantitative data can map out trajectories … qualitative data can provide an understanding of what lies behind these'. Subsequent sections of the chapter, therefore, draw upon in-depth individual longitudinal case studies, presenting analysis that enables a more nuanced understanding of how, and why, welfare conditionality structures diverse work-related outcomes for different people, over time. On one level the individual case histories offered are illustrative of the wider patterns noted in the first part of the chapter. However, the detail and depth of these 'condensed accounts' enables a shift from 'an illustrative case study towards the idea of an exploratory case history … [to] capture the essence of the interplay between agency and ecology, the particular and the general' (Thomson, 2007: 57, 58).

As such they facilitate a deep and grounded understanding of the efficacy (or otherwise) of welfare conditionality in promoting and sustaining paid employment among social welfare benefit recipients. The second part of the chapter explores how and why key components of welfare conditionality (that is, benefit sanctions, the imposition of mandatory support and their discretionary implementation) variously triggered, inhibited, enhanced and/ or sustained people's movements off welfare and into work and vice versa. The third part of the chapter highlights how the extension of behavioural requirements under threat of benefit sanctions combine with issues related to impairment, gender and ethnicity. Discussions highlight the ineffectiveness of welfare conditionality in promoting paid employment over time among the diverse groups of WSUs (including some with multiple and complex needs), interviewed. The next part then considers how low-paid workers experienced the UC regime and asks whether or not 'in-work' conditionality impeded or facilitated progression within the PLM.

Diverse trajectories: stasis, recycling and pathways into and out of work

Our aim was to conduct repeat interviews with WSUs on up to three occasions across a two-year period, revisiting each respondent at approximately 12-month intervals. Having initially interviewed 481 people at wave a, we were able to complete 339 repeat interviews with the same respondents at wave b and subsequently undertake a further 262 wave c interviews in the final part of the fieldwork. The three waves of interviews were completed between 2014 to 2017 (see methods appendix for fuller discussions). Utilising a combination of framework analysis in NVivo, in-depth reading of the transcripts generated at each wave and the construction of a work–welfare movement summary table in Excel, it was possible to map and explore the different employment trajectories of the 339 WSUs interviewed on two or more occasions. Figure 4.1 offers a numerical presentation of the types of change in employment status (or lack thereof) that occurred for the individuals who took part in the study. This chart clearly illustrates that across the timeframe of the repeat interviews, *stasis*, that is, an absence of significant and sustained change in employment status, was the most common outcome for the substantial majority of WSUs.

The majority of WSUs (that is, 137 out of 240 people) within the stasis group were subject to welfare conditionality and the lack of change in their employment status over time equated to being out of work at wave a and remaining outside paid employment at each subsequent interview they took part in. Further analysis of the stasis group also revealed that an additional 75 WSUs were not subject to work search requirements or welfare conditionality. The vast majority of these 75 people were allocated to, and remained in, the 'Support Group' of Employment Support Allowance (ESA) across the study. A further small number of people were lone parents with infant children, full-time carers for disabled people or individuals who for reasons that could not be clearly ascertained were also not compulsorily required to seek work to retain eligibility to their benefit.[1] The inertia of these

Figure 4.1: Employment trajectories of 339 welfare service users interviewed two or three times over a two-year period

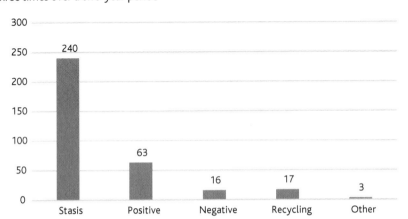

WSUs could perhaps be read as indicative of an appropriately functioning social security system in which disabled benefit recipients (and certain exempted others as noted) are not required to actively seek, or prepare for, paid employment as a condition of continued benefit receipt. However, this assumption is out of kilter with the experiences of large numbers of disabled respondents, who following a Work Capability Assessment (WCA), were initially found fit for work or work-related activity, and subject to varying degrees of sanction-backed conditionality; despite having long-term mental and/or physical impairments. Many of these respondents also spent considerable time and energy challenging (with varying degrees of success), the outcome of initial WCAs and/or reapplying for ESA often with the support of their doctors as episodic illnesses 'flared up' or new impairments arose (Dwyer et al, 2020). Finally, a further 28 respondents included in the stasis group reported maintaining the same employment status across each wave of repeat interview. Paid employment here ranged from working permitted part-time hours while in receipt of certain benefits, to full-time employment for a minority of respondents. This form of stasis, a lack of change in WSUs' type and level of employment, potentially may be interpreted as positive, rather than negative, as these individuals reported retaining their paid employment status at each repeat interview. However, among these 28 respondents, substantive 'progression' within the PLM, as envisaged in the Department for Work and Pensions' (DWP) theory of change for improved labour market outcomes (see, for example, DWP, 2016: 11), was almost entirely absent.

Beyond stasis, consideration of the employment statuses reported by a further 63 people who took part in repeat interviews warranted a broadly *positive* interpretation of their work trajectories over time. The overwhelming majority of this group were unemployed at their wave a interview and had subsequently entered paid employment and/or reported maintaining or further improving their working hours at wave b or wave c interviews. However, this should not be interpreted as indicative of the unequivocal success of welfare conditionality in triggering and sustaining movements off benefits and into full-time employment. Within this group, an analysis of the employment status achieved by each individual shows that 27 people achieved full-time employment, 13 part-time work, eight working variable hours and five becoming self-employed; with the remainder variously employed on short hours.[2] A smaller number (16) who took part in the repeat interviews had *negative* employment trajectories. Two of this group managed to retain some form of paid employment but both were undertaking fewer hours while the rest were in some form of paid employment at wave a but out of work at subsequent interviews.

A similar small number of respondents (17) reported fluctuating employment experiences at their repeat interviews. They outlined oscillating work–welfare trajectories, whereby periods of work gave way to unemployment, followed by a subsequent short-term/temporary return to some form of paid work, succeeded by another period of benefit claim. Repeat work–welfare *recycling* is a common feature in the lives of many benefit recipients who find themselves at the sharp end of an increasingly flexible PLM (McCollum, 2012). Beyond the small number of respondents allocated to the recycling category, oscillating work–welfare trajectories had a more general resonance across the wider sample of WSUs interviewed. Further analysis of respondents' data, where individuals reported on changes that had occurred between interview waves and/or reflected on the realities that characterised their working lives in the longer term, indicated that recurrent, short-term movements between various insecure jobs, interspersed with periods of unemployment, were routine and typical experiences for many. As McCollum (2012) notes, for a variety of reasons, sustained transitions off welfare and into long-term employment among disadvantaged groups are rare, with subsequent trajectories of advancement, or progression, within the labour market even more uncommon; a reality that flies in the face of the rhetoric that is often favoured by welfare conditionality's most fervent advocates. Such sustained movements off welfare benefits and into work were only exceptionally evidenced within the WelCond study and, as the data and discussions presented in this chapter indicate, instances where either benefit sanctions or mandatory support played an identifiable role in triggering such movements were atypical and extremely rare.

In concluding this section, it is important to recognise that WelCond was a qualitative longitudinal study that utilised a purposive sampling strategy to recruit people who were subject to welfare conditionality in various settings. The numbers set out in preceding discussions are in no way statistically representative of the wider population of those in receipt of UK out of work social security benefits. That said, Figure 4.1 and its accompanying narrative offers a stark illustration of the limited extent to which movements off welfare and into work occurred for the majority of the WSUs who took part in the study. A deeper understanding of how and why, over time, welfare conditionality facilitated or inhibited such movements is enabled by the qualitative longitudinal case histories and discussed in this chapter.

The impact of welfare conditionality on work/welfare trajectories: sanctions, support and discretion

The DWP remains committed to the use of sanctions as an effective and necessary element of welfare conditionality on the grounds that they 'motivate claimants to engage with support on offer to look actively for work and thereby to move into work' (DWP, 2018b: 1). As noted in Chapter Three, evidence on the effectiveness of benefit sanctions in coaxing or coercing benefit claimants into paid employment is, at best, mixed. Analysis of the data from across the WSU sample clearly evidenced that the threat and application of benefit sanctions do little to enhance individuals' motivation to prepare for, seek or enter paid work. Rather than moving people off welfare and into paid work, sanctions routinely trigger a range of often profoundly negative personal, financial, health and employment outcomes (see Chapter Six for fuller discussions). For some, the implementation of welfare conditionality, and sanctions in particular, worked to push people further away from the possibility of future employment and caused severe hardship and, on occasions, even destitution, as Harry's case demonstrates.

Case 1: Harry: repeat sanctions, disengagement and destitution

Harry is in his 40s and has depression. He last worked in the manual sector a decade ago. Previously in receipt of Incapacity Benefit, following a WCA he was found fit for work and moved onto Jobseeker's Allowance (JSA). At our initial wave a interview, with his doctor's support, he was attempting to reapply for ESA while rough sleeping after the application of a benefit sanction led to rent arrears and ultimately eviction. Informed by Jobcentre Plus that he did not qualify for hardship payments, Harry had not received any social security benefits for several months due to the application of a six-month benefit sanction.

> '[I'm] living on the street ... then they decided I wasn't sick or whatever so they took me off Income Support, put me on Jobseeker's. Then that all went wrong and I got sanctioned and then I got made homeless. ... I couldn't pay the rent

because I was sanctioned ... you can actually claim Housing Benefit without Jobseeker's, but then no one tells you that. So then my rent ended up backing up and because my head was all over the place I just couldn't deal with it. ... They made me go to a Work Programme [WP]. ... You go in, they give you a nice sales pitch about all the wonderful things they're going to do and then say "Right, off you go, find a job" and that's it basically it. ... I got sanctioned because I missed appointments with them.' (Wave a)

Told that if he returned to attend the WP then the sanction might be lifted he attempted to re-engage with the WP, but again missed some appointments because of other pressing priorities. "[I] lost interest then because you've got no money and I have to spend most of my time running around trying to find something to eat." Harry was clear that:

'Sanctions only hurt. There's no good in them. I know they might wheel the odd person on the BBC and say "Look this man if it wasn't for sanctions", but the reality is no they're just harmful, they just hurt. And support, are we talking governmental support? ... Like I say the only real support is charity.' (Wave a)

Unable to find Harry after 12 months, we managed to track him down two years later for a second (wave b) interview. In the interim period, following a further benefit sanction he had lost another tenancy and was again rough sleeping. Subject to repeat and escalating benefit sanctions Harry had completely disengaged from the social security system to avoid the stresses that sanctions and welfare conditionality triggered which, in turn, exacerbated his depression.

'I just can't be arsed with the stress for £70 a week. It's just not worth it. Every time you go in, you're on hooks, like, what's going to happen now? ... Then they send you on stupid courses. ... I don't claim benefits at the moment. I just don't want to know. Too much of a headache. You know, you never know from one week to the next whether you're getting paid and it's just proper stress ... it's pointless. "Do it. If you don't, you're sanctioned." It's nuts! The only thing it has done is make it more difficult basically. They say, like, it encourages people to go to look for work. No, it doesn't.' (Wave b)

At wave b, Harry was destitute and reliant on charitable provision for food and peace of mind.

'I can be quite lucky sometimes. ... I get my breakfast at [Charity]. I work here all day and lunch here. Evenings, there's different places dotted about where you can get something to eat. ... The only place you get any kind of help are charities. Everywhere else is a waste of time. ... [Doing voluntary work] it's just helping my state of mind really more than anything.' (Wave b)

On one level, Harry's case is an extreme example of both stasis and the inefficacy of welfare conditionality in promoting work norms and enforcing engagement with paid work. He was out of work, homeless and destitute when first interviewed and in the same position two years later. Certainly, the implementation of repeat sanctions meant he was no longer reliant on social welfare benefits (having disengaged from the social security system because of the stress it caused), but he was also further away from the possibility of undertaking future paid work. Although, not having engaged in paid work for a decade, previously the social security system had at least enabled him to maintain a social housing tenancy and feed himself. It was the implementation of welfare conditionality after being found fit for work, despite his depression (specifically, the imposition of compulsory job search followed by benefit sanctions for non-compliance), that set him on the path to abject poverty and 'state endorsed destitution' (McKeever and Walsh, 2020).

More generally, beyond cases like Harry which detail the severe outcomes that ensues for some, analysis of the repeat interviews revealed that benefit sanctions were consistently perceived and experienced as overtly punitive in intention and effect. Significantly, in the context of this chapter, which focuses specifically on exploring the efficacy of using benefit sanctions to move people off welfare and into paid work, the overwhelming majority of respondents stated that their implementation was more likely to undermine future engagement of paid work rather than enhance it. Ivan's story explains why benefit sanctions can often inhibit rather than enhance transitions into paid work.

Case 2: Ivan: a successful transition into work despite poor support and multiple sanctions

At his wave a interview Ivan was living in homeless accommodation after his parents were evicted from their family home for rent arrears. Six months previously he had been made redundant when his full-time warehouse work (where he was employed on a zero hours contract), ended abruptly. Like many others interviewed, Ivan outlined a fluctuating employment history with a string of short-term, insecure or temporary jobs punctuated by time in between on JSA.

> 'The Jobcentre I've been in and out of it the same as I have been with work because I've done from butchers to window fitting to working on a market. I've done all sorts, plumbing to bricklaying but it's just never been permanent work.' (Wave a)

Actively seeking work, he was unimpressed with what he perceived as the ineffectual support offered by his DWP Work Coach and he firmly believed that Jobcentre Plus was primarily focused on monitoring work search requirements and sanctioning people for non-compliance rather than helping them into work.

'No adviser has ever helped me look for work. They tell you to do things and if you don't do it then they're stopping your money. It's like "Sign up to an agency" but that's just any normal thing. ... I have to go on Universal Jobmatch[3] daily. I have to ring up jobs daily, send off for work daily, go down to your agency ... and they don't think you've done anything. ... It's in the Jobcentre. The name job adviser. You'd think that they'd advise you for jobs but they don't ... just sign your book ... and advise you if you don't do this your money gets stopped ... a little bit of help would be nicer than no help at all.' (Wave a)

Ivan had been sanctioned several times, "four weeks ... then 13 weeks one time" for not doing his job search properly (despite unsuccessfully arguing his case), and then missing an appointment. He was clear that, in his case, benefit sanctions reduced the likelihood of finding future employment and, simultaneously, pushed him away from engaging with Jobcentre Plus.

'[Sanctions] did actually bring me down ... not going to have money for a month and then the second time knowing that I'm not going to have money for nearly two and a half months. It's crazy. You're pulling your hair out. What do you do? How am I going to look for work if I haven't got any money to go out and look for work. ... It's given me a different view on the Jobcentre. It hasn't improved anything to do with getting work because I'm still doing the same thing. It's not improved it but it's just given me more hate for the Jobcentre really, personally.' (Wave a)

'It is tough when your money does get stopped and you've got no money. There's no motivation whatsoever – some people get in a dark place and I was nearly getting there, a dark place from just being there.' (Wave b)

At wave b Ivan had moved into full-time, permanent employment with a logistics company and was living in rented accommodation with his partner. He had found his new job through his personal contacts.

'It was an agency. ... I went down and in two days I was in the warehouse working with a friend that told me about the job. So yes, it worked out really quickly, it really changed actually, and was successful. ... I've been trained up onto a Forklift licence.' (Wave b)

Ivan's case study demonstrates both the routine ineffectiveness of benefit sanctions in helping people into paid work and also counters welfare conditionality advocates' claims about the necessity of benefit sanctions as a tool to end people's reliance on social welfare benefits. Following his redundancy, like many of his counterparts, Ivan was actively seeking work. His successful transition into work was achieved through his own endeavours, in spite of rather than because of, mandatory engagement with Jobcentre Plus or the application of benefit sanctions.

More widely it was exceptional for WSUs to state that the application of a benefit sanction had triggered a movement off benefits and into work. The standout example was Jacob (Case 9). Elsewhere another respondent stated he had chosen to become self-employed in order to escape the unremitting 'hassle' associated with claiming benefits: "I hated the Jobcentre ... that was one of my main motivators to really find some way away from the whole Jobcentre, Work Programme and sanctions" (male ex-offender, wave c). However, it is important to emphasise that across the sample of 481 WSUs interviewed, no more than a handful of respondents spoke of benefit sanctions triggering movements off benefits and into work. The effectiveness of the other core component of highly conditional social security regimes, that is, mandatory engagement with work search and employment training activity, in helping people into work are considered next.

Poor support: mandatory work search and employment training

As previously noted, beyond receipt of benefit per se, the support made available to UK social security benefit claimants subject to behavioural conditionality has several dimensions. Broadly conceptualised, such support (depending on personal circumstances) may include access to discretionary loans and alternative benefit payment arrangements, reductions in a person's specified work-related responsibilities through the use of easements, and the provision of mandatory work search and employment training (see, for example, Stinson, 2019a, 2019b; Chapter Two, this volume). Ensuing discussions highlight two key points. First, the shortcomings of much of the mandatory work search and employment training that individuals are required to engage with as a condition of their benefit receipt. Second, the importance of how DWP Jobcentre Plus Work Coaches and WP staff respond to a client's circumstances when implementing policy. Indeed, street level bureaucrats' (SLBs) decisions about how to exercise their discretionary powers were often highly salient in structuring claimants' future opportunities.

Only a small minority of respondents reported being supported into work through their interactions with Jobcentre Plus and even then, as Peter's case shows, respondents often had reservations about both the support they received and the perceived preoccupation of Jobcentre Plus with work search compliance.

The majority of WSUs interviewed were often highly critical of the mandatory support they received from the Jobcentre. Although guidance emphasises the importance of tailoring an individual's Claimant Commitment to a person's particular needs and changing circumstances (DWP, 2020c), Work Coaches routinely have large caseloads and limited time for each

Case 3: Peter: job search first, employment support second

Peter is a young man with a previous history of retail work. Three months prior to his wave a interview he had left his last job following a disagreement with his employer and was claiming UC. Like Ivan he felt that the system primarily prioritised monitoring job search activities above and beyond effectively supporting people into work.

> 'They're pretty hopeless down there [Jobcentre Plus] to be honest. They took everything out like all the phones, all the machines so that you can look for work, it's all gone. You have to go online to be able to do it and obviously I had no internet so it's even harder.' (Wave a)

> 'There's only so much you can apply for especially in [Location]. 35 hours each week means you're applying for the same job each week technically ... if you don't do the amount of work then you're going to get sanctioned, you won't receive your money.' (Wave a)

Significantly, undertaking 35 hours' job search had become 'work' for Peter (see also the counterproductive compliance section in Chapter Six), who also mentioned that he was starting the Construction Skills Certification Scheme (CSCS) which he hoped would boost his chances of finding work.

When interviewed 12 months later, Peter was working variable hours and had worked during the previous year on several different short-term contracts as jobs became available. He also detailed how the CSCS course paid for by the Jobcentre helped trigger his initial move back into employment.

> '[Jobcentre Plus] got me the [CSCS] card, I did the training, did the test. ... Normally it would cost quite a bit of money to do all of that, and I managed to get it free, so that was a bonus, and it's got me into work. ... I got a job straightaway when I had that card. Literally, on the day after I received that card I was in work [but] ... I had to ask. Because I want to go onto site, and my mate told me about it, he said, "Look, there's loads of work round there, it pays more than working in a shop", so I asked. They were like, "Yes, we've got this, actually, just starting next week. Do you want to do it?" I was like, "Oh, all right then. Why didn't you tell me this before?"' (Wave b)

By facilitating the CSCS course, the Jobcentre undoubtedly widened Peter's future employment options and helped him secure construction work. Nonetheless, it is noteworthy that providing tangible support did not appear to be a priority – the CSCS training opportunity, which ultimately proved helpful, was only offered after Peter had prompted his Work Coach.

appointment (Scullion and Curchin, 2022). Such time constraints, combined with a 'work first' approach, severely limit the UK regime's capacity to deliver the personalised and intensive support necessary to help those with multiple and complex needs effectively address their issues and move into work (Dean, 2003). Respondents routinely reported brief and perfunctory meetings between themselves and their Work Coach at the outset of a claim. Rather than a negotiation about how best to tailor work-related requirements to individual situations, WSUs recalled conversations dominated by the threat of benefit sanctions for non-compliance with specified work-related requirements. Having 'agreed' their Claimant Commitment, many detailed subsequent meetings in which meaningful support in finding work was often lost within a system that prioritised perpetual job search accompanied by evidence of repeated applications for work. Rather than promoting successful employment outcomes Work Coaches were regularly viewed as prioritising and monitoring claimants' work search requirements and the instigation of sanctions against those deemed to be breaching their commitments (see Chapter Six). When individuals were mandated by their Work Coach to attend outsourced job search and employment training delivered by WP providers, WSUs regularly stated that the support available was of limited use in improving skills or enhancing future chances of employment. Much of the training was criticised as being of poor quality and too generic to help people overcome the barriers that prevented many them from working. The majority believed their attendance was more about enforcing acquiescence and conformity with their Claimant Commitment conditions rather than boosting chances of employment. Such preoccupations are perhaps to be expected within advanced, 'work first' regimes that have become increasingly focused on 'hounding delinquents' (Novak, 1997) and arguably reoriented on punishing poor people and forcing them off welfare benefits rather than ensuring a basic level of social security (Fletcher and Wright, 2018).

Case 4: Joy: supported into work

Joy entered the UK via the asylum system. Subsequently granted refugee status she quickly found employment in a call centre before being made redundant and initiating a JSA claim. In her wave a interview she told us about being mandated by her Work Coach to undertake a basic English course; despite migrating from an Anglophone country and being able to read, write and converse fluently in English. On completing the course, she was then required to attend further compulsory training on job searching and CV preparation. Although the training was inappropriate and offered little of value in helping her find work given her existing level of education, she did as instructed to retain her right to benefit and avoid a sanction. Reflecting the counterproductive outcomes (discussed in Chapter Six), it was evident that some of the mandatory requirements had deflected Joy from meaningful job search and her ultimate goal of employment.

> 'I didn't have a choice. ... I was like, I already know English. I come here every single Thursday and I think I've executed whatever you've required of me. So for you to doubt that I know English? ... [Work Coach] "You have to attend the two eight week courses and, if you don't we will sanction you, so it's compulsory, Monday to Friday, 9:30 to 3pm". So that's like a full-time job when it's on.' (Wave a)

> 'Jobcentre first before anything else. ... I've got this online diary, whereby every single day I have to write out my activity history and say today I did this, this, this. ... It's just too much of a commitment, energy being directed to the wrong area rather than looking for a job and also getting a job. ... It is very difficult and I feel that they put more pressure [on me] ... than help me get a job.' (Wave a)

However, at wave b she was happy to be working full-time, having found employment as a direct result of being mandated (five months after initially signing on), to attend the WP and, more importantly, assigned to a personal adviser who proactively prioritised supporting Joy to identify suitable employment opportunities.

> '[WP provider] have a larger database when it comes to employers. ... They helped me with positions that I wasn't aware of ... never under pressure like at the Jobcentre. ... I felt really comfortable not just with the organisation but with the individual allocated to assist me. ... February, I had an interview, got the job. ... So excited, 35 hours per week and a permanent position. ... I passed my probation in three months so I'm now full-time and permanently employed. It's been going great.' (Wave b)

At her final wave c interview Joy remained employed with the same company. She had received a pay rise and, while far from financially comfortable, she was managing to pay her rent and support herself. Reflecting on her experience of sanction and support (she was sanctioned at the outset of her JSA claim because she did not understand the system properly and failed to attend a meeting), it was clearly the tailored support offered by the WP adviser that she was assigned to, and not the sanction she had previously received, that enabled her movement into work and subsequent progression.

> 'Being signed up with that organisation was a blessing in disguise. ... Initially, I just thought, oh, the Jobcentre's just trying to get rid of me. ... I felt listened to, I felt assisted ... in my journey to get a job, and yet the sanctions were a total opposite, so definitely the support was much appreciated, was more useful. ... It got me the job.' (Wave c)

Having outlined the perceived shortcomings of the work search and employment and skills training provided by Jobcentre Plus and WP providers it needs to be acknowledged that on certain rare occasions, mandatory support did play a key role in enabling a very small number of WSUs into work. Joy and John's stories both clearly illustrate the importance of supportive engagement by Work Coaches and WP providers with clients if individuals are to achieve positive employment outcomes. Both cases also highlight the significance of how SLBs exercise their discretionary powers (see Chapter Three for previous discussion of Lipsky [2010 (1980)] and so on) in structuring different employment outcomes.

It is important to reiterate that Joy's case is atypical. This story of mandatory support triggering a positive movement off welfare benefits and into sustainable paid work was very much the exception rather than the norm. John's case details another rare example of a successful transition from welfare to work over time, but again illustrates the limitations of a system built around compulsion and sanction.

Case 5: John: sanction, support and the importance of discretion

John is a man in his 50s with a prior long-term history of paid work who became addicted to hard drugs later in life. With his life 'spiralling out of control' he detailed how he lost his job, house, partner and children. Unemployed for approximately three years he had ended up rough sleeping, before securing a hostel place and subsequently supported housing as he attempted to turn his life around.

> 'I got made redundant and I started to dabble ... doing a few things that maybe I shouldn't have to make a bit of money and to be honest it was quite exciting and it sort of all snowballed.' (Wave a)

At his wave a interview John outlined how his journey to recovery was enabled in part by the positive support of a particular Work Coach at Jobcentre Plus who had engaged with him when he was at his lowest and supported his claim for JSA and then subsequently helped facilitate a move on to ESA because of John's long-term impairment.

> 'After I'd lost everything I had to then sign on again. My adviser this time was absolutely fantastic. I couldn't praise him up enough. ... I explained my situation. I said "look I'm a drug addict and I'm doing my best to get clean. I'm in recovery" and he was just really supportive. He wasn't on my case. He was encouraging, brilliant. ... He hasn't just let me get away with it. He's been "What about this training course? Go for that." ... He could have sanctioned me on numerous occasions.' (Wave a)

His journey back into paid work had also been facilitated by support offered at two homelessness support organisations that helped him overcome his addiction and had given him work, first as a volunteer and then, via competitive interview, on a paid apprenticeship scheme. Two things mattered greatly to John. First, that people had gone the extra mile for him. For example, he talked about a senior worker coming in on a Sunday to help him with his apprenticeship application. Second, he also commented on the fact that many of the workers in the organisation had been homeless themselves so they didn't judge him adversely on his past, but rather, supported him towards a more positive future.

> 'Before I came here all I was interested in was drugs. ... I was at rock bottom, I had no family, no friends, I had nothing apart from the clothes on my back. I can honestly say that this place [Homelessness support organisation] saved my life. ... That's no exaggeration it's really just turned my life around completely.' (Wave b)

By the time of our third and final interview John reported he had recently got a permanent job in another city and was living in shared rented accommodation. He didn't have much money because his housing costs had increased but he was proud to be working full-time again. He still had medical issues to address, but he was back in charge of his life and planning for the future.

Interestingly, John also expanded on his experience of a benefit sanction that he had received following an appointment with another adviser on an occasion when his regular supportive Work Coach was away. John arrived early for his Jobcentre appointment but was told by the security guard to wait downstairs. He did as required and was allowed in at his allotted time.

> 'Sat there for 20 minutes. Now, by the time somebody come and got my card, the woman she said, "You're late", I said, "Well, no, I'm not, I was downstairs 15 minutes early, the guys wouldn't let me up and when I come upstairs, nobody took my card." She said, "Well, I don't believe you." I said, "Well, come and ask the security guards." She said, "No, I'm sanctioning you." ' (Wave c)

Refusing to accept this outcome, John was adamant he would not leave until he saw a manager. He was next informed that if he did not leave the police would be called but he refused to move. In time the manager appeared who said he had spoken to security and that he believed John's account and apologised, but then stated that "Unfortunately, because she sanctioned you, I can't overrule it". John left the building and relied on homeless charities to feed himself and survive for the next few weeks without benefit.

Support was clearly the key to ensuring John got his life back on track but his case also illustrates inconsistencies in the way different Job Coaches implement welfare conditionality and the wider issue of the inappropriate application of benefit sanctions and the negative impacts that they routinely trigger. His resilience and the support of non-statutory providers stopped him from being deflected from turning his life around positively. Although much emphasis has been placed on the need for benefit claimants to change their expectations and behaviour, Joy and John's cases clearly demonstrate the need for some of those charged with administering frontline policy to change their own behaviour and use their discretionary powers to genuinely support people as and when required. To borrow Djuve and Kalvi's (2015) terminology, without 'Carers' (that is, SLBs who implement policy empathetically and adapt systems to support rather than punish people), it is unlikely that either John or Joy would have been able to overcome the significant barriers they faced to make the successful transition, over time, from reliance on benefits to sustained employment. When individual SLBs choose to operate simply as bureaucratic 'Clerks' implementing regulations (for example, when sanctioning John inappropriately, or in making Joy unnecessarily undertake basic English language and numeracy training), the mandatory 'support' offered delays and/or impedes people making positive progress in their personal and working lives.

Dealing with difference: conditionality as a panacea for labour market inactivity

A key feature of welfare conditionality within contemporary social security systems has been the incorporation of increasing numbers of both disabled people and lone parents under its remit. Especially in 'work first' welfare regimes it is no longer deemed acceptable for the majority of those with long-term impairments and/or significant informal, familial care responsibilities to be exempt from the responsibility to search for, and undertake, paid employment whenever possible. Within the UK, successive governments have seen it as appropriate and necessary to apply the twin mechanisms of mandatory engagement with specified employment training/support and sanctions to spur those in receipt of incapacity benefits and lone parents into paid work (see Chapter Two). The two longitudinal case studies that follow offer explanatory insights into how, and why, simply extending welfare conditionality fails to remedy labour market inactivity among disabled people and those with caring responsibilities.

Case 6: Stacey: inflexible compulsion exacerbates illness, reducing the likelihood of paid work

Stacey is a lone mother with a long-term, episodic, mental health condition. She last worked before the birth of her children a decade ago. At wave a, allocated to the ESA Work Related Activity Group (WRAG), she was subject to benefit sanction for failure to undertake mandatory work-related tasks. With the help of her doctor, she was attempting (unsuccessfully) to resist being assigned to the WP.

> 'I have [mental health impairment] but they put me in the WRAG. ... We appealed, it took over six months for them to go through the appeal process. Then a phone call saying "No you're going to be in the WRAG group" ... a leaflet saying with this group you will get the support ready for when you want to go back to work and it will be done at your pace. Then within a week I got a letter saying that I had to attend a two-week mandatory programme and then another week mandatory programme otherwise I'd be sanctioned. ... It really causes a lot of stress and pressure with my [condition] which means I don't sleep which affects my mood which then obviously has a knock-on effect with my home life and my children.' (Wave a)

A year on, Stacey remained out of work in the WRAG and reported worsening mental health due to work-focused requirements, which she felt were being applied with little consideration of either her impairments or responsibilities as a lone parent.

> 'I can't control my [condition]. I wish I could, but still you're getting that push, push, push. ... All they want is to hit their targets and for me to do their training and get back to work. They were sending me out appointments for two weeks at a time where I was supposed to be in every day for nearly six hours at a time. One, I have children. The times you want me in I can't do. Two, I can't sit in front of the computer for nearly four hours a day. I can't meet what you want and it was a case of if you don't then you could lose your benefit. ... It got worse due to benefits ... the work-related part of ESA ... pushing and pushing ... but with my mental health and things I relapsed really badly and it caused me to crash.' (Wave b)

At wave c Stacey continued to contest her WRAG allocation and her health had further deteriorated. She is awaiting a date for a new WCA but was fearful of the outcome.

> 'I was being pushed too hard by [WP], the support that is supposed to help you get into work, and my GP just said at the minute with your health the way you are you're deteriorating, I just don't feel you should be in that group. So he sent a letter to the Jobcentre with a sick note and asking for me to be moved over to the Support Group ... got a letter a month later saying I'd have to have another medical.' (Wave c)

'In the two years, I've had about eight or nine [WP] support workers because they just pass you around left, right and centre. ... You were just a number or a name on a form for them to get their bonus at the end. ... They just didn't look at the condition ... doing all of that made me ill. ... If I fail the assessment ... I'm going to have to go back to looking for work and things like that and I just know that even if I got a job I probably wouldn't be able to keep to it. So I'll end up going round in circles or even being sanctioned, so is it going to change me? No, because I've got disabilities. I can't help that.' (Wave c)

Over the two-year period of our study Stacey's employment prospects had diminished due to worsening mental health triggered largely by the imposition of mandatory work-related requirements. The problems detailed in her case; the failings of the WCA system, compulsion inherent in behavioural conditionality exacerbating existing illness and the disregarding of long-term and/or episodic impairments as legitimate reasons for not engaging in work-related activity have been widely noted elsewhere. Extensive evidence now details the inappropriateness, ineffectiveness and harms set in train by extending welfare conditionality to disabled people (Newton et al, 2013; Hale, 2014; Barr et al, 2016a, 2016b; Oakley, 2016; Moth and Lavallette, 2017; Patrick, 2017; Dwyer et al, 2018, 2020; Davis, 2019; Stewart, 2019; Mehta et al, 2021; Williams, 2021).

As the final quote in Amy's case shows, the implementation of conditionality and compulsion solved none of the dilemmas and issues she faced. Although some lone parents interviewed recounted sympathetic and caring Work Coaches and WP advisers, the majority reported inadequate consideration of their informal caring responsibilities within a system which they perceived as pushing individuals into often low-quality, low-paid work regardless of familial commitments and a lack of appropriate, affordable childcare (Johnsen and Blenkinsopp, 2018).

Case 7: Amy: work and welfare recycling and the limitations of 'work first' for lone parents

In receipt of JSA at wave a, Amy had sole caring responsibilities for her three school-aged children. Stressing a willingness to work she spoke of two job offers that she could not take up due to parental responsibilities.

'WP provider found me two jobs. ... I went for it and the guy was "I'm really happy" ... the hours which was ten to two so it was a brilliant little number so I was quite happy. Told me I had to do a week training. ... I said to them, who pays for the training? They didn't know. Then I went back to the Jobcentre and asked them who paid for my week's training because even though I was going to get 70 per cent off with my childcare when it did come through there was still going to be a week missing because they didn't want to pay for the week's training. So I was still going to be left with a bill of £230. Basically I couldn't start that job because of that. ... Then I went for another job interview. I was told that they would fit the hours around me. ... I found out I was going to start at two and end at eight o'clock at night, childcare only runs to quarter to six, and then you had to work like once every Saturday but there's no childcare on a Saturday.' (Wave a)

Aside from a lack of access to affordable childcare and unsuitable working hours, Amy outlined how mandatory work search requirements undermined her role as a mother.

'Usually the children are in school nine until three ... so you've got that to look for work but then when the children are off. ... They want to go to the park and they want to go here and they want to do that and you're saying no. ... The summer holidays was a nightmare, how you had to try and sign on, had to look after children, try and look for a job, try and get all these appointments ... and then little ones are not allowed in [WP] either.' (Wave a)

At wave b Amy detailed that she had worked briefly for two companies in the previous year. Pushed by the WP she initially took on 20 hours per week employment at a call centre leaving after the unscrupulous employer failed to pay her due wages and would not confirm her period of employment, which led to a Housing Benefit suspension.

'I felt I was kind of pushed. ... I don't think I really had like a choice in the matter. ... I worked there for like five weeks. ... I then I had to go back to the [WP adviser] and told him basically he hadn't paid us ... and then we got paid £203 for like the five weeks work. ... I was supposed to get £120 a week. ... Stopped my Housing Benefit and all that because this guy wouldn't give me a letter to say I worked there to get the Housing Benefit. ... So the housing wouldn't like sort it out and it would go on and on and on for months.' (Wave b)

Unable to evidence her employment for Housing Benefit purposes, Amy fell into rent arrears and quickly took on employment to try and make ends meet.

'I had to like take the nearest job that came ... travelling there and travelling back with the bairns ... up in the morning dragging the bairns out a way over there. Then coming back, because like I had to get the seven minutes past train and then back for ten to three for the bairns. So I ended up myself off with stress. I had the housing phoning me all the time. ... I was told it was going to Court for the housing ... because I ended up owing £2,000 in arrears. ... I was scared

I was going to actually lose my house ... how do I explain to my three little ones I don't have a house when I went out to work at that point? I just broke down in the doctors. ... I ended up on anti-depressants. ... It's not been a good experience to go back to work.' (Wave b)

Unsupported and fearful of eviction, despite her best efforts to combine parental and paid work responsibilities, Amy became seriously unwell and ended up claiming ESA. At her final wave c interview, following a WCA, she was found 'fit for work'. Amy was out of work and back on JSA. Variations in the employment 'support' she had received were evident as she reflected on her experiences over the previous two years

'When I first had to sign on, I had a dreadful woman. ... It was just, "Oh, you will – these jobs are out at this, but you'll have to look." The one I've got now is understanding. ... She put me on a computer place. ... She always gives me a ten o'clock meeting time ... so I can get the [school] run done if either of them are not well, then that's you and you're trying to catch up later on at night on the phone.' (Wave c)

Essentially, Amy was back where she had been two years previously; out of work, juggling 20 hours' compulsory job search and training, alongside caring for her children and facing unresolved childcare barriers.

'Childcare. That's my problem, definitely childcare. ... Because you just always need to be there for your kids and you give your kids everything and – I just think I've let myself down. Oh, my God, maybe I shouldn't have took that job. Maybe I should have just stayed on the giro and not went into that job, but then at the time, I had to take that job. I went to the adviser and they said I had to, so I *had* [stresses word] to take the job, but at that time, in my head, I was like, no, I shouldn't have took it.' (Wave c)

More widely, evidence suggests that highly conditional social security systems fail to address issues of difference adequately. Although Work Coaches are supposed to adjust individual claimants' work-related responsibilities to their personal circumstances, the systemic disadvantages routinely faced by disabled people and lone parents (the majority of whom are female – see Wright, 2022 for fuller discussions of conditionality and gender) are often overlooked especially in 'work first' welfare systems. Furthermore, as evidenced by several of the case studies in this chapter, a benefit system built on sanction and mandatory support is ill-equipped for the delivery of effective welfare or employment outcomes for people with multiple and complex needs (Dean, 2003; Bauld et al, 2012). Similarly, ethnic difference and disadvantage is routinely ignored, despite evidence of 'welfare chauvinism' whereby 'harsher policies have been introduced and implemented more eagerly when the target group for activation reforms has been immigrants' (Breidahl, 2012: 119). Previous research indicates discriminatory and racialised, sanction and support decision-making occur within Scandinavian (Breidahl, 2012), US (Monnat, 2010), German (Ratzmann, 2021) and UK (Hudson et al, 2006; Shutes, 2011) welfare systems. The deleterious impact of welfare conditionality and the UK government's wider hostility towards migrants' welfare claims, evidenced by the removal of routine interpretation services at Jobcentres and an overtly hostile 'activation-plus' regime (O'Brien, 2013), have been explored elsewhere (Dwyer et al, 2018, 2020; Scullion, 2018).

Universal Credit and 'in-work' conditionality: promoting employment progression?

Since the introduction of UC in 2013 welfare conditionality now applies to low-income workers in receipt of wage/housing subsidies and other financial support (for example, Tax Credits) alongside unemployed people and those in receipt of long-term sickness and incapacity benefits. The implementation of 'in-work' conditionality is premised on the idea that extending mandatory work search requirements (with benefit sanctions for non-compliance), will enhance low-paid workers' progression within the PLM and reduce their reliance on social security benefits. As Jones et al (2019) note, the ill-defined notion of 'in-work' progression means that workers in receipt of UC can be variously required to increase their hours and/or look to make progress with their current employer, seek further additional work elsewhere (for example, simultaneously take on multiple part-time jobs), or seek new alternative work elsewhere (DWP, 2018c). In practical terms this effectively makes low-paid workers' continued receipt of UC conditional on individuals achieving full-time work with earnings above the stated conditionality threshold (Wright and Dwyer, 2022). However, as Sharon and Jacob's cases illustrate, ensuring 'in-work progression', that is, supporting people into better paid and more sustainable work, appeared to be consistently absent when the UC claimants interviewed by WelCond interacted with Jobcentre Plus staff.

Case 8: Sharon: Universal Credit and the pursuit of progression

Sharon is a young woman with an employment history, starting in her early teens with a Saturday job in the family shop and then working with animals in various roles. She is dyslexic and has lived with a long-term serious physical health condition since late childhood which causes recurrent fractures and ongoing pain. She has undergone several major operations and at the time of her wave a interview was waiting for further surgery.

Allied to her physical disability she also takes medication for her mental health. At her wave a interview she explained how she spent three weeks claiming JSA before (very briefly) taking her last part-time post; leaving due to a work accident which linked to an existing impairment.

> 'Got a job, but because it was 15 hours, I was still told I had to sign on. I did that, broke my leg and then I got a phone call saying, "You missed your appointment." "I'm in hospital, I've broken my leg and I'm waiting for an operation tonight." They basically turned round and went, "Well call us back when you're out of hospital, we'll put you on ESA." ... "Okay. What is ESA?" She explained to me and I'm like, "Why has nobody told me this? I could have had that all that time I actually needed it to now." ' (Wave a)

Subsequently, Sharon was placed on ESA for a short period but, despite her ongoing impairments, was found fit for work following a WCA and transferred onto UC. Needing income but not wanting the hassle of constant job applications for unsuitable work she found her next job through a family friend:

> 'So I got off of it pretty sharply, because I was working Sundays and Mondays. Then it [pain] got so bad that they literally spread them. ... I had a longer period between the Wednesday and the Sunday and the swelling went down completely, but of course then it would swell back up, so it was always in constant flux.' (Wave a)

The fluctuating hours of her employment contract, allied to her ongoing impairments, complicated her UC claim:

> 'A zero hour contract. Basically you go in, if they've got nobody in they'll call you up and you go in. I was due to work six days that week. ... [UC] kept saying, "Right, just tell us how many hours you're doing per week we will take that amount, and weigh it up and then pay you whatever is left." And I was like, "Okay", but I wasn't, I was going to do a full week, then I knew I wasn't going to get any money, much money. Then I was cutting it down because I wanted to see if I could do a full week, and if I could do a full week, I could carry on doing that and I could get off UC.' (Wave a)

Unable to continue working, her doctor provided a sick note which the Jobcentre accepted. However, as a UC claimant, she had to continue actively searching for work, despite being ill.

> '"Come in and you can look for jobs." ... I do it every two weeks. ... She was talking about moving me to once a month, because I'm off work and I can't work. ... Overall, it's okay. ... When I was looking for jobs they were like, "You're doing excellent, but do more." ... I was on my mum's laptop for about five hours

a day. ... I was always looking for the newest ones, applying, and nobody was getting back.' (Wave a)

Twelve months on, at wave b, Sharon was living with her partner and part of a joint UC claim. She remained out of work and her partner was in low-paid work. In line with the intended design of UC, the couple's benefit money fluctuated as his hours and pay packet increased or decreased each month. Unable to make ends meet and confused about how UC worked, Sharon's partner reduced his working hours, expecting 'her' UC benefit payment to increase. At this point her Job Coach,

'[t]urned round and said, "Well that means you've got to get a job for 20 hours." ... I turned round and went, "At the moment love it's hard enough getting out the door."' (Wave b)

Rather than aiding progression in the PLM, Sharon's perceived experience of "UC screwing up my claim and me not having any money" (wave b), worsened her anxiety, triggering panic attacks.

At wave c, Sharon reported she had been employed for the previous eight months; initially working 14 hours per week but more recently only six hours, following advice from her doctor. Nonetheless, the Jobcentre continued pushing her to increase the hours she worked contrary to medical advice.

'I saw it online ... they were doing interviews at the Jobcentre, so I was like, "Oh, put me down for an interview. I can't go wrong." Basically everything that I've known – I've worked in shops ... a merchandiser. I got the job. ... My doctor says because I'm still having trouble with [recurrent physical impairment], that I shouldn't really be doing more hours. ... When he found out I was doing 14 he turned round and said, "Don't push yourself." ... Now I'm doing six hours, he's not worried as much. ... When I told him what the Jobcentre wanted he said, "You've just cut down to the right amount of hours and they want you to find another job?" And he turned round and said, "Just tell them to piss off. ... Tell them to phone me."' (Wave c)

Sharon's case offers insights into the complexities of UC's supposedly simplified system (Summers and Young, 2020) and evidences the hardships that can occur when sanction-backed work search requirements are extended to encompass low-paid workers who are expected to evidence 'in-work progression' while working in the lower echelons of an increasingly flexible and demanding PLM. Jacob's case further highlights many of the impacts of conditionality within UC.

Case 9: Jacob: experiences of sanction and support within Universal Credit

Jacob is a young man with a history of employment in the hospitality sector. A UC claimant, he became homeless and unemployed nine months before his wave a interview, following a split with his personal partner, who was also his work manager. At wave a he outlined how a benefit sanction, which he had unsuccessfully appealed against, had directly worsened his mental health and financial position.

> 'I've been suffering from depression, but I'm trying to get it sorted. ... I got sanctioned by the Jobcentre because I didn't have a note from the hospital stating that I was in hospital after trying to take my life. They're supposed to help people get work, but they don't. ... I'd gone from £240 to £30 a month. That wasn't even enough to feed myself. ... Which sends me back down into a downward spiral. And, it's just [slight pause] I don't understand how they can get away with it. ... My behaviour was just fine. I mean I can't help having to be in hospital after having a mental breakdown. ... I would love to work, but obviously part of me, because of my mental problems at the moment, doesn't think it's a good idea.' (Wave a)

A year on, Jacob was back working in the hospitality sector. "I'm now in permanent work. Up until recently I was working two jobs" (wave b). However, by his final wave c interview, he had recently become unemployed again, having resigned following a dispute. His new partner was supporting him financially in the short term and, given his previous experience, he was confident of getting another job soon. Adamant that he would only reclaim UC as a last resort, he held particularly negative views of the support he had received from the Jobcentre.

> 'Absolutely fucking God awful! Excuse my language. ... The Work Coaches at the Jobcentre are useless because all they do is sit in front of the computer typing away, offering no support whatsoever, putting you on courses that you don't actually need to be on.' (Wave c)

Reflecting further, he emphasised how being in work helped his mental health and, surprisingly, commented on the positive effect of previously being sanctioned.

> 'Working gives me something to focus on, it takes my mind off my problems, it keeps my mind active. If I'm feeling low then I don't like being sat around doing nothing. ... [The sanction] gave me the kick up the arse I needed to get a job ... it made me more determined in finding a job, working my arse off and being a better person than what the Jobcentre made me out to be.' (Wave c)

Both Jacob and Sharon's cases are important for several reasons. First, they evidence the oscillating work–welfare–work trajectories typical for many in insecure jobs at the lower end of the PLM. As previously noted, this recycling pattern was a feature of many WSUs' employment biographies across their longer-term working lives. Second, the cases highlight the wider shortcomings of the support made available to UC claimants, in relation to both delivering a consistent level of social security and appropriate and effective job search/employment training activities. Third, the narratives demonstrate a systemic disregard for the disabling effects of impairment and how these may negatively impact on an individual's ability to engage in the work-related requirements demanded of increasing numbers of social welfare recipients. Fourth, Jacob's final comment, about how being sanctioned played a role in him seeking work is thought-provoking; especially because at wave a he had initially been extremely angry, believing its application was both inappropriate and ineffective. Given Jacob's (and indeed Sharon's) evident willingness to work, it is highly questionable that he needed either a 'kick up the arse' or the debt and stress that his benefit sanction created in order to make him engage with paid work. Further, analysis of his longitudinal interviews reveals that Jacob found each of his successive jobs through his own endeavours. Jacob did not require the stick of compulsion to work. What he, and others like him, need is access to an adequate level of benefit when periodically unemployed and/or unwell. His statement that he would "work his arse off" in an attempt to "prove himself a better person" is redolent of benefit recipients accepting and internalising over time the 'self conditioning' logics of welfare conditionality whereby '[p]erceptions about the necessity of work – and the individual's responsibility not only to find work but to have a life shaped by work – become embedded and ultimately "assumed"' (Dwyer and Ellison, 2009: 65).

Finally, both these cases evidence the limitations of 'in-work progression' when implemented in tandem with sanction-backed welfare conditionality among low-paid workers who have had little contact with the DWP previously (Finch, 2016). More recent research outlines the myriad failings of an ill-conceived approach that appears to inadequately serve the needs of both workers and employers.

> Rigid expectations placed on individuals to increase hours or pay are at odds with the realities of working life in the UK labour market. ... [Employers'] overriding priority would continue to be their 'bottom line' and keeping labour costs low. ... A 'work first, then work more' approach, focused on placing conditions on individual workers continues to neglect the 'demand side' of active labour market policy – it fails to consider long-standing issues of poor work quality and management practices, and broader issues

relating to the needs of workers outside of the paid labour market. (Jones et al, 2019: 16)

The importance of progression for those in low-paid work should not be disparaged. Indeed, a recent government funded report by the In-Work Progression Commission (2021) sets out how it might more meaningfully be enabled. It highlights the twin barriers of inadequate transport and childcare provision that will need to be addressed if those trapped in low pay (disproportionately women, minority Black and ethnic, and disabled people), are to move forward in their working lives. It also identifies the provision of appropriate support as key to enabling future in-work progression for low-paid workers. That said, it largely ignores the conditionality issue, mentioning sanctions only once within its 92 pages, but does recommend the use of incentives to reward progress rather than penalties to punish failure.

Conclusions

Returning to the question posed at the start, the key finding emerging from the qualitative longitudinal analysis presented in this chapter is that welfare conditionality within social security systems (particularly those orientated to a 'work first' model), are routinely ineffective in enabling people's entry into, or progression within, the paid labour market over time. Stasis was the most common outcome. For those who did find periods of paid employment, 'work was often experienced as elusive or transitory – more like a moving target than a destination' (Wright et al, 2018a: 1). The UK's current highly conditional benefit system, where sanction for non-compliance with behavioural work search responsibilities appear to be prioritised over supporting people into employment, means that key structural barriers to entry into paid work, often linked to issues of impairment or familial care responsibilities, are unlikely to be adequately addressed. Likewise, it is highly unlikely to assist people with multiple and complex needs to move closer to, or into, paid employment (see also, Dean, 2003, Bauld et al, 2012).

Our longitudinal interviews demonstrate that benefit sanctions do not work to move people closer to employment, rather they triggered profoundly negative outcomes (see Chapter Six for further discussions), that were likely to push people further away from future work. Much of the compulsory work search and training support offered by Jobcentre Plus and WP providers was identified by many WSUs as too generic and of poor quality. Those mandated to attend courses frequently experienced them as punitive rather than empowering. That said, as the exceptional case studies of successful entry into sustainable work highlight, the provision of personalised support is clearly pivotal in enabling successful transitions into paid employment. Here empathetic use of the discretionary powers available to SLBs is crucial in facilitating peoples' entry into paid work. The introduction of 'in-work' conditionality within UC broadened the definition of 'dysfunctional' welfare dependency to include low-paid workers. Rather than deliver 'in-work progression' this extension of welfare conditionality appears to have cemented a 'coerced worker claimant' model at the heart of UK social benefit policy. This approach fails to meet the employment and social security needs of claimants while simultaneously undermining the requirements of employers (Wright and Dwyer, 2022). It is unlikely to motivate people into better paid and more sustainable employment over the long term.

Notes

[1] Such individuals were typically in receipt of Income Support or Carers Allowance. See Turn2us (2021a, 2021b) for the rules that pertain under UC in respect of carers, and so on.

[2] We recorded full-time work as anyone working on average 25 hours plus per week, part-time between 16 and 24 hours and short time as 1–15 hours.

[3] Universal Jobmatch was a website commissioned by the DWP. Unemployed people were required to sign up to the website and Job Coaches regularly used the site to monitor their clients' job search and application activities. Following criticisms that many advertised jobs breached the website's terms and conditions and that fake jobs were being posted (Mason, 2014), it was closed and replaced in 2018 by 'Find a Job', https://www.gov.uk/find-a-job.

FIVE

Welfare conditionality and problematic or antisocial behaviour

Beyond social security the use of mandatory engagement with specified systems of support and associated sanctions for non-compliance to tackle the problematic conduct of certain individuals and families is now firmly established within social housing, antisocial behaviour (ASB), family intervention and criminal justice policies, especially with the UK (see Chapters Two and Three). Here discussions focus on the efficacy and impacts of welfare conditionality in triggering and sustaining behaviour change among citizens with more complex needs such as people experiencing homelessness, criminal justice system offenders and individuals and families whose actions have seen them subject to ASB or family intervention policies (FIPs). In order to capture a broad range of interventions within the WelCond study, each of these groups was initially separately purposively sampled. However, analysis revealed that many individuals within these three groups shared common histories in terms of their overlapping vulnerabilities and involvement in various types of behaviours that were perceived as harmful and/or antisocial. Many had previously experienced and/or continued to be vulnerable to street homelessness. Substance misuse and addiction, although not universal, was also a recurrent feature in some respondents' lives. Alongside this, large numbers also discussed ongoing long-term mental and physical impairments, for which some were receiving various medical and therapeutic treatments while others were not. Across the three groups of people experiencing homelessness, offenders and people subject to ASB and/or FIPs, a total of 82 welfare service users (WSUs) took part in two or three repeat interviews. Of these, 77 people were not in paid employment at their wave a interview and remained out of work at their subsequent repeat interviews. Given the often complex and multi-faceted issues and barriers these people routinely faced, it is perhaps not too surprising to report that welfare conditionality within the social security system overwhelmingly failed to trigger movements off welfare and into work among these often highly vulnerable respondents.

Having previously discussed the limited efficacy of welfare conditionality in moving people into paid work (Chapter Four), the first part of this chapter explores the impacts and effects of welfare conditionality when operationalised as an attempt to curb problematic ASB. The second part moves on to define and consider the notion of 'compound conditionality'.

Here discussions focus on how welfare conditionality, when implemented separately within distinct policy areas (for example, social security benefits, ASB interventions, social housing policy), often then intersects to impact negatively on individuals who are simultaneously subject to behavioural requirements in more than one aspect of their lives.

The efficacy of welfare conditionality in addressing antisocial behaviour among people with complex/multiple needs

Debates about the tension between care and control that exist within welfare policy are long-standing. Various mechanisms of sanction and punishment have long been used to control the conduct of poor and vulnerable people and/or exclude them from basic welfare provisions before the notion of the welfare state emerged (Goroff, 1974; Mann, 1992). Marxist scholars have also highlighted that rather than simply offering benign support to vulnerable people, 'welfare capitalism' (that is, the welfare state) also acts as an essential prop that enables late modern capitalism to function and generates inequality (Offe, 1982). Additionally, others have detailed how the rise of welfare conditionality has proved to be a powerful tool for simultaneously controlling the behaviour of social welfare recipients and advancing the assertions of neoliberal ideology (for example, Novak, 1997; MacGregor, 1999; Dean, 2000, 2001, 2002; Larkin, 2007; Grover and Piggott, 2013; Jordan, 2014; Edmiston, 2016; Nethercote, 2017; Brown, 2017). More specifically, Larkin notes that policies which emphasise conditionality are likely to engender 'at least quasi punitive effects particularly on those vulnerable members of society who arguably are in more need of state assistance than sanctions on vital resources' (Larkin, 2007: 319). Rather than signalling benevolence, where welfare conditionality dominates, social welfare arguably promotes forms of social control which structure 'situations in which individuals either have no viable options available to them in making decisions or are required to conform to a specific classification or perform specific actions or desist from specific actions in order to obtain that which is an entitlement to resources and/or services' (Goroff, 1974: 19).

In the decades since, the extension and consolidation of sanction and compulsion, the two key elements of welfare conditionality routinely associated with changing behaviour (see Chapter Three), add further weight to Goroff's assertion. Certainly, in the UK, coercive welfare measures that combine an 'enforcement-plus-support' approach have been asserted as effective in controlling a wide range of ASB, including street-based prostitution, drink and drug use and begging, and so on (see Flint, 2009b; Johnsen and Fitzpatrick, 2010 for fuller discussions). Critics, however, question the extent to which such policies may help people engage in positive behaviour change. For example, Phoenix (2008) argued that the use of Antisocial Behaviour Orders (ASBOs)[1] to tackle prostitution further criminalises street-based sex workers and increases their chances of prosecution within the criminal justice system but offers little in terms of help and support. Conversely, others have noted local variations in the interpretation and implementation of national policy and argued that enforcement type measures designed to tackle 'problematic street cultures' can lead to positive outcomes for some vulnerable street users and the wider general public alike (Johnsen and Fitzpatrick, 2010). The qualitative longitudinal case studies and accompanying analysis set out in this chapter explore and explain how mechanisms of sanction and support (control and care) variously impact on the lives of individuals with complex needs whose behaviour is deemed as requiring remedial intervention. Discussions offer grounded insights into how, and why, the efficacy of welfare conditionality in challenging and changing ASB, varies over time. Initial consideration of Linda's and Keith's cases highlights both the possibilities and limitations of welfare conditionality for triggering and sustaining positive behaviour change.

Case 10: Linda: choosing to change – taking control and the importance of support

Linda is a young woman who lives alone in social rented housing. An ongoing long-term mental health condition, diagnosed in adolescence, alongside physical impairments, have prevented her from working throughout her adult life. She remained in the ESA Support Group across the three waves of repeat interviews and is supported by her mother, who acts as her carer.

In her youth, her 'problematic' behaviour initiated ASB interventions, experiences of homelessness and, in due course, repeat custodial sentences.

> 'I was a toe-rag. I was always on the drink and I used to take drugs and I got into a lot of trouble from when I was eight … kept getting into trouble. … [I was] given an Acceptable Behaviour Contract [ABC][2] at first … but I kept getting letters saying that I was going to get one [ASBO]. Then I got called into the office. … They handed me the ASBO. … I wasn't allowed in the area so basically I couldn't see my friends and family; I'd have to stay outside. Then I breached it and breached it again so they gave me an ASBO for the whole of south [City].' (Wave a)

Linda discussed how the ASBO had a detrimental effect on her health and triggered further problematic behavioural outcomes but had limited impact in curbing her antisocial and criminal behaviour.

'It made my illness worse. ... I was always depressed, I was always self-harming. ... I couldn't see my family and things and I felt like I was isolated because I was always out of the way. ... [The ASBO] never worked for me back then. ... I just thought I'll go to jail and didn't bother.' (Wave a)

'I know a few people that have had an ASBO and I know it didn't help them either. It didn't help me because I was always breaching it, so it's just basically sitting there, it's not doing anything.' (Wave c)

Ultimately, several factors combined to prompt Linda's decision to change her behaviour. Struggling with the harsh realities of prison alongside recognition of the detrimental affect her actions were having on both herself and her family Linda made a personal choice to cease offending and seek the support necessary to address her problematic behaviour.

'My mum got really depressed. ... It was tearing my family apart ... seeing me in there, hurting myself, taking overdoses, trying to hang myself. ... I was always in and out of the hospital. It just wasn't nice so I went and got the help, I got help from a psychiatrist. Now I see a psychologist, I get help for panic attacks. ... From thereon I turned the corner. ... I was going down the wrong routes. ... I chose to move on. It was my own choice.' (Wave a)

'When I was in clink, doing my [X]th jail sentence and I couldn't do it anymore and my mum came in to visit and I just broke down. I said, "I can't do it and I won't be back" and she said, "Well I'd need to see that" and I've never been back. It's been nearly nine years. I never looked back.' (Wave b)

On release from prison, she moved back to live near her mother (facilitated by the lifting of the ASBO for staying out of trouble), cut off contact with her former peers, joined a sports club and engages in regular exercise which "helps with my anger, helps with my panic".

Case 11: Keith: the limitations of welfare conditionality in cases of ongoing substance addiction

Born into a financially secure family, Keith had a long history of paid employment in various roles. He had last worked three years previously, becoming unemployed because of alcohol dependency. He was assigned to the Support Group of ESA and his benefit status remained unchanged across the two-year span of our repeat interviews. At wave a Keith stated he was in supported recovery for his addiction. Having rented out his privately owned flat to raise some money, his tenant had not paid him the rent, so he lived in his partner's accommodation. Keith admitted committing a number of offences, including domestic violence against a previous partner; all of which had been committed under the influence of alcohol. Keith further detailed how two years earlier he had been served with an ASBO due to noise and other nuisance in his flat, some of which was caused by a friend he was allowing to stay.

> 'I was getting drunk and it was my fault. ... I think in that [same] week with the police confiscating my stuff, so I couldn't play loud music anymore ... and that's when the ASBO thing happened. So, I had to tell [Friend] not to come round.' (Wave a)

Reflecting on his situation, Keith identified the ASBO and an ensuing court appearance, which in turn led to the offer of an alcohol abstinence programme, as significant in addressing his alcohol-induced problematic behaviour.

> 'When I think back at it, I suppose, yes, the ASBO did have some sort of positive effect ... made me calm down and really think about what I was doing wrong and basically it all ended up as drink. ... I needed to get that sorted out. ... The ASBO didn't stop me from doing it. The court offering me [Abstinence programme], that's what was different. They actually offered me three months of therapy ... the ASBO it made me start.' (Wave a)

A year later Keith had gained repossession of his own flat. While undergoing residential treatment for alcoholism he had allowed his (then homeless) son to move into the flat. Returning home to chaos he relapsed and started to drink heavily again.

> 'His pals were all there. They were all smoking bongs ... they'd all got beers. The last thing I needed was to be going into a situation like that and I just flipped. I actually relapsed that day after ten days of being sober. So that was me for about another three months.' (Wave b)

His son continued to engage in criminality and ASB in the flat. As the owner, Keith was threatened with a further ASBO until he managed to convince the authorities he was not responsible. Having 'trashed' the flat, and facing various criminal and nuisance charges, his son abandoned the property and disappeared, leaving Keith to pick up the pieces. Keith declared himself bankrupt, handed over the management of his finances to a charity and was trying hard not to relapse again.

> 'Oh, how the mighty have fallen. It feels like I was doing okay and now I'm just right at rock bottom again. I decided to take [medication], which makes you really ill if you drink on it, as a deterrent, a sort of failsafe. ... It's really hard.' (Wave b)

At wave c, a year later, Keith's drinking had escalated, leading to the instigation of a breach of the peace charge for ASB.

'Drinking much more, just in the last couple of months though ... stress and the court really. ... Watch telly, get pissed at the moment. ... The police arrived with this social worker and they threatened to give me an ASBO and I just burst out laughing "Why are you giving a middle age man an ASBO? I'll hang it on my toilet door." ... The more she got irate, the more I kept laughing.' (Wave c)

Asked to reflect on the likely impact of the new ASBO he was potentially facing, he stated:

'Absolutely pointless. ... If you get an ASBO you should get support along with it as a social worker, a psychotherapist, a Community Psychiatric Nurse otherwise it's not going to work.' (Wave c)

Without accompanying, ongoing support to help Keith address his ongoing alcoholism, positive and sustained behaviour change moving forward appeared highly unlikely.

Some common ground can be found across Linda's and Keith's cases. Both highlight the limitations of punitive sanction-based approaches in reducing ASB among those whose lives are structured by multiple and overlapping forms of disadvantage. The futility of prioritising sanction-based approaches as effective behaviour change mechanisms and the ensuing damage which they may then generate is clearly evidenced. Linda's ongoing breach of the escalating ASB interventions to which she was subject over time triggered homelessness, further undermined her mental and physical wellbeing, distanced her from familial support and failed to reform her behaviour in any meaningful way and led to repeat offending and periods of imprisonment. Conversely, it's also possible to argue that criminal justice sanctions were important in triggering positive behaviour change for Linda and Keith. Certainly, Linda wanted to break away from the cycle and pressures of repeat incarceration, but the wish to reconcile with her family and avoid causing future hurt to loved ones (compare Bowpitt et al, 2011) was also key in motivating her to seek professional support to manage her mental health issues moving forward. Considering the ineffectiveness of her ASBO, Linda commented "that with more support" her earlier decade of offending and self-harm may well have been averted. Similarly, for Keith, court proceedings linked to his ASBO directly led to the offer of therapy which helped him, albeit temporarily, to manage the drinking that underpinned much of his problematic behaviour. However, it was support, not sanction, that most effectively triggered positive behavioural change for both. For Amy, the ongoing support she received from both professionals and her family enabled her to sustain long-term positive behaviour change. Keith's period in supported recovery, although short-lived, was enabled by appropriate support. Given the multiple issues many were dealing with, such setbacks were common among those WSUs subject to various ASB interventions. Behaviour change for these respondents was often complex and non-linear with periods of progress often followed by relapse (Batty and Fletcher, 2018; Flint, 2019).

Analysis of Jimmy's story further reiterates the importance of providing effective support for marginalised individuals subject to the implementation of ASB sanctions. Unlike Keith who, as an owner-occupier, was insulated from the threat of eviction, Jimmy's housing security was under threat due to the ASB behaviour of others in and around his flat (see also Sinead's case 13).

Case 12: Jimmy: punishing the victim of antisocial behaviour?

Jimmy is an older man in his 60s. In his wave a interview, following previous experiences of homelessness, he had lived in a housing association flat for 18 months. He is unemployed and last worked a decade ago and managing an ongoing mental health issue for which he is receiving therapy. In receipt of Housing Benefit, he was claiming benefits to maintain his National Insurance credits but had taken the decision not to claim Jobseeker's Allowance (JSA) to avoid being forced to search for work without "any help from the Jobcentre". He had recently been issued with an ABC following complaints about noise and ASB associated with his flat.

> 'I had someone ... staying temporarily, I suppose, living with me, but they were causing trouble and antisocial behaviour. They decided to have an ABC with me – which I breached, basically. ... You sign an agreement saying what you will or will not do and if you keep to it, it's okay. If you don't then they can get an eviction. ... I used to go off and do my things and leave them in the flat. ... It's not my behaviour, no, but I thought I was being blamed for things that were beyond my control. ... They say it's my responsibility, my tenancy ... just get the police in, but with this person that isn't always easy. ... Because they just take the phone off me. I've had to buy five phones this year already.' (Wave a)

Worried and unable to stop the visits of the person causing the ASB, Jimmy felt unsupported by his Housing Officer who took the side of the complainant and simply reiterated the need for him to take control of the situation. Concerned that he may face eviction, Jimmy turned to a homelessness project worker who continued to support him.

> '[Homelessness project worker] got me onto social services, who have recommended me for sheltered housing, which I think would be much better for me. ... I said I'd go anywhere; I'm not going to refuse an area. ... I've got to keep proactive about my assertiveness, things like that, so I've got to work on that. Self-care has got to be priority number one.' (Wave a)

However, Jimmy was unable to access older people's sheltered housing because he did not meet the age threshold. A year on at wave b he expanded further on his problems and outlined how the support he received in the interim period had enhanced his ability to take back control of a situation he felt previously unable to address.

'I went to social services and got help there. ... I've been to psychotherapy which I'm still going. ... I'm stricter with myself and more aware of the situation and able to put a stop to it. ... It was someone who knew me from some time ago, kept coming round and taking money or taking things I bought, I had to replace them. ... I was giving it to this person and so obviously I didn't pay my bills, so my debt went up and then it took me ages to get back to normal. ... I was aware that if I didn't succeed in stopping it from happening, I'd be on the street and I wouldn't get any help.' (Wave b)

At his wave c interview Jimmy reiterated the importance of the ongoing help he received from the homelessness charity in managing his own situation and also supporting others through the voluntary work he now undertook.

'I'm more aware of things now, and also because of the voluntary work I do at [Homelessness Charity] my self-esteem is much higher. I'm more determined to sort it out. ... When I have a problem I have acquaintances at [Homelessness Charity], some staff, that I can always speak to if I need to, so I see people every week when I go in for voluntary work.' (Wave c)

Jimmy's case raises interesting questions. First, this is a vulnerable older man who, having experienced homelessness in the past, desperately wanted to retain his tenancy and live peacefully. The reality of his situation is that he is being dominated and bullied by another person; a woman who takes his money and whose behaviour on gaining entry into Jimmy's flat is the root cause of the reported ASB. Predictably perhaps, given the complaints received from other tenants, the landlord's response is to instigate an ABC with the tenant (Jimmy), backed up by the threat of eviction if breached. Although essentially a victim rather than a perpetrator of ASB, the landlord's response is simply to threaten sanction and tell Jimmy to deal with it or face the consequences. Research elsewhere highlights that once complaints are made and ASB procedures set in train, those identified as perpetrators often have difficulty in accessing help from landlords to deal with underlying ASB they themselves may face (Cameron, 2022a). Understanding Jimmy's predicament, both the homelessness charity and social services initially try to resolve the situation by attempting to move Jimmy beyond the reach of the person who is mistreating him and also the actual perpetrator of the ASB. When this fails, the support they put in place to equip Jimmy with the personal resources to better assert himself to prevent future exploitation by others is central to improving his self-worth and managing the problematic behaviour that undermined him and caused wider nuisance. Second, in his wave b interview Jimmy revealed how he managed to survive financially without claiming JSA solely because an ascendant relative had recently bequeathed him a modest weekly income in their will. By not claiming JSA this enabled him to circumvent the behavioural requirements and associated pressures now inherent within highly conditional benefit regimes; something he had in common with Linda and Keith (and certain others in this chapter), who were exempt from mandatory work search and benefit sanctions due to their placement in the Support Group of ESA. Such cases highlight how the absence of the threat of compulsion and benefit sanctions through the operation of welfare conditionality within social security systems is important for individuals who are experiencing multiple and complex needs and who are looking to stabilise their lives. This lack of further conditionality in relation to necessary income is significant because where it is present it routinely exacerbates the problems faced by multiply excluded people (see the section on compound conditionality in this chapter).

The differential impact of family intervention policies

Despite inflated claims about the success of FIPs (for example, DCLG, 2015), the case studies that follow illustrate and explain the variable effectiveness of FIPs in addressing the behaviour of families whose lifestyle and behaviour have been deemed as problematic. Understanding the reasons why these interventions may succeed or fail is a difficult task. However, as ensuing discussions indicate, successfully tackling the wider contextual factors at play in families' lives, alongside the continued availability of a dedicated support worker to coordinate a family's interactions with the (sometimes myriad) other agencies involved are often key to securing positive behavioural outcomes (Batty and Flint, 2012; Bate, 2016). Let us first consider a successful family intervention.

Case 13: Sinead: enabling progress – a successful family intervention

Sinead is a young lone parent with no formal educational qualifications. At wave a[3] she was in receipt of Income Support and had never undertaken paid work but expressed a desire to do some employment training once her youngest child was in nursery. She had been issued with an ASBO because of ASB emanating from youths congregating around a flat which she had shared with a former partner.

'Their behaviour is down to us because they're visiting our property. ... A lot of complaints about swearing and things that the youths were doing. ... They'd sent me a warning letter prior obviously, noise nuisance letters and things like that and then it was a letter that I received with an interview for me to go into the housing office. ... That's when [I got] the ASBO. ... One of the things on the ASBO was that my name would get taken off the housing register for a year, so I wouldn't be able to put any bids on any houses. ... Which obviously was a problem with me wanting to be moved anyway. If the things kept on going while the ASBO was issued to me, then it would lead to eviction, so basically everything had to stop. ... These youths were obviously putting my housing situation at risk, so I started telling them that obviously you're going to have to clear off. ... That's when the youth that we did have the problem with at the time smashed my window and, because I had social services as well at the time, I then phoned social services.' (Wave a)

Paradoxically, in attempting to comply with the ASBO, and preserve her future right to a social tenancy, Sinead herself became a victim of ASB. Supported by her social worker she was ultimately allowed to relocate to a new area where she was allocated to the local Family Intervention Team (FIT).

'At the beginning, there were lots of different things I needed help with; money management, rent paying, getting rehoused, nursery ... because obviously, at the time, I was still in temporary accommodation. ... [FIT worker] has access to my rent account, so he can check it to make sure it's getting paid. ... [Child] starts nursery on Monday and then I'll be starting my training which is everything we've planned to do more or less done.' (Wave a)

'[FIT worker] when we first met, he discussed things. He asked me to put things in my words. ... [They] do a support plan with you ... some things you don't actually think about and then, once it's suggested to you, oh yes, perhaps that is a good thing. ... It makes you think more. ... I want to improve myself ... prove to people that I am capable.' (Wave a)

When interviewed for a second time 12 months later, Sinead's life had improved significantly. Her child was attending nursery and regular payments reducing the rent arrears owed on her previous tenancy were ongoing. Sinead had also applied for voluntary work. Her progress was such that she had recently been 'signed off' by the FIT.

'Bills are the first thing on a pay day. My rent, gas, electric; once they're on, shopping. ... Social services are no longer involved as well. ... [FIT worker] made me think a lot more into what I was actually doing ... what were my main priorities ... being that intense, really helped me along, it just gave me that kick up the bum!' (Wave b)

'Maybe it does take something like [FIT] or social services to make you realise that the way you're living your life isn't right. When you do look at it yourself ... from an outsider's point of view. ... It does hit you in the face and you do realise yes, maybe things should change. ... I'm thinking a lot more about the place I'm living in and obviously to respect neighbours and rent needs paying. ... I've changed quite a lot in that way. I've done a basic maths course. ... Currently waiting for a Criminal Records Bureau check to come back because I'm going into voluntary work for the elderly because I'm wanting to become a carer.' (Wave b)

Additionally, Sinead reported a recent, very positive meeting with Jobcentre Plus (JCP) who were keen to support her endeavours to find future employment.

'Over a child's age of one, my local Jobcentre do a work-focused interview. I had one of those, I mentioned what I'd like to do and that I'd possibly like to do some work experience. Within two weeks they'd got back in touch with me and found a place that I could work as a volunteer. ... They are very understanding about if you have got children especially if you're a single parent. ... They said if I needed to be in voluntary work more than 15 hours they could supply me with childcare costs. ... The interview was compulsory, but no, I didn't feel any pressure.' (Wave b)

Reflecting on the positive changes to her life that had occurred in the previous year, Sinead was optimistic about her future:

'My self-esteem's a lot better ... my parenting. ... I'm happy with where my life's at the minute thanks to the support and things that I have had. ... Yes, I think I'm able to do it now, definitely. Like I said, now I've had that kick up the bum I think I've got the ball rolling now.' (Wave b)

Although Sinead admitted that the jolt of the ASBO, and its potential consequences, initially scared her, the intensive support she subsequently received from her dedicated FIT worker was fundamental to her reflecting on, and improving, her life moving forward. Sinead specifically highlighted her FIT worker's non-confrontational, partnership approach ("He doesn't just drill it at you") and how he advocated on her behalf in multi-agency meetings as significant in helping her progress. It is the absence of compulsion when interacting with the FIT, and more recently with JCP staff, that have enabled her to address problematic aspects of her previous behaviour and simultaneously moved her much closer to the possibility of paid work. Sinead's story provides further evidence of the potential for frontline family intervention teams to look beyond the unhelpful labelling of 'problem families' to provide practical support to help families address problematic aspects of their behaviour and enhance their future aspirations (Batty and Flint, 2012; Parr, 2017).

Sinead and Jimmy's cases raise important wider issues about the identification of ASB and the effectiveness of the policies routinely used to tackle it. The boundaries between victim and perpetrator of ASB are often blurred and may be subject to change overtime (Cameron, 2022b). Although Sinead accepted that aspects of her lifestyle were problematic and needed to change, it was the behaviour of others (the youths in the vicinity of her flat) that triggered her being issued with an ASBO. Subsequently, this led to her becoming a victim of the youths' ongoing ASB which, simultaneously, jeopardised Sinead's attempt to bid for a new social tenancy and enhanced the possibility of eviction. Being rehoused elsewhere was clearly a key initial step in helping address Sinead's issues. In her wave b interview she noted the significance of making a conscious decision to distance herself from former 'friends' once she had been moved. Relocation undoubtedly improved Sinead's situation (although ultimately the youths' ongoing ASB remained unresolved). Furthermore, without the support of the social work team, who were involved in Sinead's life for other reasons, it is highly unlikely that Sinead's initial relocation to emergency accommodation would have been secured.

Case 14: Freya: the limits of 'family' intervention

Freya is a middle-aged mother of three children. She previously worked for over 20 years before an accident and the onset of depression ended her long-term relationship and triggered a mental health crisis. These events led to unemployment and a close relative becoming guardian of her children. On finding a new partner her relative subsequently left the children to fend for themselves and Freya moved into the house and resumed care of her children. Because the tenancy was not in Freya's name the family were evicted, ending up homeless and living in bed and breakfast accommodation. Following referral by social services, because of her son's violent behaviour, the FIT became involved. At wave a with the support of the FIT and a homeless charity the family had been rehoused and the son's behaviour improved.

> 'The woman from Family Intervention, she was the one who helped me move both times. They come and visit me once every week. ... Since we've been in the house, he's settled; his behaviour has calmed down. ... We don't argue or row at all now and we have a laugh. ... We went out bowling yesterday afternoon; that was lovely and it was the first time that I'd been out with the kids together and they didn't row. ... My work with the FIT has finished and obviously [Homelessness Charity] has nearly finished. ... That all these services are going is a good thing. ... They can see that there is no need for them anymore because we are starting to become like a proper family should be.' (Wave a)

Twelve months later Freya's initial positive summation of the FIT's impact had changed. Despite everybody's best efforts, and the FIT's willingness to become involved, she reported that the underlying causes of her son's behaviour remained unresolved and violence continued to blight the family's lives.

'I got [FIT], my son didn't turn up for the meetings, so it was pointless. ... He's not ready to talk about his issues yet. ... [FIT] can't really do anything for him because until he's ready to actually address the issues that make him angry because it is a big thing. ... He does try so hard, so hard not to get so mad. As you noticed, I've got holes in my door, I've got dents in my fridge, his bedroom.' (Wave b)

At wave c, the situation had further deteriorated. Her son had left the family home, become homeless and was in trouble with the police.

'I had the social services on the phone asking would I have him back or could he come back to me. ... Because of all of his violence and how angry he is. I just can't, I love my son to bits, I really do and I don't like the fact that I had to say no. ... Not because he isn't welcome but because I just don't want him living here, I've got to think of her [daughter] and the violence.' (Wave c)

When contemplating the overall effectiveness of the FIT, Freya's response offered insight into the positive potential and the wider limitations of behavioural interventions that are unable to offer solutions to the wider issues associated with living in poverty.

'There was a difference for a while but once they all go. ... I just think that [son's] problems were not explored enough. ... His problems don't stem from necessarily me; they stem from what he went through when he was temporarily housed with my [relative] because I had a breakdown. ... It was more I had to do it than wanted to do it. ... We did action plans. Luckily enough the worker I had, she was lovely. ... They all said, oh he will settle down but he didn't, he just got worse.' (Wave c)

'He got in with this kid and his father and this boy's dad has criminal tendencies. ... [Freya's son] was thinking it was going to be great. ... He was genuinely interested in what [FIT worker] did with him, the bike project. ... But I think the influence from his friend, of shall we say the limelight sort of thing, the money, "I could earn lots of money from doing this." ... I think that was more of a pull because I'm on benefits and I haven't got the means to get all the things that I might need for him to be in a rugby team and he didn't like the stigma of being the "benefit child".' (Wave c)

As Freya's case shows, FIPs can improve certain aspects of families' lives over time. For example, the FIT were instrumental in supporting Freya's transition into a new home following homelessness. This, alongside referral to several specialist educational projects, also led to initial improvements in her son's behaviour. The personal commitment of individual FIT workers to support the family and try to address the son's behaviour is also evident across the two years of interviews. However, it is apparent that cessation of her son's violent behaviour was temporary and, ultimately, the intensive support available failed to address the underlying causes of the son's behaviour; leaving a young man who appears to have embarked on a pathway to offending as the best solution to his ongoing problems.

Case 15: Jeanette: focusing on the wrong issue?

Jeanette has poor physical health and significant debts. She last worked in retail a couple of years previously, giving up her job because her mother who became seriously ill could not continue providing childcare. The FIT first became involved because her daughter, who Jeanette indicated was being bullied, failed to regularly attend school. Initially, a FIT worker visited daily, helping establish a routine for her daughter and build Jeanette's confidence. At wave a her daughter was attending school, but Jeanette believed the level of intervention and focus on her parenting skills was inappropriate.

> 'It was purely her attendance, not because of my parent skills or anything like that. ... I'm actually signed off now. ... It's prompted me to be harder on my daughter with things like her going to school. ... I can't afford another fine and I'm definitely not going to prison. ... I appreciated the help ... [but overall] I think it was pointless. ... Don't get me wrong, I enjoyed meeting them and that but nothing has changed for [Daughter] at all. Only the fact that I've been harder on her. ... I think they could do wonderful work with people but in the right situation but, to me and my situation, well, it didn't need that sort of intervention. ... I don't think I needed the sort of work that they thought I needed, to be quite honest with you.' (Wave a)

At wave b Jeanette's daughter had started high school and was once again refusing to attend. The FIT became involved for a second time and her daughter was awaiting an appointment with Child and Adolescent Mental Health Services (CAMHS). Frustrated and demoralised, Jeanette resented the FIT's perceived focus on her insufficient parenting skills and felt that she was being coerced into attending inappropriate support:

> 'They referred me back over and apparently if I wouldn't have accepted their [FIT's] help anyway then social services was the next step. But I just don't know what they think I can do. I mean it's been like it since reception. I've done everything they've asked me to do.' (Wave b)

> '[FIT] not helpful at all. They've put me on a parent group the first one was for babies. She's not a baby. They were talking about babies, so I refused to go. Then she set me one up there for teenagers, because obviously she was going to big school. ... I went every week like I was meant to but no, that didn't really help either. ... I wouldn't change how I've brought up my daughter. The only thing, like I said, is her schooling. But that's not my problem. ... Like I said, she is a very,

very bright child. It's such a shame. I don't want her to waste that, because as she gets older I suppose she will get her confidence. ... I want her to be able to have a good job.' (Wave b)

'I'm not going to another parenting group. There's no point. It's just useless. Like I said she's not a naughty child. ... I want them [FIPs] to go away, because it doesn't matter, she won't go to school.' (Wave b)

A year later at wave c Jeanette reported that things had dramatically improved for her daughter who, through the intervention of CAMHS, had been referred to a specialist school to support young people dealing with mental health issues.

'It was basically CAMHS that got [Daughter] in school. ... She went up there for a few meetings and had like a one-to-one session with the worker. ... She's now in a hospital school [Location] and she absolutely loves it. The change in her is amazing ... she's made so many friends. ... I've seen a really, really big difference. It just makes me happy to know that she's happy and she is really happy.' (Wave c)

Regular non-attendance at school has been recognised as having serious negative impacts on children's future life chances and parents who do not ensure their child's attendance (or provide appropriate home schooling), face a range of legal sanctions (gov.uk, 2021) and Jeannette had herself been subject to a court imposed fine. However, Jeanette's increasing frustration across the three longitudinal interviews with the FIT's focus on her perceived parental deficiencies, is apparent. She consistently argued that her child's refusal to attend school would be resolved once her daughter received specialist help. Ultimately, it was only when CAMHS diagnosed the daughter's anxiety, were able to offer ongoing treatment/support and referred her to an appropriate educational setting that the situation improved. Problematic parental behaviour can be a significant factor in children's non-attendance at school and, given the FIT's remit, it is perhaps predictable that they should seek to address the issue in hand by seeking to remedy what they perceived as Jeanette's poor parenting skills. However, research has also identified chronic anxiety in children as a causal factor in school refusal (Finning et al, 2019). Rather than attempting to resolve Jeanette's perceived poor parenting behaviour the solution to such cases may lie in providing more adequate funding for children's mental health services and ensuring young people and their parents are better supported in managing their mental wellbeing (Children's Commissioner, 2020).

Compound conditionality

Beyond the conditionality evident within the social security system, for many people experiencing homelessness, offenders and others seen as engaged in antisocial or problematic activities, eligibility for the receipt of various services are often contingent on specific behavioural requirements, as highlighted in this chapter. For example, individuals may be required to simultaneously engage with interventions in relation to social tenancies, enforcement approaches designed to combat rough sleeping and ASB and FIPs or face various sanctions (for example, removal of benefit, access to a support service, loss of social tenancy and/or a fine or imprisonment) if they fail to meet specified behavioural standards or responsibilities (see Batty and Fletcher, 2018; Batty et al, 2018; Johnsen et al, 2018b for further discussions). As such, certain people, often those with multiple and complex needs, are subject to 'compound conditionality'. This occurs when a person is subject to the imposition of behavioural requirements (and accompanying sanctions for non-compliance), in relation to two or more aspects of their life and the exercise of such conditionality combines to intensify (that is, compound) the problems and social exclusion that they then may face.

Case 16: Alan: compound conditionality in action

Alan had previously worked in various manufacturing and hospitality jobs. He had been unemployed for several years, largely due to long-term substance misuse, which had also led to street homelessness. Alan was on a methadone maintenance programme and was also receiving further medical treatment for a serious long-term physical health condition. Because of ongoing physical and mental health impairments he was in receipt of ESA in the Support Group across the three waves of interviews (but had previously been on JSA). Following a couple of years in hostel accommodation, at wave a he was living in social housing but threatened with eviction for repeated complaints about his behaviour.

> '[Social landlord] said that they're still getting complaints I'm smoking weed, the smell of weed coming from mine. I've once again totally denied it. I said to [housing officer] "This is 18 times, you're not finding nothing, when's this going to stop?" ... I've had enough of it. And they've said to me if they get another complaint in the next two weeks they're going to take legal action to get me out. And also they're going to pass all this information as well on to the police again.
> ... I do smoke weed but I don't smoke in my flat, and I'm telling you that now.
> ... You get told by police don't smoke it on the street, smoke it in your house. So what are you meant to do? Break the law, go on the streets, smoke it where you're going to get nicked? The police tell you to smoke it at home.' (Wave a)

Asked how the threat to his tenancy affected him, Alan detailed the negative impact it generated in relation to his opioid treatment regime before also reflecting on the consequences of being issued with a benefit sanction when previously in receipt of JSA:

> 'I'm not going to any of my appointments anymore. I've just messed up my script because of it. ... Because I missed my doctor's appointment, because of all this shit going on. ... I'm having to go back to fucking supervised consumption in a chemist and that pisses me off that because it's embarrassing. ... I never went to the interview because of what's going on in the flat. Because of all this shit. It's doing my head in.' (Wave a)

Commenting on the impact of his benefit sanction:

> '[Jobcentre] said I missed an appointment. But I never, I phoned up about the appointment and cancelled it. But even so they said I missed it and it was the third appointment that I'd missed so they sanctioned me. I had nothing. ... They shouldn't just take money off people and leave them with nothing. ... I had to go out robbing when they done that. ... I didn't do the food banks then. I had to go out robbing. That's not good though, do you know what I mean? To leave people with nothing and destitute and no electric.' (Wave a)

At wave b complaints about cannabis persisted. Alan told how he received a further six or seven home visits and several letters from the landlord and expanded on how he worried about what would happen if he lost his home:

> '"Under your tenancy, you're not permitted to smoke cannabis in the building" and blah de blah, "If this persists we will take you to court and apply for an eviction". That's what I keep getting through the door and I'm not doing anything for them to do that. I'm not smoking weed in my gaff, I'm not. ... It gets me depressed. Part of why I'm on the sick is depression anyway. I don't need it, I'm thinking I'm going to lose my gaff; I'll end up back on the streets, back on the gear. I can't handle that, I couldn't.' (Wave b)

Additionally, Alan's financial situation had worsened. He found himself stuck in a 'catch-22' situation due to the implementation of the Spare Room Subsidy Housing Benefit rules implemented in 2011 (see Chapter Two):

> 'There's the bedroom tax, which is putting me into debt and eventually I'll lose my gaff over it because it's building up and building up. ... I've asked to be moved, but because I'm in arrears they won't move me. If they move me the arrears will stop building up and I'll be able to pay them off.' (Wave b)

At wave c, two years after his first interview, compound conditionality continued to undermine Alan's attempts to desist from the harmful behaviours that characterised his past. Sanctioned once again by the Jobcentre, this time erroneously for non-attendance at a work-focused interview, which, as a member of the ESA Support Group he did not have to go to, and subject to ongoing pressures related to the repeated but unproven complaints of ASB, his situation had deteriorated:

> 'It was a difficult five weeks. ... I had to pay back what I borrowed and then when I did get the money, I had to pay it back so I didn't have no money again. ... [The block of flats] is full of old people, I said "obviously I'm not liked; move me". They won't, they won't do nothing ... they want me out; that's what they want, but they're not getting me out. I'm not doing nothing wrong. ... I'm a lot more distant now from everyone in the block. ... I'm being horrible the way I speak about them as well ... I used to be on heroin for years; I've been off it for [x] years. I done well to get off drugs and I'm being accused of something that I'm not. It winds you up. When it first started I nearly relapsed and I nearly went back to heroin ... by accusing me of this is they're isolating me even further. ... I've been depressed and when I'm like that I don't want to do nothing; I'm not bothered about anything. I'm at risk of going back to square one.' (Wave c)

Frustrated by the landlord's persistent monitoring of his behaviour, without instigating further action and facing mounting rent arrears (because of his inability to make up the shortfall in his reduced Housing Benefit), Alan repeated his request to be rehoused elsewhere into a one-bedroom flat. This would simultaneously solve the ASB complaints of his current neighbours and stop the ongoing accumulation of further rent arrears; both of which threatened the progress he had made in addressing the most problematic aspects of his life. As noted, this would not occur while rent arrears remained against his name.

Case 17: Eddy: back 'on track' in spite of benefit sanctions

Eddy outlined how he had either been in prison or homeless for most of his young adult life. At wave a he was in receipt of ESA in the Support Group due to long-term mental health conditions and was taking medication for anger management issues. He had just got a new tenancy. Two years previously, in his late teens, he had initially been served with ASBOs and then faced subsequent fines and custodial sentences for street drinking, nuisance and criminal activity, which he believed were ineffective in changing his behaviour.

> 'I didn't give a fuck about anything. I'd rob anything. What I wanted I just took. Then the police started giving me ASBOs. ... I wasn't allowed on a certain area

of my own street. ... Every shopping mall I wasn't allowed in ... [ASBOs made] no difference. I'm still me. The coppers can't tell me what to do. ... I don't see myself, when I'm sat up there, causing trouble. I don't. I'm just sat there having a laugh with my friends. ... As soon as the police come, move you on ... the beer starts winding you up, because of the police, and you're going off kicking wing mirrors off or fighting your next man.' (Wave a)

Eddy also outlined how the imposition of a benefit sanction triggered rent arrears, a period of homelessness and survival crime:

'Because I went to the mental health hospital, I got sectioned. ... They stopped my money. ... I get a sanction, bloody hell; that's more pain and hard work. ... I tried applying for Hardship. ... I filled everything in I needed to and didn't receive anything. Then they stopped paying Housing Benefit. All it did was put me in debt.' (Wave a)

'I had to adapt. ... I've got no family whatsoever. ... I wasn't allowed to come into this place. ... I had to commit crime and stuff, it was the only way. ... I only stole because I needed food. It wasn't like I needed drugs or drink or fags. I just needed something to eat. I got done, I got arrested for nicking a sandwich.' (Wave a)

Keen to take responsibility for his behaviour Eddy was trying to address his behaviour and break the cycle of offending, arrest and jail that had characterised his life so far:

'The courts and police, they've known me since I was a child. ... I'm not proud of it but it's like my behaviour, I can't help it. It's like I've always been on [medication] for [mental health impairment]. ... It's nobody else's fault. It's always my choice. ... Daft people I knocked about with when I was young but I don't do some of the stuff that I used to do ... rob houses and cars. ... I started to grow up a bit and get a bit wiser. ... I just had enough of going back in and out of jail ... going in and starting over and going back, starting all over.' (Wave a)

When interviewed at wave b 12 months later, Eddy reported he had been assessed as fit for work, moved off ESA onto JSA and assigned to the Work Programme. He had received a further six-month benefit sanction for not completing his job search requirements and was angry towards JCP and Work Programme staff who he believed had failed to appreciate his literacy problems or offer appropriate support. This was contrasted with the help provided by a charity support worker.

'Yes, you have to fill that out and my writing is not good ... so much will be good and then it starts going mad and then I just fucking rip it up because I get really angry easily. ... Since I had the interview with you I think I've had two payments ... thank fuck I'm getting housing benefits. ... [Work Programme] they're just arseholes, mate, they're fucking rank.' (Wave b)

> '[Charity support worker is] a right good guy and always helps me if I need something to be read and that. ... He doesn't judge you, he doesn't fucking look at you to say that you're lying and things like that. ... He listens, he doesn't look down at me.' (Wave b)

A further 12 months on at wave c, the importance of the charity support worker's intensive help in managing Eddy's problems and enabling him to avoid relapse into offending behaviour is apparent. Eddy has resumed a supervised medication regime and was awaiting further therapy. He was undertaking some voluntary work and hoped to commence basic catering training in the near future. The charity worker had worked with Eddy to initiate a Personal Independence Payment claim and, importantly, liaised with JCP to alert them of Eddy's issues and his ongoing efforts to turn his life around. This has broken the cycle of anger, non-compliance and sanction that characterised Eddy's prior relationship with JCP.

> 'It's got much better now. Now I'm on track and the [JCP] adviser knows what's what. So, I have to go in there, quick sign and then I'm out. ... They're on about putting me on ESA. I had a different adviser. He met me outside, bless him. He was all right. He was only a young lad, but he understood me.' (Wave c)

> 'I needed help because I was going off track again. ... All I need now is just to see this psychiatrist. [Charity support worker] helped me, got me back into going to the gym, stopped smoking. ... He helps me all the time with that [job search requirements]. He helps with everything like my shopping and stuff ... comes down and just checks on me and that because I'm on [medication]. So I get that once a month. ... Yes, a hell of a lot better. ... Out of the gutter, from the fucking street onto my feet.' (Wave c)

Individuals with multiple and complex needs are routinely subject to behavioural requirements, compulsion and sanction in relation to multiple aspects of their lives. Alan and Eddy's cases show how compound conditionality regularly operates. When progress in managing or desisting from problematic behaviour occurs, usually through engagement with appropriate support services, it can be easily undermined by the application of sanctions elsewhere.

Conclusions

The use of welfare conditionality is far from a cure-all solution to antisocial and problematic behaviour. Its implementation may trigger a range of consequences. These include positive behaviour changes ranging from episodic engagement with support services in times of crisis (which provides the space for temporary cessation of harmful activities), to the more meaningful improvements in people's self-esteem and the individual agency required to achieve transformative, sustained desistence from antisocial or criminal behaviour. More negatively, welfare conditionality, especially 'compound conditionality', may promote disengagement from support, further destabilise already marginalised individuals and trigger worsening behavioural outcomes (Batty et al, 2018; Batty and Fletcher, 2018: Watts and Fitzpatrick, 2018a).

As Batty and Fletcher note, 'change starts with the individual' (2018: 3); people need to possess the motivation and personal capacity to change their own behaviour. Motivations for seeking help among those with multiple needs and vulnerabilities are often complex. Factors such as a desire to reconnect with family, personal recognition of harm to self and others, and the development of enhanced self-worth are all important. Decisions to change may also be triggered by more negative events; imprisonment, personal injury, or a more general tiring of the ongoing threats to housing, personal freedom and even life itself that persistent harmful behaviour or repeat offending may bring. However, not everyone is equally able to make such decisions. For example, those experiencing substance addiction, facing hunger, or a housing or mental health crisis are often unlikely, or unable, to prioritise changing their behaviour over and above meeting basic daily survival needs. Nonetheless, the priorities of those engaged in antisocial or harmful behaviours are not fixed in stone but evolve over time with their changing experiences and circumstances (Bowpitt et al, 2011). It is therefore vital that when people seek to change their behaviour, that suitable support from a range of actors (statutory, non-statutory, family [if appropriate]), is available to help them try to move forward with their lives. Those who are supported to develop their self-esteem and empowered to take back personal control are more likely to make substantive progress in getting their lives back on track and desist from harmful activities (McNeill and Bowpitt, 2021). However, any support must be continuously offered alongside a realistic recognition that, among those facing multiple challenges, progress may be temporary, with relapse a recurrent reality; something that is out of kilter with the decontextualised, linear 'rational actor' models of behaviour change that dominate behaviour change models in policy circles (see Chapter Three).

As evidenced by the longitudinal case studies in this chapter, the most effective interventions in tackling those behaviours that are deemed harmful prioritise care over control. For example, FITs that are able to proactively work with families and provide intensive support and curtail the imposition of further sanctions are most likely to enable people to reconsider aspects of their conduct and improve the lives of family members and those around them (Batty and Flint, 2012). In contrast, while welfare conditionality, whether it is deployed within social security or ASB regimes, remains wedded to sanctions as the default response to individual non-compliance (that is, a personal failure to meet the required behavioural conditions), it is more likely to impede, rather than facilitate, the personal progress required to reduce those behaviours that are considered harmful or antisocial.

Notes

[1] ASBOs were a new form of civil court order, introduced in the Crime and Disorder Act (1998). They granted local authorities or the police the powers to stop an individual from acting in an antisocial manner and/or to exclude them from their home or other specified locality. Breach of an ASBO may lead to imprisonment. They continue to operate in Scotland but have been superseded in England by measures introduced in Crime and Policing Act (2014). See further discussions in Chapter Two.

[2] An Acceptable Behaviour Contract (ABC) is 'a voluntary written agreement which is signed by an individual committing antisocial behaviour. In signing the contract, the individual is agreeing to abide by the terms specified and to work with the relevant support agencies' (ASB Help, 2021: np). Breach of an ABC can trigger further ASB interventions, legal proceedings and/or ultimately eviction.

[3] We were able to interview Sinead on two occasions one year apart.

SIX

Unintended outcomes? The wider impacts of compulsion and benefit sanctions in social security

Chapters Four and Five considered the efficacy of welfare conditionality in moving recipients off social security benefits into paid work and also in relation to the reduction or cessation of harmful and antisocial behaviour. This chapter sets out and explores other significant key outcomes that ensue when 'work first' welfare conditionality is extensively promoted and rigorously implemented. The use of benefit sanctions is central to welfare conditionality within social security regimes and the first part of the chapter offers a commentary on the unprecedented rise (and subsequent fall) in the number of benefit sanctions within the UK (see Chapter Two, the social security system). Discussions in the second part of the chapter then set out the WelCond project's key findings in relation to the implementation of sanction-backed social security regimes, that is, the universally detrimental impacts on the health, financial and emotional wellbeing of those subject to them. Building on this, the third part offers more detailed discussions of how, and why, compulsion alongside the threat and implementation of benefit sanctions prompt a number of unintended behavioural outcomes as people seek either to retain receipt of their benefits, or alternatively reject the imposition of welfare conditionality.

The great UK sanctioning drive

During the period 2010–16, characterised as the 'great sanctioning drive' (Webster, 2016), the routine use of benefit sanctions in the UK significantly increased, reaching an unprecedented peak in 2013 before falling away in subsequent years (see Figure 6.1[1]). Between 2009/10 and 2013/14 more than one-fifth of all those individuals who claimed Jobseeker's Allowance (JSA) were sanctioned at some point (that is, 1,833,035 of the 8,232,560 individuals who claimed JSA within the specified five-year period). It is estimated that in the year to 30 September 2014 there were approximately 895,000 JSA and Employment and Support Allowance (ESA) sanctions issued before reconsiderations and appeals (Webster, 2015). The National Audit Office estimated that in 2015 there were around 800,000 referrals for a sanction decision among claimants of Universal Credit (UC), JSA, ESA or Income Support (NAO, 2016). The Department for Work and Pensions (DWP) have argued that the reduction in the use of sanctions in more recent years is indicative of the effectiveness of sanctions and improvements in the delivery of employment support feeding into higher levels of claimant compliance. However, evidence suggests that the rapid rise and subsequent fall in sanctioning rates is most likely due to changes in government policy feeding into DWP management priorities and thus frontline practice. Webster (2016) notes an unannounced ministerial level decision in May 2010 led to significant rises in the monthly numbers of people referred for a sanction by Jobcentre Plus (JCP) staff until October 2013, when referrals began to fall at similar rates across all JCP offices simultaneously; again, suggesting a higher level shift in policy impacting on frontline priorities and implementation. Changes in the expectations placed on claimants are also likely to have important effects. Following its introduction in 2011, the numbers of JSA and ESA claimants mandated to attend the Work Programme (WP) (see Figure 6.1) increased dramatically, bringing more people under the remit of the benefit sanctions regime. Perhaps unsurprisingly, this fuelled a subsequent rise in sanctions that fell away again as the numbers referred to the WP decreased from 2013 onwards (NAO, 2016; Webster, 2016).

It would be wrong to assume that more recent reductions in the maximum duration of sanctions and their overall use within the benefit system are indicative of a more substantial principled rejection of welfare conditionality by UK governments. The financial costs associated with implementing an extensive benefit sanctions regime are substantial, but UK administrations

Figure 6.1: Estimated annual total number of benefit sanctions before challenges, all benefits

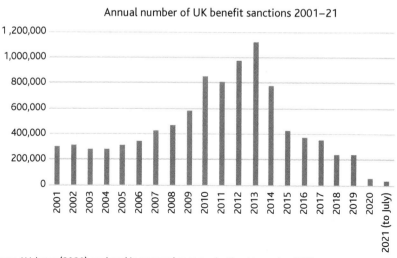

Source: Webster (2020), updated in personal communication November 2021

appear to be happy to bear such costs in order to retain sanctioning as a key part of the social security benefit system. In 2016 the DWP saved around £132 million in denied benefits due to the application of sanctions. However, the cost of administering sanctions (estimated to be between £30 and £50 million) and the £35 million in Hardship Payments subsequently made to qualifying claimants, alongside the much wider unknown costs to the public purse that accrue elsewhere due to the indirect effects their application, have to be weighed against any headline savings in a cost/benefit type analysis of sanctioning policy (NAO, 2016, 2018). Furthermore, changes instigated by the Conservative government in the Welfare Reform and Work Act 2016 illustrated a willingness to advance sanctions-backed welfare conditionality. Reductions in the child age thresholds (from three to two years old for mandatory work preparation, and from five to three years old for full work-related requirements), which govern when welfare conditionality is applied to lone parents, brought parents of ever younger children under the rubric of sanctions. The Act also abolished the additional £29.05 per week 'limited capability for work' payment previously allocated to disabled ESA/UC claimants placed in the Work Related Activity Group. Denounced by the Chancellor as a 'perverse incentive' that deterred certain claimants from exploring options to enter paid work, the government argued that its removal would encourage more disabled people into employment. Conversely, critics believed that loss of the payment would increase hardship among disabled people and push many further away from employment (CPAG, 2016).

As Figure 6.1 also illustrates, the number of benefit sanctions fell dramatically in 2020 and 2021. This was due to the exceptional circumstances triggered by the COVID-19 pandemic. Given the unique circumstances of the COVID-19 crisis and the subsequent unprecedented rise in benefit claims, the UK government introduced a number of significant temporary changes to social security policy (see Hobson, 2021 for details). In March 2020, with much of the economy in lockdown, JCP offices closed and wider freedom of movement outside the home curtailed, the DWP suspended work search/availability for work requirements and the use of benefit sanctions. However, in July 2021 sanctions-backed conditionality was reintroduced with claimants being re-contacted to review and agree personalised Claimant Commitments, which the DWP stated would be adjusted in light of any self-isolation, shielding or other COVID-19 associated requirements. In response to critics of the reinstatement of sanctions (Harris, 2020) and suggestions that the reintroduction of conditionality needed to be clearly communicated with claimants (Summers et al, 2021), the DWP emphasised that local JCP staff would be empowered to make use of their existing discretionary powers to ensure recommendations are sensitive to personal circumstances and local job market conditions and that 'a sanction will only be used where a claimant has not provided good reason for meeting the agreed requirements in the Claimant Commitment' (DWP, 2020d: np, cited in Hobson, 2021: 22). Leaving aside these pledges, independent analysis of the DWP statistics points to a significant rise in UC sanctions in the month immediately following their reintroduction, with 15,929 benefit sanctions issued in 2021 alone. A figure that if consistently repeated would equate to an estimated sanctions total for 2021 in excess of 191,000 (Webster, 2021). Despite significant falls in the number of benefit sanctions, and the DWP's abandonment of the three-year maximum sanction duration in 2019, they remain an integral part of the UK's current benefit system. The sanctions policy hiatus sparked by COVID-19 has passed and the number of sanctions implemented is again on an upward trajectory. Regardless of numbers implemented, those subject to benefit sanctions in the future will most likely continue to face similar issues and hardships, therefore, a reiteration of WelCond's key findings concerning benefit sanctions remains relevant for as long as sanctions are retained.

Among the welfare service users (WSUs) who undertook a wave a interview, 186 people discussed being subject to benefit sanctions; 104 had been sanctioned once, 69 between two and five times, and 13 had experienced more than five benefit sanctions. Numbers reduced significantly as the repeat waves of interviews progressed with 35 WSUs at wave b reporting a new benefit sanction(s) since their previous interview. Of these 29 were sanctioned once between their wave a and wave b interviews, five on between two to five occasions with a single respondent reporting in excess of five sanctions being applied. In our final wave c interviews, nine individuals reported being sanctioned on one occasion previously, with one interviewee recounting multiple sanctions. The high initial incidence of benefit sanctioning within the sample and the significant decrease across subsequent waves of repeat interviews is most likely explained by several factors. First, at wave a respondents were invited to reflect on and discuss the sanctions that they had been subject to in the years prior to their first interview. In contrast, when conducting the fieldwork for waves b and c researchers asked individuals to focus on new benefit sanctions that had been applied in the shorter 12-month period since they were last interviewed. Second, it is important to note that the three waves of repeat WSU interviews were conducted between 2014 and 2017. The high incidence of sanctions data generated in the wave a interviews therefore also likely reflects the knock-on effects of the harsher sanction regime first introduced in October 2012, that stimulated the historically unprecedented peak in benefit sanctions that subsequently occurred in 2013. The later wave b and wave c interviews were undertaken as national sanction numbers started to decline. Third, experience, or fear of, the dire consequences of a benefit sanction also prompted a number of WSUs to focus on ensuring compliance so that they avoided sanctions and their profoundly negative impacts moving forward (see the section on counterproductive compliance in this chapter).

Pernicious and punitive: the impacts of benefit sanctions

Benefit sanctions are now the dominant tool used to enforce work norms and punish non-compliance among social benefit recipients within the UK's conditional welfare state (Fletcher and Wright, 2018; Redman, 2020). Many of the case studies presented in Chapters Four and Five of this book (for example, see Harry, Ivan, Joy, John, Stacey, Sharon, Jacob, Alan and Eddy) evidence the harm and hardships that ensued when benefit sanctions were implemented. Previous analysis has also detailed the pernicious impacts generated among those respondents within the WelCond study who received benefit sanctions (Dwyer, 2018a, 2018b). In order to avoid repetition of previously published data this section presents two new case studies that outline the deeply negative impacts that benefit sanctions produce.

Case 18: Albert: sanctioned into poverty

Albert is an older man who migrated to the UK as a child 50 years ago. At wave a he had been unemployed for 18 months. He had previously undertaken a variety of jobs across his lifetime, many secured via employment agencies. Despite phoning beforehand to say he would be delayed due to a hospital appointment, Albert was sanctioned for being four hours late for a JCP meeting.

> 'I think it was rather harsh, because it's the first time I've actually missed an appointment with the Jobcentre ... not even give me a chance, and just sanction me. ... I even showed them the letters from the hospital. ... I've got to go for a hardship payment or crisis loan or something, because I've basically got no money; for electric, no money for gas. What's in the cupboard. ... I've got my tomato sauce, and that's it we've got nothing. ... If I appeal against it it's going to take longer than [a fortnight] anyway, so I'm just going to wait until I sign on again and then they're going to put me back on the JSA. It's not worth the hassle. ... I'm hungry now, I'm not going to get any food off them today.' (Wave a)

At wave b Albert remained unemployed and was having problems securing work because he had lost his UK passport and the agencies he approached had started asking for it as proof of his legal right to work. He reflected on how his previous benefit sanction had led to poverty and reduced his prospects of returning to work.

> 'By sanctioning you they're trying to say it gives you an incentive. ... That's the barrel of the gun pointing at your head, you've got to do this. So, it's a pressurised

incentive, but at the end of the day it's a very negative role in trying to help you back to work because if they sanction you that means you've got less money. ... If I got a job offer tomorrow. ... I haven't got the money to even go on the bus to get there, I haven't got decent clothes to wear. ... I can't remember the last time I bought anything apart from food. I don't buy clothes ... we've got no savings, we've got no car. The food is basically hand to mouth. ... You won't find anything in my freezer.' (Wave b)

A year later (at wave c), Albert detailed how, having resolved his documentation issue, he had registered with several employment agencies and found some short-term work in the past year. However, following a traffic accident, he again became unemployed. Once back on JSA after a period 'on the sick', he was mandated to sign on daily and then received a second benefit sanction for unsatisfactory job search.

'For three and a half months, they made me sign on every day. I rang the Jobcentre ... "You're wanting me to actively look for work, but you still want me to come to this Jobcentre which is a half hour walk from my house, you want me to come here every day and sign on?" ... "Yes, we want you to sign on every day." ... It was getting like a joke. ... "Just sign this." Sometimes I didn't even have to sign anything. ... They wouldn't say, "Do you want any help?" They just said, "Right, you can go." ... I go in of a day, are there any more new jobs come in? "Go and look on the computer." So I'd go over, go on the Universal Jobmatch, same jobs, same companies, same hours. ... All they did was use that to basically say, "You aren't looking on our Universal Jobmatch. Now we're sanctioning you." ... Thirteen weeks they've sanctioned me. ... The jobs which I receive on the Universal Jobmatch I've already applied for. ... "Well, you have to keep applying for this job."' (Wave c)

Demoralised, Albert set out how the sanction forced him to sell his possessions in an attempt to survive financially.

'They've got the misconception that I don't want a job. ... I hate being in this position I'm in now. It's making me feel depressed, it's like pressure's on you. ... When I was working it was so better, we'd save up, we'd have nice holidays, nice clothes, nice food. I've got none of that anymore. ... I've sold all my possessions ... my mountain bike, the iPad I got given by my sister, I've sold that just to get by. I've got nothing of any value; I've got no jewellery, got nothing. ... I've got no direct debits anymore because I can't afford to get anything. It's dire ... our first priority is paying the £37 a week out of our benefits towards the bedroom tax and the rent arrears.' (Wave c)

Living in a three-bedroom house, their adult children having grown up and left, Albert and his wife were also subject to the removal of the spare room subsidy (aka 'bedroom tax'). Albert noted that reductions in their benefit due to "the bedroom tax and sanctions" (wave c) left the couple with £50 per week joint income. Raising this issue at JCP he stated that he was told that his rent was not a JCP concern. On approaching his social landlord to downsize, their response was that a housing transfer was not possible because of his existing rent arrears (see also Alan in case 16); arrears that first came about due to the bedroom tax.

Case 19: Johnny: ineffective and inappropriate sanctioning

Johnny is a single, middle-age man who worked in a skilled industrial job for two decades before being made redundant four years prior to his wave a interview. Since then, he had moved in and out of various temporary jobs/zero hour contract work, signing back onto benefits for short periods when between jobs. At wave a he recounted being inappropriately sanctioned on JSA.

> '[JCP] appointment that I was due to go to at one of the offices in town. I wanted to change the appointment, the lady at the time said I couldn't do it there and then. I had to phone in or write in. … So I did all that.' (Wave a)

Nonetheless, he was subsequently sanctioned for failing to attend his original appointment and although his appeal against the decision was successful, he quickly fell into debt in the period before his benefit was reinstated.

> 'I finally got through to this lady. … They had an independent look at it and within five minutes she'd rung me back and said "Yes it should never have happened. We allow your claim" and then I got paid. … They admitted they messed up … but I got sanctioned … which really left me in the shit. … So for six weeks I was paid nothing. … The extra that I pay towards my rent I couldn't pay that. So I had to explain it to my landlord and as for food, gas, electric. … I relied on family and at one point I was getting very close to going to what they call food banks.' (Wave a)

A year later Johnny was working at a transport company in a job that he had independently found shortly after completing his wave a interview. However, at his wave c interview another year on (reflecting the ongoing cycle of the insecure work available), Johnny recounted how he had once again been made redundant and signed onto JSA for two months before, subsequently, securing another short-term contract in his current job. Beyond the financial hardship he suffered, Johnny's long-term resentment and anger at being inappropriately sanctioned was apparent. Across all three waves of interviews he strongly and consistently asserted the negative impacts that he believed behavioural conditionality engendered.

'They're [JCP] trying to force them into work, not help them find work. ... From my experience and the experience I've heard from others, it is all about the punishment.' (Wave a)

'I feel a lot better since I got this job. ... I got it myself via [a commercial website]. The threat of the sanction and actually being sanctioned had no bearing on me actually getting a job whatsoever. It was something I was doing anyway. ... [Consequently] you don't want to be cooperative. You've been sanctioned. You've got it in your head. ... Every time I went in [to JCP], "I got sanctioned". It doesn't help sanctioning anybody. ... It honestly doesn't work like that. ... If somebody takes food out of your kid's mouths or whatever you aren't going to forget. ... I'll always remember that, always.' (Wave b)

'It stressed me out and upset me. ... What they did was disgusting, truly. I don't blame a particular person I blame the system, that I'll never forgive.' (Wave c)

Reflecting concerns raised by other WSUs interviewed, Albert and Johnny's cases raise important questions about the wider behavioural assumptions that underpin welfare conditionality, while simultaneously highlighting the negative impacts of sanctions and compulsion. First, the necessity of using welfare conditionality to enforce work norms among benefit recipients is challenged. Albert and Johnny's commitment and willingness to work is evident in their prior histories of employment over the longer term. Albert had undertaken a variety of largely unskilled jobs, one after the other; with his most recent period of work ending only when he was knocked down by a car. Johnny had previously held a single skilled job for over 20 years before facing redundancy. Moving forward, using his own initiative, he subsequently independently searched for, and attained, a series of less secure jobs. Rather than lending support to those who advocate the imposition of welfare conditionality as a necessary corrective for irresponsible 'work shy' behaviour (Mead, 1982; Blair, 2006; Duncan-Smith, 2014; Dunn, 2014), Albert and Johnny's actions are indicative of many people who are trying to manage structural changes beyond their control. That is, individuals trapped in the pattern of repeat work–welfare recycling, characteristic of many contemporary lower skilled 'flexible' labour markets (see Chapter Three).

Second, the dominance and ubiquity of the logics of welfare conditionality within the UK's benefit system is further illustrated by both cases. Albert wanted help to find work and instead was placed under an intensive daily signing on regime and then subject to a 13-week sanction for failing to repeatedly apply for jobs on Universal Jobmatch that he had previously unsuccessfully applied for. Similarly, in his wave c interview Johnny recalled how during his most recent short-term period of claiming benefit between jobs, his Work Coach accepted Johnny's written evidence of a start date for his next job and fully understood he would be employed again in the near future. However, he then informed Johnny that he had to keep actively applying for further jobs, which they both knew he had no intention of taking (because of his existing job offer), otherwise his benefit would be sanctioned.

Third, Albert's case in particular highlights the limited efficacy of punitive benefit sanctions in changing the behaviour of benefit recipients. If benefit sanctions are such effective tools for moving people off welfare and into work, why is it necessary for certain people to be subject to repeat and increasing periods of sanction? Imposing ever more stringent benefit eligibility conditions (that is, a daily signing on requirement) and then implementing a second, three-month benefit sanction for non-compliance deepened Albert's poverty and moved him further away, not nearer to, the paid labour market. Fourth, as evidenced by the DWP's later decision to rescind it, the sanction Johnny received was clearly inappropriate. Across the sample there were further examples of benefit sanctions being inappropriately implemented despite individuals' efforts to avoid them. For example, 'John' (case 5, Chapter Four), was sanctioned by the actions of what he perceived as a 'hostile' Work Coach, even though he had fully complied with the conditions attached to his claim. One WSU, who had informed her Work Coach in advance that she could not attend a scheduled work-focused interview (WFI) because she needed to go to her brother's funeral in her country of origin, received initial assurances that her benefits would not be negatively affected. Nonetheless, she was sanctioned on her return to the UK; a decision that the DWP upheld on her appeal. Another woman who was for late for a JCP appointment explained her delay was due to accompanying her daughter for cancer treatment. She was informed that, as her daughter had recently turned 18 and was now an adult she could have attended alone, and a benefit sanction was applied (compare Alan, case 16 and Albert's initial sanction, case 18). More broadly the inappropriate and disproportionate application of benefit sanctions (for example, when initiated for being late for a JCP appointment), created deep resentment for many WSUs. As both Albert and Johnny's cases highlight, beyond triggering and exacerbating poverty, benefit sanctions often created an entrenched and long-standing sense of injustice among WSUs that undermined the possibility of more supportive and employment enabling relationships between claimants and JCP staff emerging in their future interactions.

The outcomes and issues that emerge from Albert and Johnny's specific cases have far wider resonance. Previously published analyses of the data generated by the WelCond study, highlight that benefit sanctions universally triggered severely detrimental financial, material, emotional and health outcomes (Dwyer, 2018a, 2018b). Our evidence suggests that sanctions-backed welfare conditionality produces punitive, state endorsed abuse that promotes forms of 'symbolic and material suffering' (Wright et al, 2020) and exacerbates particular aspects of vulnerability (see Dwyer et al, 2018, 2019, 2020; Fletcher and Flint, 2018; Jones, 2018; Scullion, 2018). Beyond our own analyses a host of other studies have detailed similar punitive outcomes generated by benefit sanctions (for example, CAB, 2013; Batty et al, 2015; Church Action on Poverty, 2015; Freidli and Stearn, 2015; Salford City Partnership, 2015; Adler, 2016, 2018; Batty, 2017; Patrick, 2017; Reeve, 2017; Cheetham et al, 2019; Redman, 2020; Veasey and Parker, 2021; Scullion and Curchin, 2022).

The compliant, the unable and the unwilling

Alongside the poverty and profound harms that benefit sanctions produce, welfare conditionality also generates and sustains a number of negative behavioural changes. Two of the most significant outcomes were the adoption of 'counterproductive compliance' (Wright and Dwyer, 2022) and disengagement from the social security system; with the latter routinely triggered because people were either unable, or unwilling, to meet the mandatory requirements placed upon them to retain benefit eligibility. The reasons why people responded differently to the compulsion and sanctions fundamental to highly conditional social benefit systems are explored in this chapter.

Counterproductive compliance

The routine use of welfare conditionality within social security systems is commonly defended on the grounds that it helps to reduce reliance on social security benefits while simultaneously promoting a work ethic and movements into paid work among benefit recipients. Leaving aside the limited efficacy of welfare conditionality in promoting entry into, and progression within, the paid labour market (as discussed in Chapter Four), the application of mandatory work search requirements under threat of sanction established a culture of counterproductive compliance for many benefit recipients. In direct contrast to the commonly asserted logic, welfare conditionality often inhibited meaningful and effective attempts to secure future employment among WSUs. This is because, as it has been extended and intensified, the primary role of JCP appears to have changed (Wright and Dwyer, 2022). Rather than assisting people into paid work, the general consensus among WSUs was that Jobcentres have primarily become focused on 'policing' the conditions attached to individuals' benefit claims and enforcing compliance through the threat or application of benefit sanctions. Such perceptions were common across the sample. For example:

> 'Well it's not their job to help you to find a job really. All their job is, is to see if you're actually applying for jobs on their website [Universal Jobmatch]. ... Has he done enough job search, that's all they're interested in, nothing else.' (Jobseeker, wave a)

> 'The kind of process of constantly having to sort of feed the system, to tick the boxes, actually gets in the way of doing the genuine progress towards employment.' (Lone parent, wave a)

On occasions some WSUs even spoke in terms of evidencing mechanistic, mandatory job search activity, rather than applying for jobs they had a realistic chance of obtaining, as their primary responsibility. In some cases (as in the following quote; see also 'Peter', case 3 in Chapter Four), respondents even spoke of undertaking their mandatory job application/work search requirements as a full-time occupation: "My job was solely to prove to that woman [Work Coach] that I had applied for so many jobs, and that was it. ... Whether they were suitable for me, whatever, it didn't matter" (UC recipient, wave b). Although the mindset voiced in this quote appears to be counterintuitive to the stated aim of using welfare conditionality to move people off benefits and into paid work, it is a logical, if somewhat unintended, outcome of a policy that demands intensified work search responsibilities of claimants. Governments that make intensive work search activity a central tenet of continued social security benefit receipt (for example, "you will be expected to look or prepare for work for 35 hours a week, depending on your circumstances" [DWP, 2020c: np]) should not be surprised when claimants ensure they do as they are instructed to avoid a benefit sanction. The pressure to evidence ever more demanding and extensive levels of job search and application, in tandem with WSUs' strong desire to avoid the punitive effects of a benefit sanction for non-compliance, led to some respondents applying for jobs that both they, and their Work Coaches, knew they had no realistic chance of getting.

> 'I was looking for jobs that I had no training in. ... I've never worked in a kitchen. ... "Have you got any experience?" "No." "Well sorry." ... They wanted to get me a job in a care home. I'm like, "They wouldn't give me a job in a care home." "Well ring up for it and I'll be checking" but the first thing I said to the woman was, "I'm going to have to tell you the truth I'm not long out of prison," and she said, "Well we can't employ you but thanks very much for telling me." Basically, my job adviser was saying, "Apply for it just so I can see you're applying for jobs."' (UC recipient, wave C)

Elsewhere one man was instructed to apply for a driving job when he did not hold a driving licence, and another was required to apply for a job in a library despite having a history of construction work and no qualifications related to the advertised post. Others, like Fred, learned to do as they were instructed 'the hard way'.

Case 20: Fred: learning lessons in compliance

Fred is an older man in his 50s with an extensive employment history across his working life. However, at his wave a interview he had been unemployed for approximately six months and in and out of work intermittently over the past two years. He was sanctioned for making an insufficient number of job applications.

> 'It was when they first brought out this new [Universal Jobmatch] system. The Job Coach punched in details. I live in England. ... Four jobs in Wales. ... I'm on foot or I'm on the buses and because I didn't apply for those jobs they sanctioned me. ... I had no money, no food. ... It put me in debt with risk of losing my abode.' (Wave a)

At wave b, a year later, he remained unemployed and continued to struggle financially but reassured the interviewer he had learned the necessity of compliance in order to survive.

> 'Not [got] enough to get by on with deductions for rent arrears and past fines etc. I don't get paid till tomorrow. I'm out of food. That's the main thing. I'm out of gas. Hot water has gone. ... I've not been sanctioned [since] because I do what they ask me to do and that's it, that's what you've got to do. You've got to play their game.' (Wave b)

At his final wave c interview, replicating the sentiments of other WSUs, Fred clearly resented the high levels of surveillance and counterproductive compliance that the system generated.

> 'They were checking up on you because [they think] we're all skiving and cheating the system. That's what I felt. ... I used to lose sleep on the Thursday before I'd go and sign on. ... They didn't help me. I've done everything they asked me to do. I did not want to get suspended or sanctioned. I'll be honest with you, I was applying for jobs that I knew deep down I was never going to get. ... I was doing that so that I could say that I'd applied for a job.' (Wave c)

It is important to note that counterproductive compliance by benefit recipients should not be understood as evidence of superficial acquiescence by individuals who are keen to prolong a life of passivity reliant on social welfare. Rather, it represents a rational response to the imposition of compulsion among those potentially subject to benefit sanctions. The necessity of meeting the specified responsibilities of their benefit claim above more meaningful and effective job search activities, in order to avoid a punitive benefit sanction, is enforced on benefit recipients. Counterproductive compliance should be properly understood as a form of coerced agency demanded of those who must retain benefit eligibility to ensure their basic needs are met. Fred's case also lends weight to previous discussions about the ineffectiveness of enforcing constant, and on occasions, meaningless job application under fear of sanction. At his wave c interview Fred described how he had recently obtained a permanent full-time job as a direct outcome of more enabling JCP support.

> 'I know the light is at the end of the tunnel. … There's a lovely woman that works at my Jobcentre and she put me onto it [his new job]. … In the last year, the woman that dealt with me never even mentioned sanctions. … We'd look together at work. We'd discuss things. She had a much better way with people. … My aspirations were just to find work. Simple as that. I've worked most of my life.' (Fred, wave c)

In contrast to previous Work Coaches who prioritised compliance and sanction, Fred's most recent Work Coach focused on identifying substantive employment opportunities and supporting him into work. The provision of effective employment support rather than the threat of sanction enabled his move off benefits (see also Joy, case 4, who was similarly supported into work by a WP adviser). Such variations in the approaches of Work Coaches further emphasises the importance of street level bureaucrats' discretion in shaping the effects of welfare conditionality (see discussions in Chapters Two and Three). As previously noted we were not given permission by the DWP to conduct focus group interviews with Work Coaches. For that reason, it is unfortunate that we cannot include their perspectives in our analysis within this book.

Disengagement from social security

In contrast to those WSUs who prioritised compliance, a minority of respondents disengaged from the social security system in response to the persistent stresses and demands that welfare conditionality placed on individuals. Certain WSUs with additional and sometimes complex needs, linked to issues such as homelessness, alcohol/drug dependency and physical and mental health impairments, reacted to the inherent compulsion of conditionality by withdrawing from the social security system altogether. Some of those unable to cope with the demands placed on them, and the entrenched poverty that repeat sanctioning triggered, fell into destitution. Harry (see case 1, Chapter Four) is one such example of this type of extreme outcome. Others, rather than rely on charitable provision like Harry, reacted to a sanction by turning to begging and survival crime, such as low-level drug dealing. This was especially the case among those with a history of offending, antisocial behaviour and/or homelessness, where benefit sanctions worked to undermine individuals' recovery journeys, desistence from criminal activity and attempts to sustain positive change. (see Colin case 21, and see Batty and Fletcher, 2018; Batty et al, 2018; Johnsen et al, 2018b for further discussions).

Case 21: Colin: turning to survival crime

Colin is in his late 30s. At his wave a interview he was a recovering drug addict, living in a hostel and in receipt of ESA (Work Related Activity Group). Throughout his life he had rarely worked and described himself as a "commercial burglar". Last released from prison four years prior to his first interview, he was trying to break his previous cycle of reoffending. At wave a he admitted supplementing his benefit income through 'odd days' of informal work.

> 'All my family ... they've all worked on building sites ... but it just wasn't for me at the time – the money was better in criminality. ... I do a bit of cash-in-hand ... painter and decorator ... like £70 a day ... without that money ... I would be financially struggling. I don't know, I'd probably be back out there, criminality again, to be quite truthful.' (Wave a)

Twelve months later at wave b, Colin outlined how he had been given a benefit sanction in the interim period for missing a WP appointment; despite claiming to have phoned his WP provider in advance to explain why he could not attend. He was particularly aggrieved because he had volunteered to take part in the WP. Colin felt depressed and indicated that he might use drugs again (despite being 'clean' for over three years) and hinted that he was considering resorting to crime again.

> 'I'm waiting for the appeal to come back sometime next week ... if it isn't the six weeks, it's going to be the 13 weeks I get sanctioned. So now I'm hand to mouth. ... My mum, family they're scraping by, family can only help you so much. ... Like today, now I went and borrowed money off my mum. ... It stresses me out. ... These are the things that push me in that other direction because I think, oh bollocks, why bother? I'm better off just going and doing crime, getting money,

take the consequences because I can do the time. ... I was going to walk around to a friend of mine who's a criminal and borrow some money but then where does that put me? It puts me in their pocket.' (Wave b)

At our final interview another year on, Colin admitted he had temporarily resumed criminal activities to cope with the loss of his benefits due to the sanction.

'Thirteen weeks with no money and food vouchers, I had to go and do things I didn't want to do ... do things with people that I didn't really want to get involved with again ... commercial burglaries basically.' (Wave c)

Perhaps the most harrowing example of the negative outcomes that disentitlement to benefit can cause emerged in an interview with a young woman experiencing homelessness who we only managed to interview on one occasion. She outlined how loss of her right to ESA due to her failure to attend a Work Capability Assessment interview left her penniless. This had led her to engage in sex work where she was a victim of violent assault.

'I was on zero income. Zero Housing Benefit, zero Council Tax Benefit. Towards the end I put in a nil income form, which activated my Housing Benefit temporarily. But I think once I had nil income for four and a half months. ... I turned to prostitution. It was the most horrific time of my life. ... I got [hesitates] beaten up, raped and buggered, trying to [hesitates] earn money via prostitution. I was working with [two support organisations]. They were liaising with the benefits as well. It made no difference.' (Disabled woman, wave a)

This woman had a series of complex needs due to experience of domestic violence, drug dependency and the associated offending that addiction often involves for those with limited incomes. Highly conditional, work-first social security regimes are poorly equipped for meeting the needs of marginalised people with multiple and complex needs (Dean, 2003). Researchers have also noted that welfare conditionality is likely to establish an environment in which those with complex needs are 'set up to fail' because of an inability to understand and comply with the behavioural requirements necessary to avoid sanctions and/or retain benefit eligibility (Reeves and Loopstra, 2017). This was certainly the case for this young woman. Other WSUs interviewed also reported struggling, or being unable to meet the requirements placed upon them because of ongoing issues in their lives (for example, on impairment see Stacey, case 6; homelessness, John, case 5; ongoing addiction, Keith, case 11). Additionally, for various reasons some WSUs did not understand why they had been sanctioned. For example, a number of migrant respondents had very limited understanding of the conditions attached to benefit receipt and the consequences of a failure to meet them.

> '[Through interpreter] Because he was new to the country he didn't know all the systems, how it went, so it was very difficult for him. ... But one day he missed his appointment to sign and when he went the next day they sanctioned him for a month, he wasn't paid for a month so that time was very difficult. He'd not anything even to eat.' (Migrant, wave a)

More generally, many WSUs reported that they were initially unaware that they had been sanctioned and/or did not understand the reasons why a sanction had been applied. In such cases, where people do not comprehend what is happening, they are unable to respond as required and the justification for using sanctions as a behaviour change tool is undermined. These shortcomings have been acknowledged elsewhere with the Oakley Review of JSA sanctions noting that '[i]f communication is ineffective and understanding poor, a wide range of evidence shows that compliance with the system will be lower and, overall, the system will be less effective at moving claimants from benefits into work' (Oakley, 2014: 7).

Disengagement from the social security system was not solely an issue for those WSUs with multiple and complex needs who were unable to understand and comply with the work search requirement placed upon them. Across the two-year period of repeat interviews some respondents became 'worn down' by the incessant pressure to evidence work search and job application with little success, despite their best efforts. Over time people like Billy (case 22), the antithesis of 'cynical manipulators' who play the benefit system for personal gain (see Fletcher et al, 2016), became unwilling to accept the surveillance and compulsion of conditionality and made an active choice to disengage from the social security system.

Case 22: Billy: the jobseeker who disengaged from Universal Credit

Billy is in his 60s. At wave a he had given up his last job 10 months previously because he could no longer cope with the physical aspect of the work due to his age and an ongoing health issue. Expecting to be assigned to JSA, Billy was placed on UC as he lived in one of the pilot areas for the then new benefit. Since becoming unemployed he had legally undertaken a couple of occasional days' work when available. A committed jobseeker Billy outlined how he had signed up to two job clubs and was actively seeking work across the entire week.

'[Employment agencies] phone you up and say, "Two days' work here, two days' work there." ... I do a few speculative letters as well. ... Very helpful in the work club. ... I wasn't referred. ... Here its only on a Monday, Wednesday and a Thursday, so I go up there on the Friday, and I go to the Job Centre to do my job search on a Tuesday. So, I cover the whole week.' (Wave a)

Twelve months on at wave b, Billy was disillusioned. He had attended many job interviews but was unsuccessful in finding work. When he felt pushed to do even more work search, he walked out of a meeting with his Work Coach and was then sanctioned. With no money to live on, offended by the treatment he had received at JCP, he took the decision to stop claiming UC.

'On UC I did all that was required of me, attending work clubs, applying for jobs each week and also learning new skills on the computer, which I enjoyed. ... I went along as usual to the Job Centre with my work activity history. ... My adviser kept on at me what I was applying for and should be applying for more. ... I said to him, "I'm not going to argue with you and I'm trying my best." ... With that I left the Job Centre and I've not returned. ... I was sanctioned ... no money at all to live on. ... I decided I'm not putting up with this performance any longer and I no longer wish to claim UC. When asked why, I replied, "I'm so disgusted at the way this system treats people."' (Wave b)

At wave c, two years after we first interviewed Billy, he remained registered with an employment agency to try to find work and was still not engaging with JCP. Because he refused to claim UC, his local authority has significantly reduced his rent supplement and he was reliant on a friend to help meet his private tenancy costs.

'Staggering on with my life. ... I received a letter from the council ... cut to half the amount of the housing benefit. ... "We're assuming you could be applying for benefits." ... [I get] help from a friend with my rent. ... I just manage the little bits that I have and my friend, she gives me my meals. ... At the moment I'm with [Agency] and they're trying to find me something. ... I wouldn't go back to the Job Centre! ... How many times have I done 35 hours and still haven't got work? I got fed up arguing with these people. I'm not an argumentative person. ... The way they operate, if you can't find work, they should've sat me in a place to try to help rather than stop your money. ... When I came off it, I felt like a burden had been lifted off my shoulders. ... Now not far below homeless, to be honest ... because of the sanction and the council.' (Wave c)

Struggling financially and facing potential homelessness, it is ironic to note that in one sense Billy who started out as a 'dutiful' citizen with good intentions to fulfil his work search responsibilities had been defeated by the system of welfare conditionality that supposedly should operate to compel individuals to move off welfare and into work (see Mead, 1982). As previously noted, intensified welfare conditionality also pushes some people further away from collectivised systems of support and into deep poverty and even destitution (Crisp and Fletcher, 2008; CAB, 2013; Watts et al, 2014; Loopstra et al, 2015).

Additionally, the introduction of UC (2013) saw low-paid workers become subject to sanctions and compulsory work search requirements for the first time. Such workers, some of whom had more than one job simultaneously, often deeply resented being subject to 'in-work' conditionality. This required them to search for better paid or additional work until their earnings reached the 'conditionality earning threshold' (see Chapter Two). Many such employed UC claimants, having already demonstrated a commitment to paid work through their ongoing job(s), were frustrated at having to attend WFIs and undertake mandatory work searches under the scrutiny of JCP. Consequently, they regularly reacted by relinquishing their rights to the rent and low-wage supplements payable through the UC system. Cathy's case study explains how this kind of disengagement can occur.

Case 23: Cathy: giving up on 'in-work' benefits

Cathy is a middle-aged woman. At her wave a interview she was working a total of 29 hours a week on two part-time cleaning jobs. She obtained both contracts via employment agencies and they were scheduled to end in the near future. Previously she had undertaken various retail and cleaning jobs, claiming JSA when unemployed. She was recently moved onto UC. Her adult son lives with her and is in receipt of ESA. Although working, she is struggling financially due to low wages and substantial deductions from her monthly UC payment required to pay off rent and council tax arrears and to payback a UC Advance Payment she required in the month before her first benefit payment arrived. Cathy's monthly UC payments are also subject to further deductions due to 'bedroom tax' rules. As a low-paid worker in receipt of UC she is also subject to 'in-work' conditionality.

> 'I had to go on Universal Credit and it was like 35 hours a week jobs searching. Constantly on your case, constantly trying to sanction you. It's an absolute nightmare. ... I'm doing 29 hours, but [Work Coach] still wants me to go and do another nine hours' job search. ... I'd do it off my own back anyway. ... I'm still trying to get full-time work at the end of the day. I'm always pecking my boss's head at work.' (Wave a)

Despite working and doing her job search she had been threatened with a benefit sanction three times; most recently after phoning up to say she would be delayed because the bus was late.

> 'Just finished work ... go to the library to do the job search and then to the Jobcentre. ... The bus has bloody turned up late, what do you want me to do? It's just stupid stuff like that. They just want to sanction. Anything they can do to try and stop your money, they'll do it.' (Wave a)

A year later at wave b, Cathy reported she had been employed on variable hours throughout the previous 12 months, managing to retain a single 20-hour per week cleaning contract all year. However, in line with the fluctuating availability of work on offer, she had, intermittently, taken on additional contracts up to full-time hours, as and when they became available. Periods of full-time working then interfered with her ability to attend WFIs at JCP interviews as required. At the time of her wave b interview she was no longer in receipt of UC and, consequently, had lost access to the Housing Benefit component of UC and was struggling to make ends meet.

> 'I do contract cleaning ... when that building's done, you're off, basically ... you're waiting for the next job to come up. ... So that's where Universal Credit came in handy for me because it works up and down. So I rang them up to say that I couldn't come in because I was working full-time. So they said that was all right. Then I got a letter saying I'd missed my interview and they've taken me off Universal Credit. So I thought, you know what, just stuff you. I can't be bothered with them anymore. So, basically, mostly I've struggled because I just can't be doing with them. Just going in there for them to look down at you. ... I'm living off 20 hours for the past couple of months and I'm paying full rent. ... It wasn't as if I wasn't working and I wasn't job searching.' (Wave b)

At wave c Cathy explained that in the last year her employer had increased her contract to 40 hours a per week and, although only in receipt of the minimum wage, her financial situation had improved. She had no desire to engage with UC again if her hours reduced, unless it became an absolute necessity.

> 'If I wasn't working I don't know what I'd bloody do to be honest. I'd rather be working than searching for jobs day in, day out, and getting knocked back every five minutes. ... It's a lot of pressure, isn't it, because they're making you – forcing you into doing stuff rather than letting you do it yourself. ... I'm full-time now, aren't I, so don't bloody need them. They can stick it up their backside [laughing].' (Wave c)

For Cathy, the decision to distance herself from the behavioural requirements of a UC claim have limited financial consequences while she continues to work full-time hours. Indeed, in line with how UC has been designed, as a monthly variable benefit payment that can be reduced or increased depending on a claimant's previous monthly earnings from paid work, it is highly likely that Cathy's UC payment would be reduced to zero while in receipt of full-time wages. Also having met the 'conditionality earnings threshold' (that is, equivalent to 35 hours per week paid at the UK National Living (Minimum Wage[2]), she should no longer be subject to in-work conditionality requirements. However, should her hours reduce again she may well have to initiate a new claim for UC to meet her housing and other costs and she will then face the assessment period for first payment (often referred to as the 'five-week wait'), and be required to meet ongoing work search conditions under threat of sanction, both of which will reduce her financial security.

On one level Cathy's case study could be read by some as a conditionality success story. Cajoled into action, Cathy increases her working hours and moves off (in-work) benefit dependency and progresses into full-time paid work and financial independence. However, her fluctuating and the recent availability of increased full-time hours have little to do with sanction-backed compulsory job search. She became a full-time worker because of increased employer demand and not because the stick of compulsion changed her behaviour. One final significant, counterproductive and presumably unintended outcome, produced by the introduction of 'in-work' conditionality, is also evidenced by Cathy's case, that is, that its implementation can actually inhibit individuals' ability to undertake more paid work. Several of the 'in-work' UC recipients we interviewed reported they were unable to attend a WFI, and were subsequently sanctioned by JCP, because they were required by their employers to be at work. In building a rigid system of 'in-work' conditionality around the assumption of a 35-hour full-time working week, the UK government has failed to acknowledge the reality of the requirements of both employers and workers who are increasing operating in a highly flexible contemporary labour market (Ingold, 2020; Wright and Dwyer, 2022).

Conclusions

The compulsion and sanction inherent within social security systems premised on welfare conditionality frequently triggers profoundly negative personal, financial, health and wellbeing outcomes among social security benefit recipients. Leaving aside debates about the efficacy of welfare conditionality in triggering and sustaining movements into paid work (see Chapter Four), for a substantial number of people its use also instigates and sustains a variety of negative behavioural responses and impacts. The punitive effects of benefit sanctions and welfare conditionality more generally are now widely documented and acknowledged (for example, CAB, 2013; Church Action on Poverty, 2015; Salford City Partnership, 2015; Adler, 2016, 2018; Patrick, 2017; Cheetham et al, 2019; Redman, 2020; Veasey and Parker, 2021: Scullion and Curchin, 2022). The analysis presented here provides further evidence that one intended outcome of benefit sanctions is to discipline and punish those who are unable or unwilling to comply with the mandatory work-related requirements specified as conditions of their continued eligibility to claim (Reeve, 2017; Fletcher and Flint, 2018; Fletcher and Wright, 2018; Wright et al, 2020).

Beyond its punitive impacts, welfare conditionality propagates a culture of counterproductive compliance whereby the application of compulsory full-time employment/work search requirements coupled with claimants' strong desire to avoid the punitive effects of a sanction often gets in the way of more meaningful and effective attempts to secure employment. This is surely an unintended outcome for a policy approach purportedly introduced with the aim of enhancing labour market activity among social welfare benefit recipients? 'Rather than promoting what could be considered "positive behaviour change" ... experiencing sanctions sparked an all-consuming crisis and fight for survival. Often, fear of sanctions provoked unnecessary anxiety and depression and at worst a hypervigilance provoked by anxiety over being sanctioned' (Stewart and Wright, 2018: 7).

When sanctioned, the most vulnerable people interviewed in our WelCond study often had little option but reliance on financial and material support from friends and family (if available), or charitable providers, to meet their basic needs. A minority eschewed this option, choosing instead to engage in survival crime as an alternative. Additionally, welfare conditionality prompted deep resentment among WSUs, leading to some disengaging from the social security system. Such actions exacerbated the daily challenges and poverty that many people already faced, with individuals with multiple and complex needs often suffering the most. Furthermore, the advent of 'in-work' conditionality has established the absurd possibility that someone may have their benefit sanctioned for non-attendance of a mandatory WFI because they are required to simultaneously be at work. This has seen low-paid workers relinquish rent and low-wage supplements in order to avoid the aggravations that in-work welfare conditionality brings. As Fletcher and Flint note, the UK benefit system now overtly stigmatises social security benefit recipients (even those who are in low-paid work) and focuses on coercing 'marginal groups into work that fails to provide a meaningful stake in mainstream society' (2018: 787), removing basic rights to social security if individuals refuse to comply. Given this approach we should not be too surprised if some people then decide to disengage entirely. Perhaps this is an intended outcome of welfare conditionality after all?

Notes

[1] Data for this table was provided by David Webster in response to a personal request by Peter Dwyer. We are grateful for his assistance.

[2] The National Living Wage should not be confused with the Real Living Wage. Since 2016, the former is the minimum that should be paid to those aged 23 and over in the UK. The latter is a voluntary wage based on public consultation on the real cost of living.

SEVEN

Ethical debates

Beyond previously discussed efficacy issues, welfare conditionality also raises significant ethical questions about the fairness of its use. These debates are important for two reasons. First, because welfare conditionality, by directly linking prescribed patterns of individual behaviour to the regulation of citizens' access to collectivised systems of welfare, raises profound questions about the substance and reach of welfare states. Second, because governments' use of welfare conditionality as a behaviour change tool raises deep-seated disagreements about if, when, and why governments might be justified in seeking to modify citizens' behaviour. The first part of this chapter reviews the main arguments made by proponents and opponents of welfare conditionality. It does this through a discussion of four key contested normative, ethical positions that inform the thinking of advocates and adversaries of welfare conditionality. These are *contractualism*, *paternalism*, *mutualism* and 'unconditional' *entitlement*; the latter based on either universal human rights or the more bounded universalism of national citizenship. Each of these four approaches offer differing ethical stances on the legitimacy of using behavioural mechanisms to alter and regulate citizens' conduct and the fairness of denying, or rescinding, access to collectivised welfare provisions for non-compliant individuals. These essentially theoretical discussions then facilitate empirically grounded analysis of welfare service users' (WSUs) diverse opinions on the rights and wrongs of welfare conditionality. The second part of the chapter explores WSUs' views on the fairness of a principle of welfare conditionality, that broadly asserts that access to collective welfare goods and services should be made contingent on citizens accepting state-specified, individual responsibilities. Questions about the appropriateness of UK governments extending welfare conditionality to previously exempt groups (that is, lone parents and disabled people specifically) are then considered in the third section.

Advocates and adversaries: ethical aspects of welfare conditionality

Behaviour change usually becomes a focus for policymakers' interventions when the conduct of a specific group is identified as morally reprehensible and/or a particularly significant drain on state resources (Chatterton, 2016). These themes resonate strongly among proponents of welfare conditionality who view it as a legitimate approach for changing the behaviour of 'irresponsible' citizens who are dependent on social security benefits and welfare services. In doing so they emphasise overlapping rationales to justify its use. First, the implementation of harsh eligibility requirements backed by sanctions helps deter people from making claims, thus promoting individual responsibility. Second, arguments about the inherent moral value of paid work (over and above other forms of social contribution such as informal, familial care work), alongside the legitimacy of utilising various mechanisms of social control to correct the moral failings of the 'idle and irresponsible' are endorsed. A third set of 'utilitarian or fiscal rationales' that defend conditional welfare interventions by reference of the need to reduce, or contain, public welfare costs are asserted (see Watts and Fitzpatrick, 2018a for fuller discussions of *utilitarianism*). Fourth, 'contractual, quid-pro-quo' rationales that demand that welfare recipients must agree to give something in return for the collectivised benefits and services they receive, are regularly foregrounded (Paz-Fuchs, 2008).

As Griggs and Bennett (2009) note, drawing on diverse rationales, advocates of welfare conditionality make a number of important assumptions and assertions. First, that policies that seek to promote unconditional entitlement to social security benefits and welfare services are likely to promote unemployment and entrench 'welfare dependency' among a section of the wider population. Second, that if eligibility for receipt of welfare is made conditional on certain forms of approved conduct or behaviour, people will 'see the light' and engage with paid work and/or stop behaving irresponsibly. Proponents believe that the key behaviour change tools intrinsic to welfare conditionality can be instrumentally used to help people to 'do the right thing'. Demanding mandatory engagement with work search, training and support services (so-called carrots) will help people fulfil their civic responsibilities and also variously steer them towards making better life choices. Linked to this, given the additional support made available to help people into work, or reform their behaviour in other ways, the use of sanctions (sticks) to remove rights to benefits and services is thus justifiable for those who do not comply with their prescribed responsibilities. Finally, supporters of welfare conditionality argue that its use helps legitimise the welfare claims of benefit recipients who are not active in the paid labour market (PLM) among the wider working population (see, for example, Mead, 1982, 1986, 1997; Selbourne, 1994; Etzioni, 1995, 1997; Dunn, 2014).

Deacon's (2004) paper, which has informed several subsequent discussions (for example, Watts et al, 2014; Patrick and Fenney, 2015; Watts and Fitzpatrick, 2018a), offers insights into three differing philosophical positions routinely used to justify welfare conditionality. First, supporters of *contractualism* believe it is 'reasonable to use welfare to enforce obligations where it is part of a broader contract between government and claimant'

(Deacon, 2004: 915). This approach is premised on the belief that the state and citizens each have reciprocal contractual duties/responsibilities. For citizens these are to actively seek work and behave in a socially responsible manner while the state should provide a safety net and support to help people to enter the PLM and desist from harmful and/or antisocial behaviour (ASB). Citing White's (2003) 'justice as fair reciprocity' approach, Deacon notes that the use of welfare conditionality as a behaviour change tool may be justified, providing the state meets its side of the welfare contract by delivering certain social rights that promote a measure of equality for citizens. According to some, this contractualist approach has clear echoes with the notion of social citizenship envisaged by T.H. Marshall and other architects of the post-Second World War welfare state, where substantive social rights were embedded in, and provided by, the institutions of the welfare state as a core element of citizenship. In short, if the state meets its side of the bargain it is seen as reasonable to expect citizens to meet their welfare responsibilities in return for their social rights; correspondingly it is legitimate for the state to intervene to challenge and change citizens' errant behaviour, by denying or rescinding access to social security benefits and services when they do not. Critics have countered this by noting that the minimum preconditions required by contemporary social democratic theorists such as White (2003) to justify welfare conditionality on contractualist, fair reciprocity grounds (that is, fair opportunity, fair reward, universality and diversity) do not exist in modern Britain or in many other contemporary states (Dwyer, 2004; Patrick and Fenney, 2015).

The second justificatory framework, *paternalism*, invoked by certain advocates of welfare conditionality, often involves a loss or reduction of the personal freedoms and autonomy that are central tenets of classic liberal philosophy. A paternalistic intervention is '[a]ny public policy which prevents or deters the performance of a self-regarding action by resort to some form of legal or quasi legal sanction. In particular, paternalism exists when a public body makes a citizen unfree to perform an action, intending the prohibition to benefit the citizens in question' (Weale, 1978: 160).

Paternalist supporters of welfare conditionality accept that its imposition may lead to coercive policies that infringe the freedoms and preferences of individuals and may also cause real hardship for some. However, they also believe that a dose of disciplinary 'tough love' through the imposition of work norms and responsible behaviour, backed by the use of sanctions for non-compliance, are acceptable; ultimately because they hold that the state is exercising its coercive power and authority for citizens' own good. Lawrence Mead is the most well-known long-term advocate of paternalistic justifications of welfare conditionality, consistently arguing that a highly conditional 'tutelary' welfare regime is a fair and effective way to change the behaviour of a dysfunctional and morally chaotic 'underclass' (Mead,

1992). He argues that people's claims to greater equality and social justice can only be considered if they themselves accept the obligations placed upon them to behave responsibly. In contrast to contractualism, paternalists do not require governments to improve services or create better opportunities for disadvantaged populations. They simply assert that the state knows best, and demand that people meet the conditions placed on them or face the ensuing negative consequences of any sanctions implemented for non-compliance (Deacon, 2004).

Mead's unapologetic defence of welfare conditionality has seen him identified by several authors (Ben-Ishai, 2010; Taylor et al, 2016; Whitworth, 2016) as the 'standard bearer' for a dominant, neoliberal-inspired form of 'hard' paternalism that 'hopes to patch society together again with a mix of exhortation and intervention into the lives of the poor and the deviant' (MacGregor, 1999: 95). It is seen by some as ironic that neoliberals, who identify individual autonomy and freedom of choice as core values, have endorsed highly coercive interference into the lives of citizens in an attempt to make them change their ways because their chosen behaviours are deemed not to be in their best interest (Whitworth, 2016). This is contrasted with the so-called 'soft' or 'libertarian paternalism' of Thaler and Sunstein (2008) who advocate the use of 'nudges' to steer people towards making optimal decisions (see Chapter Three). Nudges are seen as an additional tool that policymakers can utilise to change behaviour beyond the traditional instruments of economic incentive, information provision or compulsion through the use of sanction. As Curchin (2017) notes, Thaler and Sunstein view nudges as preferential because they do not invoke the use of coercion. However, 'hard neoliberal' and 'soft libertarian' paternalism share some common ground. They both commonly assert people cannot always be relied upon to behave in ways that serve their best interests. To remedy this, both approaches offer paternalistic justifications for challenging and changing citizens' behaviour on the grounds that the benefits of state intervention outweigh any harms they might engender, such as interfering with individuals' autonomy. The key difference between the two positions is that whereas 'hard' paternalists advocate '[s]upervision which will prevent people from acting against their presumed best interest. This denies them the right to make the wrong choice. By contrast libertarian paternalism does not forbid any options. People remain free to make suboptimal choices if they wish' (Curchin, 2017: 241).

Mutualism provides a third justificatory frame for supporters of welfare conditionality. It builds from a position 'that people have commitments and responsibilities towards each other that arise independently of the claims they make on the state' (Deacon, 2004: 917) and draws upon communitarian/ civic republican traditions most recently enunciated by so-called 'new communitarians' (see Chapter One). Mutualism demands a deeper commitment and bond to the communities that people inhabit, beyond the more abstract agreement between individual and central state that underpins contractualist thinking. It prioritises the collective responsibilities and duties that community members must hold for each other. Any collectively organised and financed welfare benefits and services are seen as particular and conditional privileges to be bestowed only on active, responsible citizens who contribute to the communities that sustain them. The denial of access to collective welfare provisions for those who refuse to behave as required under community norms, through mechanisms such as welfare conditionality, is therefore viewed as unproblematic and inherently fair.

These three differing ethical frameworks variously used by advocates to defend the implementation of welfare conditionality hold little sway among those opposed to its imposition. Indeed, adversaries of welfare conditionality raise a number of counter-arguments. First, and fundamentally, they argue that welfare conditionality undermines the notion of 'unconditional' entitlement based on need and the idea that all should have minimum rights to basic social welfare derived from either the bounded *universalism* implied by social democratic notions of citizenship or commonly asserted universal human rights. For example, Dean (2013), Adler (2018) and Dermine and Eleveld (2021) all offer interesting human right based rebuttals of welfare conditionality.

As noted in Chapter One, very few social rights are totally unconditional; welfare states deliver welfare according to a mix of competing principles and priorities. Critics argue that the emergence and consolidation of a principle of welfare conditionality that demands specific behavioural requirements of claimants to retain eligibility to even basic social provision is not a renewal of the social democratic vision that emphasised status-based rights to welfare. Rather it heralds in a new 'obligation orientated welfare regime' in which 'social citizenship is extensively constructed on the basis of contractual duties rather than rights' (Ervik et al, 2015: 206). This can promote social exclusion rather than inclusion and, significantly, undermines the promise of social citizenship to deliver even a modicum of decommodified benefits and services as substantive rights.

Second, adversaries critique the focus on individual behaviour as the primary cause, and the solution to, labour market inactivity and antisocial or problematic behaviour. Such thinking fails to recognise wider structural causes of unemployment including a lack of available work, the differential capabilities of individuals, and other barriers to labour market participation that lie beyond personal control. For example, an impaired person may want to work but be prevented from doing so by wider disabling environments and practices. Third, adversaries highlight that people do not, or cannot, always respond rationally to the 'carrots' and 'sticks' applied to trigger behaviour change because other aspects of their lives may dominate at certain times. These may be both positive or negative, for example, informal care responsibilities or substance misuse may be prioritised for very different reasons. Fourth, ethical objections linked to the wider deleterious impacts triggered by welfare conditionality are also regularly highlighted by those opposed to its intervention. This includes '[a] range of unintended effects, including distancing people from support; causing hardship and even destitution; displacing rather than resolving issues such as street homelessness and antisocial behaviour and negative impacts on "third parties", particularly children' (Watts et al, 2014: 1).

Finally, and linked to the preceding point, is the argument that welfare conditionality is unfair because it is unequally implemented. It is primarily about disciplining and regulating the behaviour of people who are experiencing poverty while largely ignoring the irresponsibility and inactivity of wealthier citizens (see, for example, Dwyer, 1998, 2004; Goodin, 2000; Freedland and King, 2003; Dean, 2007, 2013; Shildrick et al, 2012; Wright, 2012; Watts et al, 2014; McKeever and Walsh, 2020 for fuller critical discussions).

Questions of principle

Chapter One set out a number of competing principles that are used to resolve questions about who gets what, and why, in relation to collective goods and services within welfare states. In the past 40 years a principle of welfare conditionality has become more prominent in many nations. Prioritising notions of individual responsibility, prior contribution and desert, the rise of welfare conditionality relegates issues of need and the notion of citizens possessing decommodified rights to social welfare (Esping-Andersen, 1990) to secondary concerns. Instead, primacy is afforded to a particular version of reciprocity. One which not only confidently declares that welfare rights come with attendant citizen responsibilities, but also holds that they should be denied or removed if individuals fail to behave responsibly. Discussions in this section consider the extent to which the WSUs who were interviewed in the WelCond study consider welfare conditionality to be a fair principle for resolving the who gets what and why, questions that are a central element of all welfare states. Towards the end of each repeat interview conducted with WSUs we asked respondents to reflect on the ethicality of welfare conditionality. Our analysis revealed that the majority of people expressed consistent views on each of the three occasions they were interviewed with little change of opinion over time. As such we do not utilise longitudinal cases studies here (as in Chapters Four to Six), rather the empirical analysis presented explores WSUs' differing views on whether or not, and why, they consider the principle and practices of welfare conditionality to be ethically justified.

In principle, WSUs were broadly supportive of welfare rights being linked to certain responsibilities. Many accepted that it was reasonable to expect individual citizens to make some form of 'valid' contribution to society, if and when they were able, in return for collective social security benefits and welfare services.

> 'I think if you're fit for work you should be working and putting into the pot the same as everybody else, and paying your taxes.' (Jobseeker, wave b)

> 'People have got to work to pay taxes to pay benefits.' (Jobseeker, wave a)

> 'Because it's not fair if people are going out paying their taxes and you've got people like sitting on the backsides just like doing nothing and still getting money.' (Universal Credit [UC] claimant, wave a)

> 'I haven't paid tax in my life ... and it's about time I started to give something back.' (Disabled person, recovering addict, wave a)

People acknowledged that individual claims on the welfare state had to be collectively funded. Consequently, WSUs commonly accepted that everyone (who was able) had a responsibility to work and contribute by paying the required taxes and, in return, they expected that the government should keep their side of the bargain by providing welfare services. The endorsement of such contractualist arguments is not entirely unexpected. A contractualist based social insurance principle, premised on cooperation between citizen and state, where the right to claim assumed citizens' willingness of prior contribution, was a foundational principle to the UK's post-war welfare settlement (see Beveridge, 1942; Marshall, 1949/1992). Since the mid-1990s, a succession of New Labour, Liberal/Conservative Coalition and Conservative governments have all made repeated and explicit reference (for example, DSS, 1998; DWP, 2010; and see Chapter Two, this volume), to the necessity of linking 'rights to responsibilities' and a pressing need to reinvigorate the long-standing 'welfare contract' between citizens and the state. Contractual narratives and language are also an explicit element of people's everyday experience of contemporary welfare provision. For example, unemployed UC recipients have to sign a 'Claimant Commitment' that records the work-related responsibilities they must accept to continue receiving UC. Likewise, certain individuals may have to agree an Acceptable Behaviour Contract if they have been engaged in ASB. Therefore, for some WSUs who subscribe to contractualism, welfare conditionality was seen as a common sense and fair organising principle. Allied to this, when behavioural requirements had been clearly set out, sanction (loss of benefit or service) was deemed as a legitimate response because individuals understood the deal on offer and had broken their side of the bargain.

'They're not sanctioning people just to punish them. They're sanctioning people because certain people aren't doing what they've actually signed up to. ... When you sign up for Universal Credit, it is a contract basically and you have to do 35 hours a week of actively seeking work.' (UC claimant, wave a)

'You're signing a contract that you'll be looking for work. You'll attend all your appointments. You'll be on time. So with me being late, that's me broke my contract. Sanction. ... That was it. Black and white. Black bold letters. "You were late. You broke your contract with us. Your fault. Docked a week's wages."' (UC claimant, wave b)

'Part of the contract with the Jobcentre is you have to send off for other jobs as well.' (Jobseeker, wave b)

For these respondents, welfare conditionality merely simplified the contractual basis of contemporary welfare provision by making the responsibilities placed on citizens in receipt of benefits explicit.

A smaller number of WSUs accepted that the implementation of welfare conditionality was ethically justifiable on paternalistic grounds. Echoing the reasoning of 'hard paternalists' such as Mead (1992), these respondents believed welfare conditionality was a necessary and fair way to counter the irresponsibility of the minority who required 'the "tough love" interventions of ever-stronger conditionality and sanctions to push them into "responsibility"' (Whitworth, 2016: 417).

'[Sanctions are] designed for people to maybe play by rules and be disciplined. It's like an incentive for you to get work and if you don't do this, this is going to happen to you. So it's like whether the person wants to do it or not they have to.' (Jobseeker, wave a)

'There are too many people on benefits. They are having an easy life. Even my sister she's on a benefit and I complain about that a lot. ... She's got a housing association house. She's got a lot of nice stuff in her house and I'm thinking you're on benefits. Surely working is better. I think they could be a bit tougher to be honest on people as a whole, not just homeless people when it comes to benefits.' (Person experiencing homelessness, wave a)

'A lot of these people need structure, they need a reason to get up in the morning, they need a social life, you know, people outside their sort of group. The best way to do that is to get a job. ... You've got a reason to get up in the morning, you know a reason to look smart and you go out, you do your job, then you come home.' (Jobseeker, wave a)

'For the lazy, the proper layabouts that are on JSA [Jobseeker's Allowance] and are just riding it, then yeah I think that is a bit of a kick up the backside that they need.' (Lone parent, wave a)

Interestingly, with the exception of the person experiencing homelessness who was in paid work, all four of the quoted WSUs were unemployed; nonetheless, they endorsed paternalistic interventions. They believed that people who were unwilling to work, or reluctant to behave in a reasonable manner, had to accept that state interventions, even if they curtailed individual choice, were fair. Ultimately the state was seen as justified in utilising sanctions-backed welfare conditionality to enforce work norms and instil basic civility. Although these WSUs accepted that this may lead to harsh outcomes for some, state interference in people's lives, when required, was deemed fair for two linked reasons. First, whether those subject to conditionality accepted it or not, they thought paternalistic state-instilled discipline would improve the lives of errant citizens and serve the interests of wider society. Second, behavioural conditionality relieves 'freeloaders' of the possibility of unconditional enjoyment of collective welfare support. This in turn serves as a necessary corrective to the 'duty deficit' inherent in many entitlement/rights-based notions of citizenship.

In many ways those WSUs who drew on such paternalist justifications to validate sanctions-backed welfare conditionality share common ground with mutualist, communitarian orientated visions of society that view collective welfare services as privileges to be rightly reserved only for dutiful citizens who behave responsibly and accept community norms. However, mutualism was largely absent from WSUs' deliberations on individuals' welfare rights and responsibilities. When, occasionally, discussions about people having ethical obligations to members of their immediate communities emerged in the interviews, these conversations regularly centred around voluntary work and charitable giving rather than specifically invoking a duty to actively engage in community life. For example:

'I know people who are working with disabled children on school runs, mornings and evenings, only doing 15 hours a week but still getting their benefits but putting something valued into the community because it's a necessary service. There are things like that in many different areas that they could do. Voluntary work, I mean even volunteering. ... It benefits the community and means that person's doing something rather than just sitting around doing nothing.' (Disabled person, wave a)

One WSU spoke directly about becoming involved in charitable community provision directly in response to the hardships triggered by conditionality:

> 'We have that wee group [Town] Against Austerity. ... So if somebody came by and they'd no food for their bairns, we'd say to them, "What do you need?" and we'd give them stuff. You know, and it was because they'd been sanctioned by the brew [benefit system] for trivial things.' (Disabled person, wave c)

Another spoke of mutual support being vital in recovery and maintaining abstinence from substance misuse among those with drug dependency issues.

> 'It's not just to keep my behaviour the way I want, it's to help others. ... I'm going to mention Alcoholics Anonymous again, that's teamwork; helping each other, being there for one another, knowing that you can depend on that person, really depend.' (Jobseeker, wave c)

However, it was very rare for respondents to invoke mutualism directly as an ethical framework for governing individuals' access to welfare provisions. Just two WSUs appealed directly to new communitarian type thinking, which asserts that basic social provisions should be reserved only for those willing to first provide unpaid community service.

> '[Sanctions are] just driving them into poverty or begging in the street. That's not a solution. ... Something else instead of sanctions would actually be a better idea rather than just saying no, you can't have any money. Maybe instead of giving them money you do something else, like make them do community work. ... Just stopping someone's money. ... They go to food banks, is that really a good way forward? ... Something that could give back to the community rather than just making them suffer.' (Lone parent, wave b)

> 'If they can find me something useful to go and do, I'd go and do municipal work. ... I'll cut grass and pick up litter, that sort of stuff, I'd be more than happy to do if it meant that I got my benefits each week. ... I'd be more than happy to work for it.' (Person experiencing homelessness, wave a)

These views resonate with Etzioni's (1995) call to make 'social basics' (that is, residual social assistance) conditional on prior acceptance of 'community jobs'. Significantly, both these respondents saw community service as a more positive alternative to benefit sanctions. However, it should be remembered that for new communitarians community duty has 'ethical precedence over rights' (Selbourne, 1994) and they are happy to endorse loss of basic welfare services (that is, sanctions) for those who fail to comply with community norms and responsibilities.

It would be wrong to assume that the presence of the three noted narratives within WSUs' ethical deliberations signals their unequivocal backing for welfare conditionality. Many respondents drew on universalism to make arguments against the use of behavioural conditionality as a mechanism for denying or withdrawing welfare. In doing so they often appealed to the notion of basic, universal, human rights.

> 'Entitlement based on human rights ... at the end of the day. You've got to have something to live on, you can't have nothing to live on because. ... Even if you're as good as gold or you're as bad as hell you've still got rights, you need food in your belly and you really should have a roof over your head and somewhere to sleep.' (Social tenant, wave a)

> 'The basic human rights of heat, food, clothing, if you're going to sanction somebody by taking away their finances, then I think that there should be provision somehow for people.' (Disabled person, wave b)

Many opposed welfare conditionality on principled grounds. Others because its imposition lead to range of negative and undesirable social and personal outcomes and behaviours (see Chapter Six) while, simultaneously, displacing, rather than tackling, the root causes of the social issues it is meant to resolve (see Watts et al, 2014).

> 'There must be a basic welfare state ... basic needs – without sanctions. That's scandalous, to threaten people using those kinds of tactics, threatening people into doing this or doing that, you get this carrot and, "You only get this if you do that." Or, "You do what we say and you get this", it's scandalous.' (UC claimant, wave c)

> 'We're a civilised society, aren't we. ... We're meant to look after each other. ... You shouldn't be having to go to food banks or go for handouts to your relatives. I think that's degrading, if I'm honest.' (UC claimant, wave b)

> 'I still needed food in my belly whether I'm scoring or waiting for a drug dealer, I still needed food in my belly to keep me alive. Even though I'm killing myself, there's other issues that have got to be addressed, but they aren't fucking drug work counsellors, are they?' (Disabled person, wave b)

'Everybody's got to eat and that. You can't live off nothing ... you're going to try and graft it, you're going to try and nick it. So it's better to let them have a little bit of money, because then it'll stop the crime.' (Offender, wave c)

To summarise, the majority of WSUs drew on a range of ethical positions, to indicate that they were broadly supportive of the idea that welfare rights come with certain individual responsibilities attached. However, although they could support this notion *in principle*, many had strong reservations about the way in which welfare conditionality had been implemented *in practice* and the negative outcomes that it often initiated. Consequently, large numbers of WSUs were keen to endorse a welfare state in which everyone, regardless of their prior conduct or record of contribution, retained access to some form of basic universal benefits and provisions (see Watts and Fitzpatrick [2018a: 138] for fuller ethical discussions on conditionality, meeting basic needs and ensuring social justice).

Conditionality in practice: appropriate for all?

Chapter One set out the ways in which welfare conditionality has increased in its significance and reach as an organising principle for the ongoing processes of welfare reform in many nations. This is particularly the case in the UK where governments of all political persuasions over the last 40 years, influenced by the New Right's long-standing antipathy to the welfare state and their arguments about dysfunctional behaviour it purportedly propagates, have consistently enacted policies to intensify welfare conditionality and expand its reach to previously exempt groups, such as lone parents, disabled people and latterly low-paid workers (see Chapter Two). Discussions in this section explore questions about the appropriateness and fairness of extending the practices of welfare conditionality to lone parents and disabled people specifically. We have already noted the deep resentment felt by low-paid workers subject to in-work conditionality (see Wright and Dwyer, 2021) so do not repeat their criticisms here.

Lone parents

Analysis of WelCond's lone parent cohort highlights that the majority interviewed recognised the positive financial, personal and familial benefits that may ensue from appropriately remunerated employment. Correspondingly, many were highly motivated to enter paid work and welcomed initiatives designed to enhance their opportunities for employment. However, the ways in which welfare conditionality was implemented, often without due regard to the particular needs of lone parents, alongside the negative outcomes that welfare conditionality may bring, called into question the ethical legitimacy of arguments for extending its reach to encompass the lone parents of ever younger children (Johnsen and Blenkinsopp, 2018).

Practical issues such as the inconsistent implementation of easements (which allow Work Coaches to reduce the work-related conditions attached to lone parents' benefit claims in light of familial caring responsibilities), and inappropriate sanctioning, were a source of feelings of injustice for some.

> '"How am I meant to do 35 hours of job search when it's the summer holidays and I've got two kids and I'm a single parent?" She pretty much said to me, "That's just the way it is. You've got to do it", and I'm like, "What? I've got to drive my kids around job searching?" Yes, she pretty much said there was nothing that could be done about it, and when I had a meltdown and everything, she said there was something that could be done about it. You didn't have to do that much during the holidays and stuff like that.' (Lone parent, wave b)

> 'They wrote to me asking me can you provide the reason why you didn't attend this appointment with Work Programme. I wrote back saying look, I had this situation, my daughter was really sick. I explained everything in detail but regardless of my explanation Jobcentre Plus sent me back a letter that I'm sanctioned for four weeks.' (Lone parent, wave a)

The role of lone parents as sole carers for their children is increasingly undervalued within a benefit system that valorises paid work, above and beyond any familial responsibilities they may have as mothers (Andersen, 2020). This is evidenced by the incremental reduction, over the last two decades, of the child age thresholds that regulate when lone parents fall under the remit of welfare conditionality. Since 2016, once their youngest child reaches age two, all unemployed lone parents in receipt of UC can be required to engage in some form of mandatory work preparation. Those with children aged three plus are allocated to the 'all work-related requirements' group with mandatory job search and work-focused interview expectations increased on a sliding scale as the child's age increases. So, for example, those with a child aged three are expected to be available for, and search for, paid work for 16 hours each week. Those with children aged 13 plus are routinely expected to search for work for up to 35 hours per week (Turn2us, 2021b). Benefit sanctions can be applied for non-compliance.

A number of the lone parents interviewed clearly resented the way in which their parenting role, especially in relation to younger children, had been marginalised by the simultaneous lowering of child age thresholds and the increasing work search and paid employment expectations placed upon them.

'I feel a mother's job is to five years old, the most important years of a child's life. ... I'm only on it [benefit] because I must be on it. I wouldn't choose for the rest of my life to be on it. I worked 22 years. I have paid my national health. I've paid my income tax. I've done everything that I'm supposed to do. ... I'm fighting to get back into the workplace but it does no encouragement for you, because if you are a mother your children are first.' (Lone parent, wave a)

This mother believed the work-related requirements placed on her, in order to retain eligibility for her benefit, were both unnecessary and unfair. She had previously demonstrated a willingness to contribute to society via long-term employment, was committed to returning to paid work in the future and believed she had earned the right to be a mother for the period of time required to stabilise her life after the break-up of her long-term relationship. Other lone parents were not opposed to seeking paid work, or expectations that they should be subject to some forms of work search activity, provided it was proportionate to their role and responsibilities as sole carers for their children.

'Yes and no. If you can get the flexibility, if it is in school hours then yes. It's just when they want us to work all hours, because for me I've got a child that's seven. I still want to be able to take her to school and I'd still want to be able to pick her up from school and I think that's important times for her to come out of school and for her to meet me and be able to tell me the things that she's done in the day. ... I think if they're going to do that they have to really tailor it correctly.' (Lone parent, wave a)

'Depending on my hours. If my [paid work] hours are okay then obviously I get a routine. ... Because I do like to have a routine. ... So long as I can sit there, have a read with her, help her with her homework, you know, spend days with her at the weekend, or whatever, then I'm all right.' (Lone parent, wave a)

These lone parents – who were all women – clearly valued their role as mothers as much as their responsibilities to provide for their families through paid work. As lone parents they were not averse to undertaking paid work provided there was an associated recognition and acceptance that paid work had to be balanced alongside their ongoing responsibilities as parents. In Chapter Three we noted how theories and models of behaviour change have been dominated and influenced by classic economic theory and the idealised subject of 'homo economicus'; the rational, atomistic, economic being (man) acting in pursuit of their own individual self-interests. The validity of this model has been shown to be limited and flawed for understanding the motivations and actions of lone parents in respect of their decisions about undertaking paid work in combination with informal, familial care responsibilities. Previous research has highlighted the significance of lone parents' 'gendered moral rationalities', which focus 'attention onto the social relations of lone mothers (especially their position in social networks and gendered labour markets) and onto their social understandings (in particular, ideas about motherhood and children's needs)' (Duncan and Edwards, 1997: 40).

The three lone parents cited in this section utilise such 'gendered moral rationalities' when evaluating the ethical legitimacy of the demands placed upon them by a highly conditional benefit system. The increased (paid) work-related requirements placed on the lone parents of ever younger children, the resultant extension of the threat of sanctions and the inconsistent use of easements by Work Coaches highlight that economic imperatives dominate contemporary social security policy and practice for this group. At best, lone parents' familial care responsibilities continue to be subordinate to the enforcement of work-related requirements. In such circumstances it is difficult to see how the 'long progression towards ever stronger conditionality' for lone parents can be considered to be 'morally just' (Whitworth and Griggs, 2013).

Disabled people

The extension of welfare conditionality to working age disabled people in receipt of long-term incapacity benefits in the UK is a relatively new development. The introduction of Employment and Support Allowance (ESA) in 2008, was the culmination of a decade-long process of 'rewriting the contract' (Dwyer, 2017) underpinning the delivery of social security benefits for disabled people. In part this was premised on the view that certain long-term recipients of disability benefits were not, in reality, impaired and unable to work but inactive, irresponsible 'shirkers' avoiding employment (see Dwyer, 2017 for a fuller discussion). Before ESA, recipients of Incapacity Benefit (the main disability benefit that ESA replaced) had to undergo regular functional capability tests and meet certain impairment criteria to receive their benefit, but they were not subject to any work-related requirements and attendant benefit sanctions for non-compliance.

In common with the WelCond sample as a whole, disabled WSUs broadly accepted that linking individual welfare rights to certain social responsibilities, such as engaging in paid work, when fit and able to do so, was appropriate. Again, contractualist arguments were usually at the fore.

> 'I do know that if you're asking for something you've got to do something back in return. That's just normal life – you don't get owt for nowt.' (Disabled person, wave c)

However, there were also strongly expressed views, particularly among those who had contributed via the taxation system in their previous working lives, that the extension and imposition of sanctions-backed compulsion and the fulfilment of work-related requirements for disability benefit recipients was unreasonable.

> 'Taxes, National Insurance ... you have paid your dues all your life your entitled to what you are getting.' (Disabled person, wave a)

Further, ethical objections were raised on several grounds. Principled critiques denounced the use of welfare conditionality within incapacity benefit systems as punitive, coercive and unjust. Here many disabled WSUs asserted their right to receive social security benefits free from work-focused requirements and sanctions once their incapacity to work had been fairly assessed.

> 'Everybody should work if they can work but some people just can't work and the government should realise that.' (Disabled person, wave a)

> 'Some people are not well enough to work and they should not be forced into taking part in things that are not good for them. But I think it should be up to the individual. If people want to work they should be given the support.' (Disabled person, wave b)

More specific arguments were raised that related to the ways in which welfare conditionality had been implemented. Many disabled people regarded the Work Capability Assessment (the points-based, functional capability test that determines both the level of benefit paid and the extent to which an impaired person is subject to conditionality) as grossly unfair, insensitively administered and leading to inappropriate outcomes. For example:

> 'It is demeaning, condescending, it is painful, it is damaging, it actually makes your disabilities worse. ... And it is completely unproductive. It doesn't get people work. Nothing in what they've done to me has assisted me in getting back in to the employment market. So these people are paid to torture me basically, for money I don't get. ... It actively malevolent and it seeks to make you someone who won't bother they system again. It's trying to make you go away and die. That's what it's for. (Disabled person, wave a)

The majority of disabled WSUs felt unfairly treated by an incapacity benefit system predisposed towards sanction for non-compliance and ill-suited to meeting the requirements of disabled people, especially those with episodic and/or mental health impairments (Dwyer et al, 2020; Scullion and Curchin, 2022). Many of those disabled people who, often following lengthy and repeated Work Capability Assessment appeal processes, were eventually released from the threat of sanctions by placement in the Support Group were relieved to be free from what they perceived as unreasonable and unethical work search requirements. However, conversely, others placed in the Support Group felt abandoned and unsupported in their desire to enter paid work (see also Pollard, 2018).

> 'When you get put into that category that's it. You're put in a corner and forgotten about. ... I've got a disability and therefore I'm good for nothing.' (Disabled person, wave a)

As such, there was an irony that the 'Support Group' appeared to represent quite the opposite for a number of participants. Although the absence of compulsion and sanctions was a relief, membership of that group was often perceived to be accompanied by the removal of access to support for those who wanted to take steps to enter employment. For some there were also fears that by showing a desire to engage in paid work while in the Support Group, this might lead to increasing future expectations of work-related activities or the questioning of their Support Group status.

Conclusions

Discussions about the ethicality of welfare conditionality are often contentious and contested. The rights and wrongs of demanding citizens' mandatory engagement in prescribed activities and behaviours in order to access, or retain, basic rights to collectively provided welfare provokes strong arguments from both advocates and adversaries of welfare conditionality, who draw on a range of competing ethical frameworks to justify their positions. The analysis presented in this chapter evidences that the majority of WSUs interviewed were broadly supportive of idea that welfare rights should be linked to certain individual responsibilities. For practical, as well as ethical reasons, among these respondents there was a general acceptance that individual citizens should be required (when they are able) to contribute via paid work and taxation systems and in return gain access to collectively funded, state-provided welfare benefits and services. Such individuals routinely invoked contractualist arguments in support of their stance. In contrast, those WSUs who were more comfortable with the implementation of sanctions-backed welfare conditionality asserted paternalistic arguments in support of a disciplinarian state empowered to interfere in the freedoms more usually afforded to citizens. The imposition of particular responsibilities and behavioural requirements on 'errant' citizens and the accompanying removal of social security benefits and welfare provisions, and the hardships that may then ensue, were deemed to be necessary, fair and appropriate. This was because the state was believed to be exercising its coercive power and authority to improve the lives of individual, 'delinquent' citizens and the wider functioning of society in general. Only a very small minority of WSUs deployed narratives that drew on mutualistic assertions to suggest that it was right and proper to make citizens' access to basic social provisions conditional on the prior fulfilment of unpaid community service.

Recourse to the three ethical discourses noted here should not be taken as WSUs' unequivocal endorsement of the principles and practices of welfare conditionality. In a similar vein to the key informants who took part in the WelCond study, welfare conditionality was subject to a number of important caveats (see Dwyer, 2020). A large number of those WSUs interviewed used human rights-based arguments to reiterate the necessity of universally available rights to the services of the welfare state regardless of previous conduct or prior contribution records. Additionally, in our interviews with lone parents, discussion of the appropriateness of the intensifying of welfare conditionality raised questions about the ethicality of requiring and valuing activity in the PLM, over and above other socially responsible and necessary forms of contribution, such as informal familial care. Similarly, the consideration of disabled people's views on the injustices and inadequacies of extending welfare conditionality to incapacity benefit recipients who were unable to work due to their impairments raised wider concerns about the inequities and profoundly unethical outcomes generated by the operation of highly conditional welfare regimes.

EIGHT

Conclusions

Within contemporary welfare states a principle of welfare conditionality links eligibility to publicly funded welfare benefits and services to individuals' acceptance of state-specified compulsory responsibilities or particular patterns of required behaviour. When welfare conditionality is implemented in policy and practice it routinely involves the use of two core elements. First, compulsion, that is, the requirement that certain people mandatorily engage with specified packages of support, typically designed with the intention of moving them off social security benefits and into paid work, or tackling antisocial/problematic behaviours. Second, the application of various types of sanction for non-compliance. Those people who do not engage as specified face the denial, or loss, of welfare benefits and services as a consequence of their failure to comply.

Internationally, across many and various types of welfare regimes, welfare conditionality has become a key part of the process of welfare reform (for example, Cox, 1998; Dwyer, 2010; Betzelt and Bothfeld, 2011; Baumberg Geiger, 2017). Influenced by New Right thinking (Mead, 1982, 1986), policymakers and governments from across the mainstream political spectrum have become convinced that the instrumental use of various combinations of sanction (sticks) and mandatory support (carrots) can effectively change citizens' behaviour to reduce 'welfare dependency' and promote personal responsibility. In reality this instrumental behaviourism has been largely implemented in response to the conduct and dependency of poorer and marginalised citizens (Dwyer, 1998; Bray et al, 2014; Harrison and Saunders, 2016; Grymonprez et al, 2020) who rely on what Titmuss (1958) identified as 'social welfare' benefits and services to meet their needs. Enforcing behaviour change among more wealthy citizens (the consistent beneficiaries of fiscal and occupational welfare) appears to be less of a concern for governments with the preferred mode of behavioural intervention, 'nudge' (Thaler and Sunstein, 2008), less directive or potentially punitive.

Welfare states have always sought to promote particular values and specific types of preferred behaviour alongside the meeting of different types of need (Mann, 1992; Dean, 1998). The advance of welfare conditionality across a range of welfare states and policy sectors can be regarded as an attempt to resolve the long-standing tension between care and control, inherent within social welfare (Goroff, 1974; Brown, 2017), firmly in favour of the latter. The ways in which welfare conditionality is implemented varies across different nations. However, it is reasonable to argue that consecutive UK governments, in line with their counterparts in other liberal, Anglophone nations (for example, Australia, the US), have enthusiastically embraced an assertive and 'work first' (Taylor, 2017) model of conditionality in which sanction rather than support predominates. The enthusiasm with which UK governments have pressed ahead with the intensification and extension of highly conditional welfare policies across a range of fields (especially in relation to social security and antisocial behaviour) is surprising, given the international evidence base contesting their effectiveness in triggering and sustaining behaviour change (Treolar, 2001; Griggs and Bennett, 2009; Griggs and Evans, 2010; Watts et al, 2014; NAO, 2016). That said, as noted in Chapter Three, strong evidence to support the efficacy of a particular policy is not a prerequisite when certain programmes fit with existing political priorities, ideological predispositions, or are judged to be electorally popular (Griggs and Evans, 2010; Spotswood and Marsh, 2016). This certainly appeared to be the case circa 2011/12 in the UK when the WelCond project was first conceived. At that time a 'conditionality consensus' in support of linking social rights to specified individual responsibilities existed across the mainstream political parties (Dwyer, 2008) and the idea found support among large sections of the general public (Kellner, 2012). Today (April 2022), the political consensus within the UK that endorsed behavioural conditionality as an effective and appropriate tool appears to be under some strain. For example, the Scottish Nationalist Party, Liberal Democrats and the Labour Party have all recently adopted policy stances that increasingly question the extension and ubiquity of welfare conditionality within the welfare state, especially in respect of benefit sanctions (for example, Labour Party, 2019; Liberal Democrats, 2019; SNP, 2022). As noted in Chapter Two, ongoing devolution of powers in relation to social security and welfare provision may further undermine the extent to which the principles and practices of welfare conditionality prevail (see Simpson, 2022 for fuller discussions). Certainly, the national governments in Edinburgh, Cardiff and Belfast appear to have different views on the efficacy and ethicality of welfare conditionality from the current UK government in London. Indeed, the Scottish and Welsh governments are exploring the feasibility of Minimum Income Guarantees and Universal Basic Income schemes as alternatives to highly conditional social security schemes (Scottish Government, 2021; Welsh Government, 2022). However, moving forward, it would be over-optimistic to predict the demise of welfare conditionality. The current UK Conservative government remain firmly committed to welfare conditionality and benefit sanctions, reinstating both in July 2020 following their suspension due to the COVID-19 pandemic (Harris, 2020). Additionally, under the Way to Work campaign (DWP, 2022), conditionality has been further intensified. Universal Credit claimants will now have only up to four weeks (compared to three months previously) to find work in their preferred sector; after which they will face sanctions for not seeking work in other areas of employment (Webster, 2022). More broadly, if the current UK government's predilection for welfare conditionality is to change it will have to engage more fully with critical voices and research that highlights the limits and ill-effects of welfare conditionality; something which does not appear likely given the Department for Work and Pensions' reluctance to publish their own research into the effectiveness of benefit sanctions in changing behaviour (Butler, 2022).

Beyond issues of politics, discussions about the effectiveness and impacts of policy often feed into ethical debates about the fairness of governments intervening into the lives of citizens to change their behaviour. Questions about whether the denial, or removal, of rights to basic welfare benefits and services, when individuals fail to comply with specified behavioural requirements, raise strong opinions among both advocates and adversaries of welfare conditionality. Against the backdrop of the contested and ongoing debates about the efficacy and ethicality of welfare conditionality this book offers an empirically grounded and theoretically informed understanding of the effectiveness of welfare conditionality in promoting and sustaining behaviour change among a diversity of welfare service users (WSUs) over time. Additionally, it offers insights into how those at the 'sharp end' of highly conditional welfare interventions make use of competing normative frameworks when considering questions about the ethicality of welfare conditionality. The key points that emerge on these issues are summarised here.

Overall, the analysis presented in this book shows that the use of welfare conditionality within social security systems is routinely ineffective in facilitating people's movement off social security benefits and entry into, or progression within, the paid labour market over time. Across the two-year period covered by our three waves of repeat interviews, 'stasis', defined as a lack of significant and/or sustained change in employment status, was by far the most common outcome for a substantial majority of WSUs. Occasional, sustained movements off welfare and into work were evident but these were extremely rare, occurring in no more than a handful of cases. Patterns of repeat work–welfare recycling, that is, recurrent short-term movements into various insecure jobs interspersed with periods of unemployment, were typical among the minority of people who managed to find intermittent paid employment across the period of the study. These respondents' ability to access or increase their hours of paid work routinely had little to do with their behaviour; rather, their opportunities were structured by the strength of local labour markets and employers' increasing demands for a flexible workforce. For some, such as lone parents, their caring responsibilities outside of the paid labour market also impacted on their capacity to maintain or enhance paid employment. Additionally, disabled people routinely faced significant structural barriers (for example, disabling environments and discriminatory practices) when looking for paid work, with the implementation of welfare conditionality often exacerbating existing illness and impairment and further reducing the likelihood of future employment (Reeves, 2017; Dwyer et al, 2020).

More generally, the factors underpinning behaviour change, in respect of both movements off social security benefits, and the reduction or cessation of antisocial or perceived problematic behaviours are complex. Change is rarely linear and is more often characterised by periods of progression and regression. Furthermore, analysis of the repeat interviews with people recruited into the antisocial behaviour/family intervention, offender and people experiencing homelessness cohorts highlights variable and, at times, very limited effectiveness of conditional welfare interventions in changing behaviour. This was especially the case where people were attempting to address multiple and complex issues, such as ill-health, homelessness and/ or alcohol or drug dependency, simultaneously.

The implementation of welfare conditionality within 'work first' social security regimes initiates and sustains a range of negative behaviour changes and outcomes. One significant and unintended outcome is 'counterproductive compliance' (Wright and Dwyer, 2022). This occurs when, in order to avoid the severely detrimental effects of a benefit sanction, claimants become focused on, and prioritise, meeting the often extensive, mandatory work-related conditions linked to their claim at the expense of engaging in more meaningful and productive job search likely to enhance their employment opportunities. Others unable to cope with the pressures and 'hassle' of conditionality disengage from the social security system entirely, leading to increased poverty, exacerbated ill-health and, on certain occasions, even destitution. A minority of those who were prompted, by the imposition of welfare conditionality, to turn their back on publicly funded welfare benefits and services, also resorted to survival crime rather than relying on charitable or familial support when, and if, it is available.

It is clear that compulsion, and the threat or application of benefit sanctions, do little to enhance people's motivations to prepare for, seek or enter paid employment. Rather, they regularly trigger extremely negative personal, financial, health and behavioural outcomes. Benefit sanctions also play a primary role in pushing WSUs away from collective welfare benefits and services. When considering the mandatory support made available to people (with some limited exceptions), our analysis demonstrates that much of the compulsory job search, training and employment support offered by Jobcentre Plus and externally contracted providers was too general, repetitive and often of poor quality. WSUs reported that it was regularly ineffective in enhancing their skills and employment opportunities. Such systemic deficiencies are significant, as the provision of appropriate and personalised support was pivotal in triggering and sustaining, over time, both paid employment and positive behaviour changes such as the reduction of antisocial behaviour. For example, the availability of intensive and holistic support in interventions such as family intervention projects played a key role in helping some families address a range of complex needs. Unfortunately, such gains were sometimes, subsequently, undermined by the operation of depersonalised welfare conditionality within the social security benefit system.

Increased conditionality often prompts greater use of discretion within welfare systems. The use of discretionary powers by street level bureaucrats (Lipsky, 2010 [1980]) responsible for the interpretation and implementation of welfare policies in their day-to-day interactions with welfare claimants is not an inherently good or bad thing. When exercised sensitively, discretionary powers can ensure the necessary flexibility required to adapt policy to best meet clients' particular needs. Conversely, discretion can be abused, leading to 'arbitrariness and domination' (Molander, 2016). Several of the case studies and the wider discussions presented in this book illustrate the significance of discretionary judgements and practices in facilitating positive or negative outcomes for WSUs. More generally, although examples of supportive discretionary practice were evident, the flexibilities or 'easements' that are designed to suspend or reduce the compulsory requirements attached to an individual's benefit claim in recognition of particular circumstances or other responsibilities (for example, homelessness, lone parenthood, impairment or illness) were not always being fully communicated to WSUs. This often led to increased pressure on WSUs, helping to fuel the detrimental outcomes noted.

Turning finally to ethical matters, the majority of WSUs commonly endorsed the broad principle of linking welfare rights to responsible behaviour such as engaging in paid work, providing informal familial care and contributing via taxation systems. However, these general sentiments should not be taken as evidence of an unequivocal endorsement of welfare conditionality. Many people believed that it was being inappropriately implemented and that the intensification and extension of benefit sanctions, particularly to previously exempt groups (for example, lone parents, disabled people, in-work claimants) was unjust.

Closing comments

The rise and consolidation of welfare conditionality represent a more punitive turn in social policy. Policymakers' predilection for identifying individual 'idleness' and 'irresponsibility' as the key cause of social problems, and the imposition of behavioural conditionality as the preferred solution to complex issues, deflects our gaze away from the ideological and structural factors that are fundamental to understanding and responding to the poverty and other inequalities that continue to blight our societies. Welfare conditionality undermines the promise of social citizenship (Dean, 1998, 2012; Dwyer, 1998), sets vulnerable people up to fail (Reeves and Lookstra, 2017) and serves individuals with multiple and complex needs particularly badly (Dean, 2003; Bauld et al, 2012). Additionally, the COVID-19 pandemic has demonstrated something of a 'conditionality conundrum', whereby benefit claimants were still actively seeking work despite the suspension of overt work-related activity requirements (Edmiston et al, 2020); evidence that further questions the necessity of welfare conditionality as a behaviour change tool. The discussions and analysis presented in this book strongly evidence that the use of sanctions-backed compulsion (the key element inherent within highly conditional welfare states), largely fails to trigger and sustain the behaviour changes that advocates cite in its defence; instead, routinely triggering a range of profoundly negative outcomes that create new, and exacerbate existing, inequalities. Welfare conditionality is counterproductive, ineffective and unethical. It is therefore time to end the misguided obsession with behaviour change and focus on promoting meaningful employment support, genuine social security and greater equality.

Methods appendix

Introduction

As noted in Chapter One, the use of conditional welfare arrangements which aim to influence the behaviour of social welfare recipients has become an established and expanding feature of UK welfare state provision over the last three decades. Against this backdrop the WelCond project (2013–19) had three core aims. First, to develop an empirically and theoretically informed understanding of the role of welfare conditionality in promoting and sustaining behaviour change among a diversity of social welfare recipients over time. Second, to consider the particular circumstances in which the use of welfare conditionality may, or may not, be ethically justified. Third, to establish an original and comprehensive evidence base on the efficacy and ethicality of conditionality across a range of social policy fields and diverse groups of welfare service users (WSUs).

A qualitative approach

Essentially the WelCond project team were attempting to explore and understand a number of linked questions about the fairness, impacts and effects, intended or otherwise, of welfare interventions underpinned by, and delivered according to, a principle of welfare conditionality. To do this we used a range of appropriate qualitative methods (see, for example, Ritchie et al, 2014; Mason, 2017). Initially, a comprehensive literature review and mapping of theoretical and normative positions related to welfare conditionality and behaviour change was undertaken alongside a rapid review of existing quantitative datasets appropriate to the various sampled populations under consideration within the project.[1] A series of cross-disciplinary seminars convened with expert international speakers also informed the early theoretical work of the WelCond team.

To allow for a comparison of how differing legislative frameworks and political approaches might impact on the implementation and effectiveness of welfare conditionality we chose to undertake our fieldwork in England and Scotland. Before embarking on extensive qualitative fieldwork a series of consultation workshops were then undertaken with practitioners (involved in policy formation and the implementation of welfare conditionality) and WSUs. Subsequently, in order to generate new empirical data to inform our work, we undertook interviews with three sets of respondents. First, the team conducted 52 semi-structured interviews with policy stakeholders (including policymakers, senior officers from government, service provider agencies, umbrella bodies and campaigning organisations). The aim was to provide insight into the political and other 'drivers' underpinning and contesting the implementation and rollout of conditional welfare initiatives at national, regional and local levels. Policy stakeholder interviews lasted approximately one hour, the majority undertaken between November 2013 and September 2014, with a small number undertaken at later dates as issues emerged or appropriate opportunities occurred. See Table A.1 for a list of policy stakeholder interviews

Next, 27 focus groups with frontline welfare practitioners were convened. In order to explore the interaction of normative and systems orientated processes in decisions related to the sanctions and support at the heart of conditional welfare regimes we used a 'vignette' (hypothetical scenario) methodology (Finch, 1987; Schoenberg and Ravdal, 2000) and presented a series of 'typical cases' of individuals or households subject to conditionality in each welfare area under investigation. The purpose of the focus groups was to explore practitioners' views about what should happen (ethically) and what they think would happen (in practice). The vignettes were used to stimulate conversations about the range of normative and operational options drawn upon when frontline practitioners made their decisions. A total of 156 respondents took part in the focus groups which were conducted in 2014 and 2015 (see Table A.2 for details). Group discussions lasted between 90 minutes and three hours.

Our original intention was to include in our focus group discussions both those who implement conditionality in their face-to-face interactions with WSUs (including Department for Work and Pensions [DWP] Work Coaches, Work Programme staff, family intervention workers, street outreach workers, local authority housing officers, and so on) and also those who play a role in supporting people subject to the various sanctions and mandatory support that welfare conditionality implies (for example, welfare rights advisers and advocacy organisation staff). However, despite repeated attempts to access Jobcentre Plus, Work Programme staff and employees of companies involved in Work Capability Assessments the DWP decided to veto their involvement in the research project and we were unable to conduct focus groups with such staff.

At the heart of the WelCond project was a large qualitative longitudinal panel study undertaken with a diversity of WSUs subject to welfare conditionality. This generated a total of 1,082 conversations across the three waves of repeat interviews that were conducted. Qualitative longitudinal research (QLR) is a valuable methodological approach for understanding processes of behaviour change and assessing if, when, how and why it may occur overtime. QLR attempts to describe changes that may be occurring, consider how they arise, and explain how and why there may be diverse outcomes for different members of a sampled population (Lewis, 2003; Saldana, 2003; Neale, 2021).

Methods appendix

Table A.1: Policy stakeholders

Code number and agreed descriptor	Code number and agreed descriptor
PS1 Managing Director, National Social Housing Representative Organisation	PS27 Senior Representative, Homelessness Umbrella Agency
PS2a Senior Policy Manager, Community Safety, Scottish Government	PS28a Senior Representative, Homelessness Campaigning Organisation
PS2b Senior Policy Manager, Social Housing Services, Scottish Government	PS28b Senior Representative, Homelessness Campaigning Organisation
PS3 Senior Policy Officer, Complex Needs Charity	PS29 Senior Representative, Homelessness Charity
PS4 Former Government Minister	PS30 Senior Representative, Homelessness Campaigning Organisation
PS5 Spokesperson for Network of Migrant Support Organisations	PS31 Senior Representative, Lone Parent Campaigning Organisation
PS6 Labour MP	PS32 Senior Representative, Children's Charity
PS7 Integration Service Manager	PS33 Senior Representative, Social Housing Sector, UK
PS8 Legal Advisor	
PS9 Representative of Scottish National Refugee Organisation	PS34 Senior Civil Servant
PS10 Senior Policy Officer	PS35 Senior Representative, Homelessness Umbrella Agency
PS11 Coordinator, Regional Rights Organisation	PS36 Senior Representative, Homelessness Charity
PS12 Policy and Communications Manager, UK Disability Organisation	PS37 Senior Representative, Homelessness Umbrella Agency
PS13 Senior Representative, Social Housing Sector, Scotland	PS38 Senior Housing Association Stakeholder, South of England
PS14 Senior Representative, Local Government, Scotland	PS39 Senior Representative, Lone Parent Charity
PS16 Senior Representative, Social Housing Sector, Scotland	PS40 Community-based Housing Association
PS17 Senior Statutory Sector Representative, Scotland	PS41a Communities and Neighbourhoods Manager, Regional Housing Association
PS18 Senior Housing Key Informant	PS41b Head of Tenancy Services, Regional Housing Association
PS19a Offender Campaigning Organisation	
PS19b Offender Campaigning Organisation	PS42 UK-wide Welfare Rights Agency Policy Officer
PS20 Government Department	
PS21 Government Department	PS43a Faith-based Charity Campaigner
PS22 Housing Campaigning Organisation	PS43b Faith-based Charity Campaigner
PS23a Offender Campaigning Organisation	PS44 Senior Policy Stakeholder
PS23b Offender Campaigning Organisation	PS45 CEO, Private Work Programme Provider
PS23c Offender Campaigning Organisation	PS46 Project Manager, Voluntary Sector
PS24 Head, NGO Offending	PS47 CEO Membership Organisation for Employment Support Providers
PS25 Senior Representative, Homelessness Charity	
PS26 Senior Representative, Lone Parent Charity	PS50 Welfare Rights Advisor
	PS51 Housing Support Manager

Table A.2: Focus groups undertaken with practitioners

Policy area	Geographical area	Focus group code number	Focus group date	Respondent number
Antisocial behaviour	Glasgow	FG-AS-02	06/05/2015	2
Antisocial behaviour	Bristol	FG-AS-04	12/05/2015	5
Offending	Glasgow	FG-AS-01	30/04/2015	4
Universal Credit	Inverness	FG-AS-03	30/03/2015	8
Social Housing	Bristol	FG-BW-01	04/09/2014	5
Social Housing	London	FG-BW-02	27/11/2014	7
Social Housing	London	FG-BW-03	11/12/2014	11
Social Housing	Glasgow	FG-BW-04	23/01/2015	12
Offending	Sheffield	FG-DF-01	08/05/2015	2
Disability	Sheffield	FG-EB-01	08/10/2015	2
Disability	Sheffield	FG-EB-02	26/11/2015	3
Jobseeking	Sheffield	FG-EB-03	26/11/2015	4
Migrants	Bristol	FG-EB-04	04/12/2015	6
Jobseeking	Sheffield	FG-EB-05	12/10/2015	5
Antisocial behaviour	Perth	FG-JM-03	16/09/2015	18
Disability	Bristol	FG-JM-01	24/04/2015	4
Universal Credit	Bath	FG-JM-02	13/05/2015	8
Lone Parents	Sheffield	FG-JM-04	11/12/2015	6
Universal Credit	Manchester	FG-KJ-01	16/04/2015	10
Migrants	Peterborough	FG-KJ-02	05/11/2015	4
Disability	Peterborough	FG-KJ-03	05/11/2015	3
Homelessness	London	FG-SJ-01	27/08/2014	7
Homelessness	London	FG-SJ-02	14/10/2014	3
Homelessness	London	FG-SJ-03	15/10/2014	5
Homelessness	London	FG-SJ-04	25/11/2014	5
Homelessness	Edinburgh	FG-SJ-05	10/09/2015	3
Homelessness	Glasgow	FG-SJ-06	16/11/2015	4

Given that an explicit goal of welfare conditionality is to promote and sustain particular types of behaviour change it is a highly appropriate approach to use to explore, across time, the effectiveness and impacts of policies that demand WSUs' mandatory engagement with various welfare support services under threat of sanction for non-compliance.

> [QLR's] focus on change, both on how people change and on how people respond to change, is very relevant in the current policy context in which individual behaviour change is seen as key to achieving desired policy goals. ... Having people look back over time can provide insight into how they perceive and explain their actions, given the opportunity to discuss and reflect. Following people forward over time provides an opportunity to explore how and why people make the individual choices that add up to particular cumulative trajectories, and more specifically to understand the ways in which people respond to and use social and welfare services. (Corden and Millar, 2007: 529)

We deliberately chose to use qualitative longitudinal techniques to enable the development of a dynamic understanding of the impacts and effects of welfare conditionality that was firmly grounded in the experiences of those individuals who were subject to welfare conditionality in their everyday lives. The qualitative longitudinal dimension enabled an understanding of how, over time, welfare recipients' choices and actions were influenced by the application of specific sanction or support initiatives alongside changes in personal and family circumstances and how these interacted with other relevant factors such as gender, ethnicity and disability (see Millar, 2007). The repeat qualitative longitudinal sample consisted of nine different groups (panels) of WSUs subject to varying types and degrees of welfare conditionality. These were recipients of working age social security benefits (jobseekers, lone parents, disabled people and both in-work and out-of-work Universal Credit[2] claimants), people experiencing homelessness, social tenants, individuals/families subject to antisocial behaviour orders/family intervention projects, offenders and migrants. The diversity of groups sampled helped to ensure that differences according to gender, ethnicity and disability could be captured and the significance and dynamics of such factors explored. Key characteristics of the sample as recruited at wave a are set out in Table A.3.

Suitable respondents were purposively sampled according to a range of appropriate criteria pertinent to each group under consideration. For example, four sampling criteria were used when recruiting the migrant cohort. First, these respondents had to meet the United Nation's broad

Table A.3: Overview of welfare service user sample characteristics at wave a

Characteristic	Percentages
Gender	56% male 44% female
Ethnicity	81% White 19% Black and Minority Ethnic
Nation of interview	72% England 28% Scotland
Age	3% not declared 10% 18–24 63% 25–49 24% 50–65

definition of a migrant, that is, '[a] person who moves to a country other than that of his or her usual residence for a period of at least a year (12 months), so that the country of destination effectively becomes his or her new country of usual residence' (UN, 2013). Second, they had to be adult migrants who had moved to the UK from the European Economic Area, or Third Country Nationals from beyond Europe with a previous positive outcome to their claim for asylum in the UK (for example, granted Refugee Status, Discretionary Leave to Remain, Humanitarian Protection Status or Indefinite Leave to Remain). Third, migrant respondents had to be individuals with prior/ongoing experience of conditional welfare benefits or interventions. Fourth, they were required not to have been granted British Citizenship status at the time of initial wave a interview.

WSUs were interviewed up to three times at on average 12-month intervals across a two-year period. Retention rates between each wave were approximately 70 per cent. That is, of the 481 people interviewed at wave a, we were able to re-interview 339 again at wave b and 262 for a third time at wave c. See Table A.4 for specific numbers retained in each sampled group. The three waves of repeat interviews took place between 2014 and 2017 and typically lasted between 40 and 90 minutes. Interviews were undertaken in 11 locations in England and Scotland, in Bath, Bristol, Edinburgh, Glasgow, Inverness, London, Greater Manchester, Peterborough, Salford, Sheffield and Warrington. These sites were chosen to ensure a reasonable geographic spread across the two nations and to help enable access to appropriate WSU respondents through the pre-existing research networks of team members. Bath, Inverness and Warrington were added as fieldwork sites following the introduction of Universal Credit in 2013 as these, alongside Greater Manchester, were locations chosen as initial Universal Credit pilot areas.

Table A.4: Number of welfare service users taking part in each of the three waves of repeat interviews

Sampled group	Wave a	Wave b	Wave c
Disabled people	58	54	45
People experiencing homelessness	55	25	16
Social housing tenants	40	32	24
People subject to antisocial behaviour/family intervention policy interventions	40	23	18
Offenders	57	35	26
Jobseeker's Allowance claimants	65	43	33
Migrants	55	38	25
Lone parents	53	43	35
Universal Credit claimants	58	46	40
Totals	481	339	262

Ethical considerations and data handling/analysis

Two principles, informed consent and anonymity, underpinned the fieldwork. Before each interview, individuals were provided with an information sheet, given the opportunity to ask questions and made aware of their right to withdraw from the study at any time. Written consent forms were used to ensure valid agreement to interview was obtained and issues related to consent were revisited with individual WSUs prior to each wave of interviews. Interpreters and translated materials were made available as required. Interviews were conducted in places convenient for respondents including workplaces, cafés, community/support agency offices and homes. The overwhelming majority of interviews were conducted face-to-face with a small number of wave b and c interviews conducted over the phone to meet the needs of respondents. WSUs who participated in the fieldwork received a £20 shopping voucher after each interview/consultation event as a thank you for their time. All interviews and focus groups were audio recorded and transcribed verbatim. English language transcripts were then produced using a professional transcription service. Appropriate anonymised code numbers or agreed identifiers were assigned to each respondent (for example, WSU-BR-LS-012a[3]) and used as required.

Policy stakeholder and focus group interviews were analysed using cross-sectional thematic code and retrieve methods (Ritchie et al, 2014; Mason, 2017) and grid analysis techniques (Knodel, 1993). A multi-dimensional approach to analysis of the longitudinal panel study data variously enabled: cross-sectional analysis (exploring individual cases across the sample at each of the three waves of data collection); repeat cross-sectional analysis (looking for change in individual cases between particular points of time) and the generation of longitudinal case narratives, to explore how, why and for whom behaviour change did or did not occur across the time period studied (see Holland et al, 2006). The data was also analysed thematically both longitudinally and at each wave/time point, to explore key issues within individual cases and allow group comparisons to explore, commonality and difference between particular respondents and sampled groups. A repeat qualitative longitudinal panel study of the size and complexity undertaken by WelCond generates vast amounts of data. In order to enable consistent longitudinal analysis across the different respondents and groups a common coding schema was developed for application across all sampled groups and the full dataset was summarised using a framework matrix approach within a QSR NVivo software package (Lewis, 2007). This was supplemented by additional, more 'bottom up' thematic analysis, undertaken by particular teams of researchers assigned to a specific policy area according to their expertise.

Notes

[1] Much of this initial scoping work was published as Watts et al (2014). We are grateful to the Joseph Rowntree Foundation for providing additional funding to support the production of this output.

[2] When the project was originally conceived, circa mid-2011, Universal Credit did not exist. Following its introduction by the Conservative/Liberal Coalition government in 2013 we added a ninth panel to the repeat qualitative interview study.

[3] This identifies: type of respondent for example, welfare service user (WSU), location of the interview (BR = Bristol), the interviewer and the wave of interview if appropriate.

References

6, P., Fletcher-Morgan, C. and Leyland, K. (2010) 'Making people more responsible: the Blair governments' programme for changing citizens' behaviour', *Political Studies*, 58(3): 427–49.

Abbring, J.H., Van den Berg, G.J. and Van Ours, J.C. (2005) 'The effect of unemployment insurance sanctions on the transition rate from unemployment to employment', *Economic Journal*, 115(505): 602–30.

Adam, S., Brewer, M. and Shephard, A. (2006) 'The poverty trade-off: work incentives and income redistribution in Britain', *Findings*, York, Joseph Rowntree Foundation, www.jrf.org.uk/sites/files/jrf/1936.pdf

Adam, S., Joyce, R. and Pope, T. (2019) *The impacts of localised council tax support schemes*, London, Institute for Fiscal Studies.

Adcock, A. and Kennedy, S. (2015) 'Benefit sanctions', *Debate pack number CDP-0113*, 30 November, London House of Commons Library, https://researchbriefings.parliament.uk/Research Briefing/Summary/CDP-2015-0113

Adler, M. (2016) 'A new Leviathan: benefit sanctions in the twenty-first century', *Journal of Law and Society*, 43(2): 195–227.

Adler, M. (2018) *Cruel, inhuman or degrading treatment? Benefit sanctions in the UK?* London, Palgrave Macmillan.

Ajzen, I. (1991) 'The theory of planned behaviour', *Organizational Behaviour and Human Decision Processes*, 50(2): 179–211.

Ajzen, I. and Fishbein, M. (1980) *Understanding attitudes and predicting social behaviour*, New York, Pearson Education.

Alden, S. (2015) 'Discretion on the frontline: the street level bureaucrat in English statutory homelessness services', *Social Policy and Society*, 14(1): 63–77.

Andersen, K. (2020) 'Universal Credit, gender and unpaid childcare: Mothers' accounts of the new welfare conditionality regime', *Critical Social Policy*, 40(3): 430–49.

APPG-UC (All Party Parliamentary Group on Universal Credit) (2019) 'What needs to change in Universal Credit?', *Report by the All Party Parliamentary Group on Universal Credit*, London, Houses of Parliament, https://appguniversalcredit.org.uk/updates/report-summary-what-needs-to-change-in-universal-credit/

Arni, P., Lalive, R. and Van Ours, J.C. (2013) 'How effective are unemployment benefit sanctions? Looking beyond unemployment exit', *Journal of Applied Econometrics*, 28(7): 1153–78.

ASB Help (2021) *Acceptable behaviour contract*, https://asbhelp.co.uk/home-practitioners/acceptable-behaviour-contract/

Bacon, M. and Seddon, T. (2019) 'Controlling drug users: forms of power and behavioural regulation in drug treatment services', *British Journal of Criminology*, 60(2): 403–21.

Bagguley, P. and Mann, K. (1992) 'Idle thieving bastards: scholarly representations of the underclass', *Work, Employment and Society*, 6(1): 113–26.

Ball, E. (2019) 'Exploring the behavioural outcomes of family-based intensive interventions', in P. Dwyer (ed) *Dealing with welfare conditionality: implementation and effects*, Bristol, Policy Press, pp 149–75.

Ball, E., Batty, E. and Flint, J. (2015) 'Intensive family intervention and the problem figuration of "troubled families"', *Social Policy and Society*, 15(2): 263–74.

Barbier, J.-C. and Ludwig-Mayerhofer, W. (2004) 'Introduction: the many worlds of activation', *European Societies*, 6(4): 423–36.

Barnard, H. (2019) *Briefing: where next for Universal Credit and tackling poverty?*, York, Joseph Rowntree Foundation.

Barr, B., Taylor-Robinson, D., Stuckler, D., Loopstra, R., Reeves, A. and Whitehead, M. (2016a) '"First, do no harm": are disability assessments associated with adverse trends in mental health? A longitudinal ecological study', *Journal of Epidemiology and Community Health*, 70(4): 339–34.

Barr, B., Taylor-Robinson, D., Stuckler., D, Loopstra, R., Reeves, A. and Whitehead, M. (2016b) 'Fit for work or fit for unemployment? Does the reassessment of disability benefit claimants using a tougher work capability assessment help people into work?', *Journal of Epidemiology and Community Health*, 70(5): 452–8.

Barrientos, A. (2011) 'Conditions in antipoverty programmes', *Journal of Poverty and Social Justice*, 19(1): 5–26.

Bastagli, F. (2009) 'Conditionality in public policy targeted to the poor: promoting resilience?', *Social Policy and Society*, 8(1): 127–40.

Bate, A. (2016) 'The Troubled Families programme (England)', *Briefing paper number CBP 07585*, 16 May, London, House of Commons Library.

Batty, E. (2020) '"Without the right support network I'd probably be either dead or in the prison system": the role of support in helping offenders on their journey to desistance', *The Howard Journal*, 59(2): 174–93.

Batty, E. and Fletcher, D.R. (2018) 'Offenders', *Final findings: research briefing for the Welfare Conditionality project*, http://www.welfareconditionality.ac.uk/wp-content/uploads/2018/05/39273-Offenders-web.pdf

Batty, E. and Flint, J. (2012) 'Conceptualising the contexts, mechanism and outcomes of intensive family intervention projects', *Social Policy and Society*, 11(3): 345–58.

Batty, E., Beatty, C., Casey, R., Foden, M., McCarthy, L. and Reeve, K. (2015) *Homeless people's experience of welfare conditionality and benefit sanctions*, London, Crisis.

References

Batty, E., Flint, J. and McNeill, J. (2018) 'Anti-social behaviour and family interventions', *Final findings: research briefing for the Welfare Conditionality project*, http://www.welfareconditionality.ac.uk/wp-content/uploads/2018/05/39273-Anti-social-behaviour-web.pdf

Batty, S. (2017) *Social insecurity? Welfare rights and welfare reform: a summary of a qualitative study into the impact on social tenants of welfare reforms carried out as part of an MA in Social Policy at the University of York*, https://www.nawra.org.uk/2017/11/qualitative-study-on-the-impacts-of-welfare-reform-on-social-housing-tenants/

Bauld, L., McKell, J., Carroll, C., Hay, D. and Smith, K. (2012) 'Benefits and employment: how problem drug users experience welfare and routes into work', *Journal of Social Policy*, 41(4): 751–68.

Baumberg Geiger, B. (2017) 'Benefits conditionality for disabled people: stylised facts from a review of international evidence and practice', *Journal of Poverty and Social Justice*, 25(2): 107–28.

BBC (2008) 'Work or lose home says minister', *BBC News online*, 5 February, http://news.bbc.co.uk/1/hi/uk/7227667.stm

Beatty, C. and Fothergill, S. (2016) *The uneven impact of welfare reform: the financial losses to places and people*, Sheffield, CRESR, Sheffield Hallam University.

Beatty, C. and Fothergill, S. (2018) 'Welfare reform in the United Kingdom 2010–16: expectations, outcomes, and local impacts', *Social Policy and Administration*, 52(5): 950–68.

Bemelmans-Videc, M. (1998) 'Introduction: policy instrument choice and evaluation', in M. Bemelmans-Videc, R.C. Rist and E. Vedung (eds) *Carrots, sticks and sermons: policy instruments and their evaluation*, Abingdon, Routledge, pp 1–20.

Bemelmans-Videc, M., Rist, R.C. and Vedung, E. (eds) (1998) *Carrots, sticks and sermons: policy instruments and their evaluation*, Abingdon, Routledge.

Ben-Ishai, E. (2010) 'The new paternalism: an analysis of power, state intervention and autonomy', *Political Research Quarterly*, 65(1): 151–65.

Bennett, H. (2017) 'Re-examining British welfare-to-work contracting using a transaction cost perspective', *Journal of Social Policy*, 46(1): 129–48.

Betzelt, S. and Bothfeld, S. (eds) (2011) *Activation and labour market reforms in Europe: challenges to social citizenship*, Basingstoke, Palgrave.

Beveridge, W. (1942) *Social insurance and allied services*, report by Sir William Beveridge, Cmd. 6404, London, H.M. Stationery Office.

Bielefeld, S. (2015) 'Compulsory income management, indigenous peoples and structural violence: implications for citizenship and autonomy', *Australian Indigenous Law Review*, 18(1): 99–118.

Blair, T. (1996) *New Britain: my vision of a young country*, London, Fourth Estate.

Blair, T. (1998) *The third way: new politics for a new century*, The Fabian Society Pamphlet No 588, London, The Fabian Society.

Blair, T. (2006) Full text of Tony Blair's 'respect agenda speech', 10 January, *BBC News*, http://news.bbc.co.uk/1/hi/uk_politics/4600156.stm

Boland, T. and Griffin, R. (2017) 'The purgatorial ethic and the spirit of welfare', *Journal of Classic Sociology*, 18(2): 87–103. https://doi.org/10.1177/1468795X17722079

Bonoli, G. and Natali, D. (2012) *The politics of the new welfare state*, Oxford and New York, Oxford University Press.

Boockmann, B.L., Thomsen, S. and Walter, T. (2014) 'Intensifying the use of benefit sanctions: an effective tool to increase employment?', *IZA Journal of Labor Policy*, 3(2): 1–19.

Bowpitt, G. (2020) 'Choosing to be homeless? Persistent rough sleeping and the perverse incentives of social policy in England', *Housing, Care and Support*, 23(3/4): 135–47.

Bowpitt, G., Dwyer, P., Sundin, E. and Weinstein, M. (2011) 'The home study: comparing the priorities of multiply excluded homeless people and support agencies', *Extended research report*, Salford, University of Salford and Nottingham Trent University.

Bowpitt, G., Dwyer, P., Sundin, E. and Weinstein, M. (2014) 'Places of sanctuary for "the undeserving"? Homeless people's day centres and the problem of conditionality', *British Journal of Social Work*, 44(5): 1251–67.

Brady, M. (2018) 'Targeting single mothers? Dynamics of contracting Australian employment services and activation policies at the street level', *Journal of Social Policy*, 47(4): 827–46.

Bray, J.R., Gray, M., Hand, K. and Katz, I. (2014) *Evaluating new income management in the Northern Territory: final evaluation report*, SPRC Report 25/2014, Sydney, Social Policy Research Centre, UNSW Australia.

Breidahl, K.N. (2012) 'Immigrant-targeted activation policies: a comparison of the approaches of Scandinavian welfare states', in M. Kilkey, G. Ramia and K. Farnsworth (eds) *Social policy review 24*, Bristol, Policy Press and Social Policy Association, pp 117–36.

Bretherton, J., Hunter, C. and Johnsen, S. (2013) '"You can judge them on how they look…": homelessness officers, medical evidence and decision-making in England', *European Journal of Homelessness*, 7(1): 69–91.

Brodkin, E.Z. and Marsden, G. (eds) (2013) *Work and the welfare state: street level organisations and workfare politics*, Washington, DC, Georgetown University.

Brown, J. and Sturge, G. (2020) 'Tackling anti-social behaviour', *Briefing paper number 7270*, 21 April, London, House of Commons Library.

Brown, K. (2017) *Vulnerability and young people: care and control in policy and practice*, Bristol, Policy Press.

Brown, K., Ecclestone, K. and Emmel, N. (2017) 'Review article: the many faces of vulnerability', *Social Policy and Society*, 16(3): 497–510.

References

Burney, E. (2005) *Making people behave: anti-social behaviour politics and policy*, Devon, Willan Publishing.

Butler, P. (2017) 'Interview with David Webster: "benefit sanctions should be a thing of the past"', *The Guardian*, 1 August, https://www.theguardian.com/society/2017/aug/01/benefit-sanctions-thing-of-past-david-webster

Butler, P. (2022) 'Report on the effectiveness of benefit sanctions blocked', *The Guardian*, 27 January, https://www.theguardian.com/society/2022/jan/27/report-on-effectiveness-of-benefit-sanctions-blocked-by-dwp

CAB (Citizens Advice Bureau) (2013) *Punishing poverty? A review of benefit sanctions and their impacts on clients and claimants*, Manchester, Manchester Citizens Advice Bureau.

Cameron, D. (2009) 'Putting Britain back on her feet', party leader's speech to the Conservative Party conference, Manchester, 8 October, https://www.theguardian.com/politics/2009/oct/08/david-cameron-speech-in-full

Cameron, D. (2010) Prime Minister's speech on cutting the deficit, 7 June, https://www.gov.uk/government/speeches/prime-ministers-speech-on-theeconomy

Cameron, D. (2011) Prime Minister's speech on Big Society, 14 February, https://www.gov.uk/government/speeches/pms-speech-on-big-society

Cameron, K. (2022a) 'Antisocial behaviour or just unmet support needs? How intervening in nuisance behaviour impacts underlying vulnerabilities', forthcoming in *AMPS Proceedings Journal Series: Cities in a Changing World: Questions of Culture, Climate and Design*. ISSN: 2398–9467

Cameron, K. (2022b) *A qualitative longitudinal study into the perceptions and experiences of alleged perpetrators of antisocial behaviour within social housing*, PhD thesis, Department of Social Policy and Sociology, University of York.

Cantillon, B. and van Lanker, W. (2012) 'Solidarity and reciprocity in the social investment state: what can be learned from the case of Flemish school allowances and truancy?', *Journal of Social Policy*, 41(4): 657–75.

Carter, E. and Whitworth, A. (2015) 'Creaming and parking in quasi-marketised welfare-to-work schemes: designed out of or designed in to the UK work programme?', *Journal of Social Policy*, 44(2): 277–96.

Chatterton, T. (2016) 'An introduction to theories of behaviour change', in F. Spotswood (ed) *Beyond behaviour change: key issues, interdisciplinary approaches and future directions*, Bristol, Policy Press, pp 27–48.

Cheetham, M., Moffatt, S., Addison, M. and Wiseman, A. (2019) 'Impact of Universal Credit in north east England: a qualitative study of claimants and support staff', *BMJ Open*, 9(7), https://bmjopen.bmj.com/content/9/7/e029611

Children's Commissioner (2020) *The state of children's mental health services*, London, Children's Commissioner for England.

Church Action on Poverty (2015) *Time to rethink benefit sanctions*, London, Church Action on Poverty, http://www.church-poverty.org.uk/wp-content/uploads/2019/06/Time-to-Rethink-Benefit-Sanctions.pdf

CIH (Chartered Institute for Housing) (2016) 'What you need to know about the Housing and Planning Act 2016', *Briefing*, London, Chartered Institute for Housing, http://www.cih.org/resources/PDF/Policy%20free%20download%20pdfs/What%20you%20need%20to%20know%20about%20the%20Housing%20and%20Planning%20Act%202016.pdf?dm_i=YRX

Clarke, A., Parsell, C. and Vorsina, M. (2020) 'The role of housing policy in perpetuating conditional forms of homelessness support in the era of housing first: evidence from Australia', *Housing Studies*, 35(5): 954–75. 10.1080/02673037.2019.1642452

Clarke, J. (2005) 'New Labour's citizens: activated, empowered, responsibilized, abandoned?', *Critical Social Policy*, 25(4): 447–63.

Clarke, J. and Newman, J. (2012) 'The alchemy of austerity', *Critical Social Policy*, 32(3): 299–319.

Clasen, J. and Clegg, D. (2007) 'Levels and levers of conditionality: measuring change within welfare states', in J. Clasen and N.A. Seigel (eds) *Investigating welfare state change: the 'dependent variable problem' in comparative analysis*, Cheltenham, Edward Elgar, pp 166–97.

Collins, J., Thomas, G., Willis, R. and Wilsden, J. (2003) *Carrots, sticks and sermons: influencing public behaviour for environmental goals*, a Demos/Green Alliance report produced for Defra, London, Demos.

Commonwealth of Australia (2007) *Changing behaviour: a public policy perspective*, Barton, Australian Government/Australian Public Services Commission.

Conservative Party (1997) *Conservative party general election manifesto*, London, The Conservative Party, http://www.conservativemanifesto.com/1997/1997-conservative-manifesto.shtml

Cooper, M. (2021) '"21st century welfare" in historical perspective: disciplinary welfare in the depression of the 1930s and its implications for today', *Sociological Research Online*, 26(2): 326–42.

Corden, A. and Millar, J. (2007) 'Qualitative longitudinal research for social policy: introduction to themed section', *Social Policy and Society*, 6(4): 529–32.

Costarelli, I., Kleinhans, R. and Mugnano, S. (2020) '"Active, young, and resourceful": sorting the "good" tenant through mechanisms of conditionality', *Housing Studies*, 35(5): 954–75.

Cox, R.H. (1998) 'The consequences of welfare reform: how conceptions of social rights are changing', *Journal of Social Policy*, 27(1): 1–16.

CPAG (Child Poverty Action Group) (2013) 'Localisation of the social fund: countdown to change', *Briefing*, 14 March, London, CPAG.

CPAG (2016) 'Changes in the Welfare Reform and Work Act 2016', *Welfare Rights Bulletin*, 252, June, London, Child Poverty Action Group, http://www.cpag.org.uk/content/changes-welfare-reform-and-work-act-2016

CPAG (2017) *Broken promises: what has happened to support for low income working families under universal credit?*, London, Child Poverty Action Group.

Crisp, R. and Fletcher, D. (2008) *A comparative review of workfare programmes in the United States, Canada and Australia*, research report 533, Leeds, Corporate Document Services, Department for Work and Pensions.

Cromarty, H. (2019) 'Rough sleepers: access to services and support (England)', *Briefing paper 07698*, 9 October, London, House of Commons Library, https://commonslibrary.parliament.uk/research-briefings/cbp-7698/

Crossley, S. (2015) 'The troubled families programme: the perfect social policy?' *Briefing*, 13 November, London, Centre for Crime and Justice Studies.

Crossley, S. and Lambert, M. (eds) (2017) 'Looking for trouble? Critically examining the UK government's troubled family programme', *Social Policy and Society*, 16(1): 81–165.

Croucher, C., Jones, A. and Wallace, A. (2007) *Good neighbour agreements and the promotion of positive behaviour in communities*, Report to Communities and Local Government and Home Office, York, University of York.

Curchin, K. (2017) 'Using behavioural insights to argue for a stronger safety net: beyond libertarian paternalism', *Journal of Social Policy*, 46(2): 231–49.

Curchin, K. (2019) 'The illiberalism of behavioural conditionality: a critique of Australia's "no jab, no pay" policy', *Journal of Social Policy*, 48(4): 789–806.

Daguerre, A. and Taylor-Gooby, P. (2004) 'Neglecting Europe: explaining the predominance of American ideas in New Labour's welfare policies since 1997', *Journal of European Social Policy*, 14(1): 25–39.

Darnton, A. (2008a) *Practical guide: an overview of behaviour change models and their uses*, London, HM Treasury.

Darnton, A. (2008b) *Reference report: an overview of behaviour change models and their uses*, London, Centre for Sustainable Development, University of Westminster.

Davidson, J. (2012) 'Single parents and the welfare-to-work agenda', *Journal of Poverty and Social Justice*, 20(3): 329–30.

Davis, O. (2019) 'What is the relationship between benefit conditionality and mental health? Evidence from the United States on TANF policies', *Journal of Social Policy*, 48(2): 249–69.

Deacon, A. (1994) 'Justifying workfare: the historical context of the workfare debates', in M. White (ed) *Unemployment and public policy in a changing labour market*, London, PSI, pp 53–63.

Deacon, A. (2000) 'Learning from the USA? The influence of American ideas on New Labour thinking on welfare reform', *Policy and Politics*, 28(1): 5–18.

Deacon, A. (2002) *Perspectives on welfare: ideas, ideologies and policy debates*, Buckingham, Open University Press.

Deacon, A. (2003) '"Levelling the playing field, activating the players": New Labour and the cycle of disadvantage', *Policy and Politics*, 31(2): 123–37.

Deacon, A. (2004) 'Justifying conditionality: the case for anti-social tenants', *Housing Studies*, 19(6): 911–26.

Deacon, A. and Bradshaw, J. (1983) *Reserved for the poor: The means test in British social policy*, Oxford, Blackwell.

DCLG (Department for Local Government and Communities) (2012) *Working with troubled families: a guide to the evidence and good practice*, London, Department for Local Government and Communities

DCLG (2015) 'PM praises troubled families programme success', London, Department for Communities and Local Government.

Dean, H. (1998) 'Undermining social citizenship: the counterproductive effects of behavioural controls in social security administration', paper to the ISSA International Research Conference on Social Security, Jerusalem, 25–28 January.

Dean, H. (2000) 'Managing risk by controlling behaviour: social security administration and the erosion of citizenship', in P. Taylor-Gooby (ed) *Risk, trust and welfare*, Basingstoke, Palgrave Macmillan, pp 51–70.

Dean, H. (2001) 'Welfare rights and the "workfare" state', *Benefits*, 30: 1–4.

Dean, H. (2002) *Welfare rights and social policy*, Harlow, Pearson Education.

Dean, H. (2003) 'Re-conceptualising welfare-to-work for people with multiple problems and needs', *Journal of Social Policy*, 32(3): 441–59.

Dean, H. (2007) 'The ethics of welfare to work', *Policy and Politics*, 34(4): 573–90.

Dean, H. (2010) *Understanding human need*, Bristol, Policy Press.

Dean, H. (2012) 'The ethical deficit of the United kingdom's proposed Universal Credit: pimping the precariat', *The Political Quarterly*, 83(2): 353–9.

Dean, H. (2013) 'The translation of needs into rights: reconceptualising social citizenship as a global phenomenon', *International Journal of Social Welfare*, 22(S1): 32–49.

Dean, H., Bonvin, J., Vielle, P. and Faraque, N. (2005) 'Developing capabilities and rights in welfare-to-work policies', *European Societies*, 7(1): 3–26.

Deeming, C. (2016) 'Rethinking social policy and society', *Social Policy and Society*, 15(2): 159–75.

Deeming, C. (2017) 'The lost and the new "liberal world" of welfare capitalism: a critical assessment of Gøsta Esping-Andersen's *The three worlds of welfare capitalism* a quarter of a century later', *Social Policy and Society*, 16(3): 405–22.

Dermine, E. and Eleveld, A. (2021) 'Protecting working welfare recipients through human rights experimentalism', *International Journal of Law in Context*, 17(4): 529–47.

Djuve, A.B. and Kavli, H.C. (2015) 'Facilitating user involvement in activation programmes: when carers and clerks meet pawns and queens', *Journal of Social Policy*, 44(2): 235–54.

Dobson, R. (2011) 'Conditionality and homelessness services practice realities in a drop-in centre', *Social Policy and Society*, 10(4): 547–57.

Dobson, R. (2015) 'Power, agency, relationality and welfare practice', *Journal of Social Policy*, 44(1): 687–706.

DSS (Department of Social Security) (1998) *New ambitions for our country: A new contract for welfare*, Green paper, Cm 3805, London, DSS.

DSS (Department of Social Services) (2015) *A new system for better employment and social outcomes: final report of the reference group on welfare reform to the Minister for Social Services*, DSS, Canberra, Commonwealth of Australia.

Duncan, S. and Edwards, R. (1997) 'Lone mothers and paid work: rational economic man or gendered moral rationalities?', *Feminist Economics*, 3(2): 29–61.

Duncan, S. and Edwards, R. (1999) *Lone parents, paid work and gendered moral rationalities*, Basingstoke, Palgrave Macmillan.

Duncan Smith, I. (2007) *Breakthrough Britain: ending the costs of social breakdown*, chairman's overview, London, The Centre for Social Justice.

Duncan Smith, I. (2014) *Speech made by Iain Duncan Smith, the Secretary of State for Work and Pensions, at Business for Britain*, 7 April, http://www.ukpol.co.uk/iain-duncan-smith-2014-speech-on-welfare-reform/

Dunn, A. (2014) *Rethinking unemployment and the work ethic: beyond the quasi-Titmuss paradigm*, Basingstoke, Palgrave Macmillan.

DWP (Department for Work and Pensions) (2008a) *No one written off: reforming welfare to reward responsibility*, London, Department for Work and Pensions.

DWP (2008b) *Raising expectations and increasing support: reforming welfare for the future*, London, HMSO.

DWP (2010) *Universal Credit: welfare that works*, Cmd 7957, London, The Stationery Office.

DWP (2012a) *Changes to Jobseeker's Allowance sanctions from 22 October 2012*, London, Department for Work and Pensions, http://webarchive.nationalarchives.gov.uk/20130627060116/http:/www.dwp.gov.uk/adviser/updates/jsa-sanction-changes/ http://data.parliament.uk/writtenevidence/committeeevidence.svc/evidencedocument/work-and-pensions-committee/benefit-sanctions/written/84015.pdf

DWP (2012b) *Impact assessment about Universal Credit introduced under the Welfare Reform Act 2012*, London, Department for Work and Pensions, www.gov.uk/government/uploads/system/uploads/attachment_data/file/220177/universal-credit-wr2011-ia.pdf

DWP (2012c), *Changes to Jobseeker's Allowance sanctions from 22 October 2012*, London, Department for Work and Pensions, http://webarchive.national archives.gov.uk/20130627060116/http:/www.dwp.gov.uk/adviser/upda tes/jsa-sanction-changes/

DWP (2016) *Universal Credit evaluation framework 2016*, London, Department for Work and Pensions.

DWP (2018a) *Guidance: new style Employment and Support Allowance*, London, Department for Work and Pensions, https://www.gov.uk/guidance/new-style-employment-and-support-allowance#history

DWP (2018b) 'Written evidence from the Department of Work and Pensions (ANC0083)' to the WPC, *Benefit sanctions*, 19th report of session 2017–19, HC 955, 549 House of Commons, Work and Pensions Committee, London, The Stationery Office, http://data.parliament.uk/writtenevide nce/committeeevidence.svc/evidencedocument/work-and-pensions-committee/benefit-sanctions/written/84015.pdf

DWP (2018c) *Employer guide to Universal Credit*, London, Department for Work and Pensions, https://www.understandinguniversalcredit.gov.uk/wp-content/uploads/2018/12/Employer-Guide-to-UC.pdf

DWP (2020a) *Guidance: Universal Credit and you*, London, Department for Work and Pensions, https://www.gov.uk/government/publications/univer sal-credit-and-you/draft-uc-and-you

DWP (2020b) *Guidance: Universal Credit for the self-employed*, updated 18 June 2020, London, Department for Work and Pensions, https://www.gov.uk/government/publications/universal-credit-and-self-employment-quick-guide/universal-credit-and-self-employment-quick-guide#the-mini mum-income-floor

DWP (2020c) *Guidance: Universal Credit and your claimant commitment*, updated 1 July 2020, London, Department for Work and Pensions, https://www.gov.uk/government/publications/universal-credit-and-your-claimant-com mitment-quick-guide/universal-credit-and-your-claimant-commitment

DWP (2020d) 'Expanding our service offer in jobcentres', *Touchbase*, 3 July, London, Department for Work and Pensions.

DWP (2022) 'New jobs mission to get 500,000 into work', *Press release*, 27 January, London, Department for Work and Pensions, https://www.gov.uk/government/news/new-jobs-mission-to-get-500-000-into-work

DWP and DoH (Department of Health) (2016) *Work, health and disability: improving lives*, Green paper, London, HMSO.

Dwyer, P. (1998) 'Conditional citizens? Welfare rights and responsibilities in the late 1990's', *Critical Social Policy*, 18(4): 519–43.

Dwyer, P. (2000) *Welfare rights and responsibilities: contesting social citizenship*, Bristol, Policy Press.

Dwyer, P. (2004) 'Creeping conditionality in the UK: from welfare rights to conditional entitlements', *Canadian Journal of Sociology*, 29(2): 265–87.

Dwyer, P. (2005) 'Governance, forced migration and welfare', *Social Policy and Administration*, 39(6): 622–39.

Dwyer, P. (2008) 'The conditional welfare state', in M. Powell (ed) *Modernising the welfare state: the Blair legacy*, Bristol, Policy Press.

Dwyer, P. (2010) *Understanding social citizenship*, Bristol, Policy Press.

Dwyer, P. (2016) 'Citizenship, conduct and conditionality: sanction and support in the 21st century UK welfare state', in M. Fenger, J. Hudson and C. Needham (eds) *Social policy review 28*, Bristol, Policy Press and Social Policy Association, pp 41–62.

Dwyer, P. (2017) 'Rewriting the contract? Conditionality, welfare reform and the rights and responsibilities of disabled people', in D. Horsfall and J. Hudson (eds) *Social policy in an era of competition: from global to local perspectives*, Bristol, Policy Press, pp 135–48.

Dwyer, P. (2018a) 'Final findings: overview', *Research briefing for the Welfare Conditionality: Sanctions, Support and Behaviour Change project*, http://www.welfareconditionality.ac.uk/wp-content/uploads/2018/05/40414_Overview-HR4.pdf

Dwyer, P. (2018b) 'Punitive and ineffective: benefit sanctions within social security', *Journal of Social Security Law*, 25(3): 142–57.

Dwyer, P. (2020) 'Questions of conduct and social justice: the ethics of welfare conditionality within UK social security', in A. Eleveld, T. Kampen and J. Arts (eds) *Welfare to work in contemporary European welfare states: legal, sociological and philosophical perspectives on justice and domination*, Bristol, The Policy Press, pp 198–210.

Dwyer, P. and Bright, J. (2016) 'First wave findings: overview welfare conditionality: sanctions, support and behaviour change', *Research report*, http://www.welfareconditionality.ac.uk/wp-content/uploads/2016/05/WelCond-findings-Overview-May16.pdf

Dwyer, P. and Ellison, N. (2009) '"We nicked stuff from all over the place": policy transfer or muddling through?', *Policy and Politics*, 37(3): 389–407.

Dwyer, P. and Patrick, R. (2021) 'Little and large: methodological reflections from two qualitative longitudinal policy studies on welfare conditionality', *Longitudinal and Life Course Studies*, 12(1): 63–81.

Dwyer, P. and Scullion, L. (2014) 'Conditionality briefing: migrants', *Research briefing for the Welfare Conditionality: Sanctions, Support and Behaviour Change project*, http://www.welfareconditionality.ac.uk/wpcontent/uploads/2014/09/Briefing_Migrants_14.09.10_FINAL.pdf

Dwyer, P. and Webster, D. (2017) 'Benefit sanctions', *Report for Labour Party Social Security Commission*, London, The Labour Party.

Dwyer, P. and Wright, S. (2014) 'Universal Credit, ubiquitous conditionality and its implications for social citizenship', *Journal of Poverty and Social Justice*, 22(1): 27–35.

Dwyer, P., Bowpitt, G., Sundin, E. and Weinstein, M. (2015) 'Rights, responsibilities and refusals: homelessness policy and the exclusion of single homeless people with complex needs', *Critical Social Policy*, 35(1): 3–23.

Dwyer, P., Jones, K., McNeill, J., Scullion, L. and Stewart, A.B.R. (2018) 'Final findings: disabled people', *Research briefing for the Welfare Conditionality: Sanctions, Support and Behaviour Change project*, http://www.welfareconditionality.ac.uk/wp-content/uploads/2018/05/40414-Disabled-people-web.pdf

Dwyer, P., Jones, K., Scullion, L. and Stewart, A.B.R. (2019) 'The impact of conditionality on the welfare rights of EU migrants in the UK', *Policy and Politics*, 47(1): 133–50.

Dwyer, P., Scullion, L., Jones, K., McNeill, J. and Stewart, A.B.R. (2020) 'Work, welfare, and wellbeing: the impacts of welfare conditionality on people with mental health impairments in the UK', *Social Policy and Administration*, 54(2): 311–26.

Edmiston, D. (2016) 'Welfare, austerity and social citizenship in the UK', *Social Policy and Society*, 16(2): 261–70.

Edmiston, D. (2018) *Welfare inequality and social citizenship: deprivation and affluence in austerity Britain*, Bristol, Policy Press.

Edmiston, D., Baumberg Geiger, B., Scullion, L., Ingold, J. and Summers, K. (2020) 'Despite the suspension of conditionality, benefit claimants are already looking for work', *LSE Politics and Policy*, https://blogs.lse.ac.uk/politicsandpolicy/conditionality-covid19/

Eleveld, A. (2017) 'Activation policies: policies of social inclusion or social exclusion?', *Journal of Poverty and Social Justice*, 25(3): 277–85.

Ervik, R., Kildal, N. and Nilssen, E. (2015) 'Contractualism and the emergence of a new welfare regime', in R. Ervik, N. Kildal and E. Nilssen (eds) *New contractualism in European welfare state policies*, London, Ashgate, pp 192–209.

Esping-Andersen, G. (1990) *The three worlds of welfare capitalism*, Cambridge, Polity Press.

Esping-Andersen, G. (2010) 'What does it mean to break with Bismarck?', in B. Palier (ed) *A long good bye to Bismarck? The politics of welfare reform in continental Europe*, Amsterdam, Amsterdam University Press, pp 11–18.

Etherington, D. and Daguerre, A. (2015) *Welfare reform, work first policies and benefit conditionality: reinforcing poverty and social exclusion?*, London, Centre for Enterprise and Economic Development Research Middlesex University in London.

Etzioni, A. (1995) *The spirit of community: rights and responsibilities and the communitarian agenda*, London: HarperCollins.

Etzioni, A. (1997) *The new golden rule*, London, Profile Books.

Family Action (2012) *Universal Credit: marginal returns? Assessing the impact of the Universal Credit on marginal deduction rates*, London, The Family Action Trust, www.family-action.org.uk/uploads/documents/MDRs%20under%20UC.pdf

Farnsworth, K. and Irving, Z. (2017) 'Crisis, austerity, competitiveness and growth: new pathologies of the welfare state', in D. Horsfall and J. Hudson (eds) *Social policy in an era of competition: from global to local perspectives*, Bristol, Policy Press, pp 187–99.

Ferrera, M. (1996) 'The southern model of welfare in social Europe', *Journal of European Social Policy*, 6(1): 17–37.

Finch, D. (2016) *Universal challenge: making a success of Universal Credit*, London, Resolution Foundation.

Finch, J. (1987) 'The vignette technique in survey research', *Sociology*, 21(1): 105–14.

Finn, D. (2011) 'Welfare to work after the recession: from the New Deals to the Work Programme', in C. Holden, M, Kilkey and G. Ramia (eds) *Social policy review 23*, Bristol, Social Policy Association and Policy Press, pp 127–46.

Finn, D. (2013) 'Opening up the "black box": what services are Work Programme providers delivering and how are they doing it', paper at Flexwork Research Conference, Amsterdam, 24–5 October, https://www.researchgate.net/profile/Dan_Finn/publication/281346540_Opening_up_the_'Black_Box'_What_services_are_Work_Programme_providers_delivering_and_how_are_they_doing_it/links/55e317ca08aecb1a7cc98f2c/Opening-up-the-Black-Box-What-services-are-Work-Programme-providers-delivering-and-how-are-they-doing-it.pdf

Finn, D. and Gloster, R. (2010) 'Lone parent obligations: a review of recent evidence on work related requirements within the benefit systems of different countries', *Research Report* 632, London, Department for Work and Pensions.

Finning, K., Ukoumunne O.C., Ford, T., Danielson-Waters, E., Shaw, L., Romero De Jager, I., Stentiford, L. and Moore, D.A. (2019) 'Review: the association between anxiety and poor attendance at school – a systematic review', *Child and Adolescent Mental Health*, 24(3): 205–16.

Fishbein, M. and Ajzen, I. (1975) *Belief attitude, intention and behaviour: an introduction to theory and research*, Reading, MA, Addison-Wesley.

Fitzpatrick, S. and Johnsen, S. (2009) 'The use of enforcement to combat "street culture" in England: an ethical approach?', *Ethics and Social Welfare*, 3(3): 284–302.

Fitzpatrick, S. and Pawson, H. (2014) 'Ending security of tenure for social renters: transitioning to "ambulance service" social housing?', *Housing Studies*, 29(5): 597–615.

Fitzpatrick, S. and Watts, B. (2017) 'Competing visions: security of tenure and the welfarisation of English social housing', *Housing Studies*, 32(8): 1021–38.

Fitzpatrick, S., Watts, B. and Johnsen, S. (2014) 'Conditionality briefing: social housing', *Research briefing for the Welfare Conditionality: Sanctions, Support and Behaviour Change project*, http://www.welfareconditionality.ac.uk/wp-content/uploads/2014/09/Briefing_SocialHousing_14.09.10_FINAL.pdf

Fitzpatrick, S., Bramley, G., Sosenko, F. and Blenkinsopp, J. with Wood, J., Johnsen, S., Littlewood, M. and Watts, B. (2018) *Destitution in the UK 2018*, York, Joseph Rowntree Foundation.

Fitzpatrick, C., McKeever, G. and Simpson, M. (2019) 'Conditionality, discretion and T H Marshall's "right to welfare"', *Journal of Social Welfare and Family Law*, 41(4): 445–62.

Fletcher, D.R. (2014a) 'Workfare – a blast from the past? Contemporary work conditionality for the unemployed in historical perspective', *Social Policy and Society*, 14(3): 329–39.

Fletcher, D.R. (2014b) 'Conditionality briefing: offenders', *Research briefing for the Welfare Conditionality: Sanctions, Support and Behaviour Change project*, http://www.welfareconditionality.ac.uk/wp-content/uploads/2014/09/Briefing_Offenders_14.09.10_FINAL.pdf

Fletcher, D.R. and Flint, J. (2018) 'Welfare conditionality and social marginality: the folly of the tutelary state?', *Critical Social Policy*, 8(4): 771–91.

Fletcher, D.R. and Wright, S. (2018) 'A hand up or a slap down? Criminalising benefit claimants in Britain via strategies of surveillance, sanctions and deterrence', *Critical Social Policy*, 38(2): 323–44.

Fletcher, D.R., Flint, J., Batty, E. and McNeil, J. (2016) 'Gamers or victims of the system? Welfare reform cynical manipulation and vulnerability', *Journal of Poverty and Social Justice*, 24(2): 175–85.

Flint, J. (ed) (2006) *Housing, urban governance and anti-social behaviour: perspectives, policies and practice*, Bristol, Policy Press.

Flint, J. (2009a) 'Subversive subjects and conditional, earned and denied citizenship', in M. Barnes and D. Prior (eds) *Subversive citizens: power, agency and resistance in public services*, Bristol, Policy Press, pp 83–98.

Flint, J. (2009b) 'Governing marginalised populations: the role of coercion support and agency', *European Journal of Homelessness*, 3: 247–59.

Flint, J. (2014) 'Conditionality briefing: anti-social behaviour', *Research briefing for the Welfare Conditionality: Sanctions, Support and Behaviour Change project*, http://www.welfareconditionality.ac.uk/wp-content/uploads/2014/09/Briefing_ASB_14.09.10_FINAL.pdf

Flint, J. (2019) 'Encounters with the centaur state: advanced urban marginality and the practices and ethics of welfare sanctions regimes', *Urban Studies*, 56(1): 249–65.

References

Flint, J. and Hunter, C. (2010) 'Governing by civil order: towards new frameworks of support, coercion and sanction?', in H. Quirk, T. Seddon and G. Smith (eds) *Regulation and criminal justice: innovations in policy and research*, Cambridge, Cambridge University Press, pp 192–210.

Flint, J. and Nixon, J. (2006) 'Governing neighbours: anti-social behaviour orders and new forms of regulating conduct in the UK', *Urban Studies*, 43(5/6): 939–55.

Flint, J. and Pawson, H. (2009) 'Social landlords and the regulation of conduct in urban spaces in the United Kingdom', *Criminology and Criminal Justice*, 9(4): 415–35.

Flint, J., Batty, E., Parr, S., Platts-Fowler, D., Nixon, J. and Sanderson, D. (2011) *Evaluation of intensive intervention projects*, London, Department for Education.

Fording, R.C., Schram, S.F. and Soss, J. (2013) 'Do welfare sanctions help or hurt the poor? Estimating the causal effect of sanctioning on client earnings', *Social Service Review*, 87(4): 641–76.

Freedland, M. and King, D. (2003) 'Contractual governance and illiberal contracts: some problems of contractualism as an instrument of behavior management by agencies of government', *Cambridge Journal of Economics*, 27(3): 465–77.

Freidli, L. and Stearn, R. (2015) 'Positive action as coercive strategy: conditionality activation and the role of psychology in UK government workfare programmes', *Medical Humanities*, 41(1): 40–7.

Freud, D. (2007) *Reducing dependency, increasing opportunity: options for the future of welfare to work. An independent report to the Department for Work and Pensions*, London, Department for Work and Pensions.

Gandy, K., King, K., Streeter Hurle, P., Bustin, C. and Glazebrook, K. (2016) *Poverty and decision-making: how behavioural science can improve opportunity in the UK*, York, The Behavioural Insights Team and the Joseph Rowntree Foundation.

Garthwaite, K. (2014) 'Fear of the brown envelope: exploring welfare reform with long-term sickness benefit recipients', *Social Policy and Administration*, 48(7): 782–98.

Giddens, A. (1994) *Beyond left and right: the future of radical politics*, Cambridge, Polity Press.

Giddens, A. (1998) *The third way: the renewal of social democracy*, Cambridge, Polity Press.

Goodin, R.E. (1986) 'Welfare, rights and discretion', *Oxford Journal of Legal Studies*, 6(2): 232–61.

Goodin, R.E. (2000) 'Principles of welfare reform: the OECD experience', paper presented to the Conference of Welfare Reform, Melbourne, Melbourne Institute, November.

Goroff, N.N. (1974) 'Social welfare as coercive social control', *Journal of Sociology and Social Welfare*, 2(1): Article 3, https://scholarworks.wmich.edu/jssw/vol2/iss1/3

gov.uk (2021) *School attendance and absence*, https://www.gov.uk/school-attendance-absence/legal-action-to-enforce-school-attendance

Gregg, D. (2010) *Family intervention projects: a classic case of policy-based evidence*, London, Centre for Crime and Justice Studies, https://www.crimeandjustice.org.uk/sites/crimeandjustice.org.uk/files/family%20intervention.pdf

Gregg, P. (2008) *Realising potential: a vision for personalised conditionality and support. An independent report to the Department for Work and Pensions*, London, Department for Work and Pensions.

Griggs, J. and Bennett, F. (2009) 'Rights and responsibilities in the social security system', *Social Security Advisory Committee occasional paper no. 6*, London, SSAC.

Griggs, J. and Evans, M. (2010) *Sanctions within conditional benefit systems: a review of evidence*, York, Joseph Rowntree Foundation.

Grover, C. and Piggott, L. (2013) 'A commentary on resistance to the UK's Work Experience programme: capitalism, exploitation and wage work', *Critical Social Policy*, 33(3): 554–63.

Grover, C. and Piggott, L. (eds) (2015) *Disabled people work and welfare: is employment really the answer?*, Bristol, Policy Press.

Grymonprez, H., Hermans, K. and Roose, R. (2020) 'The discursive construction of accessibility and its implications for outreach work', *Journal of Social Policy*, 49(3): 1–18.

Hale, C. (2014) *Fulfilling potential? ESA and the fate of the Work Related Activity Group*, London, Mind, The Centre for Welfare Reform.

Hall, P. (1993) 'Policy paradigms, social learning and the state: the case of economic policy making in Britain', *Comparative Politics*, 25(3): 275–96.

Hallsworth, M. and Sanders, M. (2016) 'Nudge recent developments in behavioural science', in F. Spotswood (ed) *Beyond behaviour change: key issues, interdisciplinary approaches and future directions*, Bristol, Policy Press, pp 113–34.

Halpern, D., Bates, C., Beales, G. and Heathfield, A. (2004) *Personal responsibility and changing behaviour: the state of knowledge and its implications for public policy*, London, Cabinet Office.

Handler, J. (2004) *Social citizenship and workfare in the United States and Western Europe: the paradox of inclusion*, Cambridge, Cambridge University Press.

Handler, J.F. (2009) 'Welfare, workfare, and citizenship in the developed world', *Annual Review of Law and Social Science*, 5(1): 71–90.

Harker, R. (2022) 'Constituency data Universal Credit rollout', *Data dashboard*, 13 April, London, House of Commons Library, https://commonslibrary.parliament.uk/constituency-data-universal-credit-roll-out/#:~:text=The%20Government%20first%20launched%20UC,to%20UC%20by%20September%202024

References

Harris, J. (2020) 'The return of benefit sanctions won't help the Covid-19 jobs crisis', *The Guardian*, 12 July, https://www.theguardian.com/commentisfree/2020/jul/12/poor-people-work-british-jobcentres-labour-benefits?CMP=Share_AndroidApp_Tweet

Harris, N. (2008) 'From unemployment to active jobseeking: changes and continuities in social security law in the United Kingdom', in S. Stendahl, T. Erhag and S Devetzi (eds) *A European work-first welfare state*, Gothenburg, Centre for European Research, pp 49–77.

Harrison, M. and Davis, C. (2001) *Housing, social policy and difference: disability, ethnicity, gender and housing*, Bristol, Policy Press.

Harrison, M. and Saunders, T. (eds) (2016) *Social policies and social control*, Bristol, Policy Press.

Haskins, R. and Weidinger, M. (2019) 'The Temporary Assistance for Needy Families program: time for improvements', *Annals of the American Academy of Political and Social Science*, 686(1): 286–309.

Haux, T. (2011) 'Activating lone parents: an evidence-based policy appraisal of welfare-to-work reform in Britain', *Social Policy and Society*, 11(1): 1–14.

Heron, E. and Dwyer, P. (1999) '"Doing the right thing": Labour's attempt to forge a new welfare deal between the individual and the state', *Social Policy and Administration*, 33(1): 91–104.

Hirsch, D and Millar, J. (2004) 'Labour's welfare reform: progress to date', *Foundations*, York, Joseph Rowntree Foundation.

HMG (Her Majesty's Government) (2012) *Social justice: transforming lives*, Cm 8314 Her Majesty's Government, Norwich, The Stationery Office.

Hobson, F. (2021) 'Coronavirus: withdrawing crisis social security measures', *Commons Library research briefing*, 26 October, London, House of Commons Library.

Hoggett, J. and Frost, E. (2018) 'The troubled families programme and the problem of success', *Social Policy and Society*, 17(4): 523–35.

Hoggett, P., Wilkinson, H. and Beedell, P. (2013) 'Fairness and the politics of resentment', *Journal of Social Policy*, 42(3): 567–85.

Holland, J., Thomson, R. and Henderson, S. (2006) *Qualitative longitudinal research: a discussion paper*, London, Families and Social Capital Research Group, London South Bank University.

Hudson, M., Barnes, H., Ray, K. and Phillips, J. (2006) 'Ethnic minority perceptions and experiences of Jobcentre Plus', *Research report no 349*, London, Department for Work and Pensions.

Hudson-Sharp, N., Munro-Lott, N., Rolfe, H. and Runge, J. (2018) 'The impact of welfare reform and welfare-to-work programmes: an evidence review', *Research report 111*, Manchester, Equality and Human Rights Commission.

Humpage, L. (2014) *Policy change, public attitudes and social citizenship*, Bristol, Policy Press.

Humpage, L. (2016) 'Income management in New Zealand and Australia: differently framed but similarly problematic for indigenous peoples', *Critical Social Policy*, 36(4): 551–71.

Hunter, C. (2006) 'The changing legal framework: from landlords to agents of social control', in J. Flint (ed) *Housing, urban governance and anti-social behaviour: perspectives, policies and practice*, Bristol, Policy Press, pp 137–54.

Ingold, J. (2020) 'Employers' perspectives on benefit conditionality in the UK and Denmark', *Social Policy and Administration*, 54(2): 236–49.

In-Work Progression Commission (2021) *Supporting progression out of low pay: a call to action*, London, Department for Work and Pensions.

John, P. and Stoker, G. (2019) 'Rethinking the role of experts and expertise in behavioural public policy', *Policy and Politics*, 47(2): 209–25.

Johnsen, S. (2014) *Conditionality briefing: lone parents*, http://www.welfarecon ditionality.ac.uk/wp-content/uploads/2014/09/Briefing_LoneParents_ 14.09.10_FINAL.pdf

Johnsen, S. and Fitzpatrick, S. (2007) *The impact of enforcement on street users in England*, Bristol, Policy Press.

Johnsen, S. and Blenkinsopp, J. (2018) 'Final findings: lone parents', *Research briefing for the Welfare Conditionality project*, http://www.welfareconditional ity.ac.uk/wp-content/uploads/2018/05/39273-Lone-parents-web.pdf

Johnsen, S. and Fitzpatrick, S. (2010) 'Revanchist sanitisation or coercive care? The use of enforcement to combat begging, street drinking and rough sleeping in England', *Urban Studies*, 47(8): 1703–23.

Johnsen, S., Fitzpatrick, S. and Watts, B. (2014) *Conditionality briefing: homelessness and 'street culture'*, http://www.welfareconditionality. ac.uk/wp-content/uploads/2014/09/Briefing_Homelessness_14.09.10_ FINAL.pdf

Johnsen, S., Fitzpatrick, S. and Watts, B. (2018a) 'Homelessness and social control: a typology', *Housing Studies*, 33(7): 1106–26.

Johnsen, S., Watts, B. and Fitzpatrick, S. (2018b) 'Final findings: homelessness', *Research briefing for the Welfare Conditionality project*, http://www.welfar econditionality.ac.uk/wp-content/uploads/2018/05/39273-Homelessn ess-web.pdf

Johnson-Schlee, S. (2019) 'Playing cards against the state: precarious lives, conspiracy theories, and the production of "irrational" subjects', *Geoform*, 101: 174–81.

Jones, K. (2018) '"I've always been a grafter": older benefit recipients and welfare conditionality', *Journal of Social Security Law*, 25(3): 173–86.

Jones, K. (2019) 'No strings attached? An exploration of employment support services offered by third sector homelessness organisations', in P. Dwyer (ed) *Dealing with welfare conditionality: implementation and effects*, Bristol, Policy Press, pp 91–118.

Jones, K., Berry, C., Rouse, J. and Whittle, R. (2019) 'Universal Credit and in work conditionality: a productive turn?', *Small projects report*, Productivity Insights Network, Manchester, Manchester Metropolitan University.

Jordan, J.D. (2014) 'The rage of well-fed lions: the economic foundation of UK welfare claimant demonisation in the neo-liberal era', *French Journal of British Studies*, 19(1): 215–50.

Jordan, J.D. (2018) 'Welfare grunters and workfare monsters? An empirical review of the operation of two UK "Work Programme" centres', *Journal of Social Policy*, 47(3): 583–601.

Kaufman, J. (2020) 'Frontline managers' perceptions and justifications of behavioural conditionality', *Social Policy and Administration*, 54(2): 219–35.

Kellner, P. (2012) 'A quiet revolution', *Prospect*, March, pp 30–4.

Kelly, M.P. (2016) 'The politics of behaviour change', in F. Spotswood (ed) *Beyond behaviour change: key issues, interdisciplinary approaches and future directions*, Bristol, Policy Press, pp 11–26.

Kennedy, S., McInnes. R., Bellis, A., O'Donnell, M. and Steele, S. (2019) 'Devolution of welfare', *Debate pack number CDP-0084*, 8 April, London, House of Commons Library.

Knijn, T., Martin, C. and Millar, J. (2007) 'Activation as a common framework for social policies towards lone parents', *Social Policy and Administration*, 41(6): 638–52.

Knodel, J. (1993) 'The design and analysis of focus groups: a practical guide', in D.L. Morgan (ed) *Successful focus groups, advancing the state of the art*, London, SAGE, pp 35–50.

Knotz, C.M. (2018) 'A rising workfare state? Unemployment benefit conditionality in 21 OECD countries, 1980–2012', *Journal of International and Comparative Social Policy*, 34(2): 91–108.

Labour Party (1994) *Jobs and social justice*, London, The Labour Party.

Labour Party (2019) 'Clear evidence that sanctions do not help people into sustained employment', statement by Margaret Greenwood MP, Labour's Shadow Work and Pensions Secretary, press release, 9 May, https://labour.org.uk/press/clear-evidence-sanctions-not-help-people-sustained-employment-margaret-greenwood/

Lalive, R., Zweimuller, J. and Van Ours, J.C. (2005) 'The effect of benefit sanctions on the duration of unemployment', *Journal of the European Economic Association*, 3(6): 1386–417.

Langdon, A., Crossfield, J., Tu, T., White, Y. and Joyce, L. (2018) 'Universal Credit: in-work progression randomised controlled trial findings from quantitative survey and qualitative research', *DWP research report 966*, London, Department for Work and Pensions.

Larkin, P.M. (2007) 'The "criminalization" of social security law: towards a punitive welfare state?', *Journal of Law and Society*, 34(3): 295–320.

Leeuw, F.L. (1998) 'The carrot: subsidies as a tool of government-theory and practice', in M. Bemelmans-Videc, R.C. Rist and E. Vedung (eds) *Carrots, sticks and sermons: policy instruments and their evaluation*, Abingdon, Routledge, pp 77–102.

Leggett, W. (2014) 'The politics of behaviour change: nudge, neo-liberalism and the state', *Policy & Politics*, 42(1): 3–19.

Legislation.gov.uk (2020) *Antisocial Behaviour etc. (Scotland) Act 2004*, https://www.legislation.gov.uk/asp/2004/8/contents

Le Grand, J. (1997) 'Knights, knaves or pawns? Human behaviour and social policy', *Journal of Social Policy*, 26(2): 149–69.

Le Grand, J. (2003) *Motivation, agency, and public policy: of knights and knaves, pawns and queens*, Oxford, Oxford University Press.

Levitas, R. (2012) 'The just's umbrella: austerity and the big society in coalition policy and beyond', *Critical Social Policy*, 32(3): 320–42.

Levy, J.J. (2004) 'Activation through thick and thin: progressive approaches to labour market activation', in N. Ellison, J. Bauld and M. Powell (eds) *Social policy review 16*, Bristol, SPA and Policy Press, pp 187–208.

Lewis, J. (2003) 'Design issues', in J. Ritchie and J. Lewis (eds) *Qualitative research practice*, London, SAGE, pp 47–76.

Lewis, J. (2007) 'Analysing qualitative longitudinal research in evaluations', *Social Policy and Society*, 6(4): 545–6.

Liberal Democrats (2019) 'A fairer share for all', *Policy paper 136*, London, Liberal Democrats.

Linder, S.H. and Peters, B.G. (1989) 'Instruments of government: perceptions and contexts', *Journal of Public Policy*, 9(1): 35–58.

Lindsay, C. and Houston, D. (eds) (2013) *Disability benefits, welfare reform and employment policy*, Basingstoke, Palgrave Macmillan.

Lipsky, M. (2010 [1980]) *Street-level bureaucracy: dilemmas of the individual in public service, 30th anniversary edition*, New York, Russell Sage Foundation.

Lister, R. (2003) *Citizenship feminist perspectives*, Basingstoke, Macmillan.

Lister, R. (2004) *Poverty*, Cambridge, Polity Press.

Lister, R. (2011) 'The age of responsibility: social policy and citizenship in the 21st century', in C. Holden, M, Kilkey and G. Ramia (eds) *Social policy review 23*, Bristol, Social Policy Association and Policy Press, pp 63–84.

Lister, R. and Dwyer, P. (2012) 'Citizenship and access to welfare', in P. Alcock, M. May and S. Wright (eds) *The student's companion to social policy*, 4th edition, Oxford, Wiley-Blackwell and SPA, 255–62.

Lødemel, I. (2001) 'Discussion: workfare in the welfare state', in I. Lødemel and H. Trickey (eds) *An offer you can't refuse: workfare in international perspective*, Bristol, Policy Press, 295–344.

Lødemel, I. and Trickey, H. (eds) (2001) *An offer you can't refuse: workfare in international perspective,* Bristol, Policy Press.

Loft, P. (2020) 'The troubled families programme (England)', *Briefing paper number 07585*, 27 November, London, House of Commons Library.

Loopstra, R., Reeves, A., Mckee, M. and Stuckler, D. (2015) 'Do punitive approaches to unemployment benefit recipients increase welfare exit and employment? A cross-sectional analysis of UK sanction reforms', *Sociology working paper number 2015–1*, Department of Sociology, University of Oxford.

Lowe, S. and Meers, J. (2015) 'Responsibilisation of everyday life: housing and welfare state change', in Z. Irving, M. Fenger and J. Hudson (eds) *Social policy review 27*, Bristol, Policy Press and Social Policy Association, pp 55–72.

Lund, F. (2011) 'A step in the wrong direction: linking the South Africa Child Support Grant to school attendance', *Journal of Poverty and Social Justice*, 19(1): 5–14.

Lunt, N. and Horsfall, D. (2013) 'New Zealand's reform of sickness benefit and invalid's benefit', in C. Lindsay and D. Houston (eds) *Disability benefits, welfare reform and employment policy*, Basingstoke, Palgrave Macmillan, pp 216–32.

Maas, W. (ed) (2013) *Multilevel citizenship*, Philadelphia, Penn Press.

MacGregor, S. (1999) 'Welfare, neo-liberalism and new paternalism: three ways for social policy in late capitalist societies', *Capital and Class*, 67: 91–118.

Macnicol, J. (2017) 'Reconstructing the underclass', *Social Policy and Society*, 16(1): 99–108.

Mann, K. (1992) *The making of an English 'underclass'*, Buckingham, Open University Press.

Manning, N. (2016) 'Social needs, social problems, social welfare and well-being', in P. Alcock, T. Haux, M. May and S. Wright (eds) *The student's companion to social policy*, 5th edition, Oxford, Blackwell-Wiley, pp 21–6.

Marshall, T.H. (1949/92) 'Citizenship and social class', in T.H. Marshall and T. Bottomore, *Citizenship and social class*, London, Pluto Press, pp 3–51.

Maryon-Davis, A. (2016) 'Government legislation and the restrictions of personal freedoms', in F. Spotswood (ed) *Beyond behaviour change: key issues, interdisciplinary approaches and future directions*, Bristol, Policy Press, pp 71–87.

Mason, J. (2017) *Qualitative researching*, 3rd edition, London, SAGE.

Mason, R. (2014) 'Government's universal jobmatch website "bedevilled with fraud"', *The Guardian*, 5 March, https://www.theguardian.com/society/2014/mar/05/government-universal-jobmatch-website-fraud

McCollum, D. (2012) '"Back on the brew [benefits] again": why so many transitions from welfare to work are not sustained', *Journal of Poverty and Social Justice*, 20(2): 207–18.

McDonald, C. and Marston, G. (2005) 'Workfare as welfare: governing unemployment in the advanced liberal state', *Critical Social Policy*, 25(3): 374–401.

McKeever, G. and Walsh, T. (2020) 'The moral hazard of conditionality: restoring the integrity of social security law', *Australian Journal of Social Issues*, 55(1): 73–87.

McLaren, J., Maury, S. and Squire, S. (2018) *'Outside systems control my life': the experience of single mothers on welfare to work*, Abbotsford, The Good Shepherd Australia/New Zealand.

McNeill, F. (2020) 'Penal and welfare conditionality: discipline or degradation?', *Social Policy and Administration*, 54(2): 295–310.

McNeill, J. (2016) 'Regulating social housing: expectations for behaviour of tenants', in M. Harrison and T. Saunders (eds) *Social policies and social control: new perspectives on the 'not so big society'*, Bristol, Policy Press, pp 181–95.

McNeill, J. and Bowpitt, G. (2021) 'Paths to resettlement: understanding the interplay of work and other factors in journeys out of homelessness', *Journal of Social Policy*, 50(4): 745–63.

Mead, L.M. (1982) 'Social programs and social obligations', *The Public Interest*, 69: 17–32.

Mead, L.M. (1986) *Beyond entitlement*, New York, Free Press.

Mead, L.M. (1992) *The new politics of poverty*, New York, Basic Books.

Mead, L.M. (1997) 'Citizenship and social policy: T.H. Marshall and poverty', *Social Philosophy and Social Policy*, 14(2): 197–230.

Meershoek, A. (2012) 'Controlling access to sick leave programmes: practices of physicians in the Netherlands', *Social Policy and Administration*, 46(5): 544–61.

Mehta, J., Taggart, D., Clifford, E. and Speed, E. (2021) '"They say jump, we say how high?" Conditionality, sanctioning and incentivising disabled people into the UK labour market', *Disability and Society*, 36(5): 681–701.

MHCLG (Ministry of Housing, Communities and Local Government) (2019) *National evaluation of the Troubled Families programme 2015–2020: findings*, March, London, Ministry of Housing, Communities and Local Government.

MHCLG (2020) *Financial framework for the Troubled Families programme*, April, London, Ministry of Housing, Communities and Local Government.

Millar, J. (2007) 'The dynamics of poverty and employment: the contribution of qualitative longitudinal research to understanding transitions, adaptations and trajectories', *Social Policy and Society*, 6(4): 533–44.

Millar, J. (2019) 'Self-responsibility and activation for lone mothers in the United Kingdom', *American Behavioural Scientist*, 63(1): 83–99.

Millar, J. and Bennett, F. (2016) 'Universal Credit: assumptions, contradictions and virtual reality', *Social Policy and Society*, 16(2): 169–82.

References

Milne, A. (2007) 'Looking for anti-social behaviour', *Policy and Politics*, 35(7): 611–27.

Mizen, P. (1990) *Young people's experiences of the Youth Training Scheme: a case study of recent state intervention in the youth labour market*, PhD thesis, Department of Sociology, University of Warwick, http://wrap.warwick.ac.uk/35614/1/WRAP_THESIS_Mizen_1990.pdf

MOJ (Ministry of Justice) (2010) *Breaking the cycle: effective punishment, rehabilitation and sentencing of offenders*, Cm 7972, London, The Stationery Office.

MOJ (2013) *Transforming rehabilitation: a strategy for reform*, London, The Stationery Office.

Molander, A. (2016) *Discretion in the welfare state: social rights and professional judgement*, Abingdon, Routledge.

Monnat, S.M. (2010) 'The color of welfare sanctioning: exploring the individual and contextual roles of race on TANF case closures and benefit reduction', *The Sociological Quarterly*, 51: 678–707.

Moran, M. (2017) *The 2015 ESA trials: a synthesis*, London, Department for Work and Pensions.

Morgan, J. (2010) 'Family intervention tenancies: the de(marginalisation) of social tenants?', *Journal of Social Welfare and Family Law*, 32(1): 37–46.

Morris, L. (2019) 'Reconfiguring rights in austerity Britain: boundaries, behaviours and contestable margins', *Journal of Social Policy*, 48(2): 271–91.

Morris, L. (2020) 'Activating the welfare subject: the problem of agency', *Sociology*, 54(2): 275–91.

Moth, R. and Lavallette, M. (2017) 'Social protection and labour market policies for vulnerable groups from a social investment perspective: the case of welfare recipients with mental health needs in England', *RE-InVEST working paper series D5.1*, Liverpool, Liverpool Hope University; Leuven, HIVA-KU Leuven.

Mulgan, G. (2010) *Influencing behaviour to improve health and wellbeing, an independent report*, Department of Health, London, The Stationery Office.

Murphy, M. (2017) 'Irish flex-insecurity: the post-crisis reality for vulnerable workers in Ireland', *Social Policy and Administration*, 51(2): 308–27.

Murphy, M. (2020) 'Dual conditionality in welfare and housing for lone parents in Ireland: change and continuity?', *Social Policy and Administration*, 54(2): 185–236.

Murray, C. (1984) *Losing ground*, New York, Basic Books.

Murray, C. (1994) *Loosing ground* (tenth anniversary edtion), New York, Basic Books.

Murray, C. (1999) *The underclass revisited*, Washington, DC, American Institute for Public Policy Research.

NAO (National Audit Office) (2013) *Programmes to help families facing multiple challenges*, Report by the Comptroller and Auditor General, London, National Audit Office.

NAO (2016) *Benefit sanctions*, Report by the Comptroller and Auditor General, London, National Audit Office.

NAO (2018) *Rolling out Universal Credit*, Report by the Comptroller and Auditor General, London, National Audit Office.

Neale, B. (2021) *The Craft of Qualitative Longitudinal Research*, London, SAGE.

Nethercote, M. (2017) 'Neo-liberal welfare, minorities and tenancy support', *Social Policy and Society*, 16(1): 15–32.

Newton, B., Meager, N., Bertram, C., Corden, A., George, A., Lalani, M., Metcalf, H., Rolfe, H., Sainsbury, R. and Weston, K. (2013) 'Work Programme evaluation: findings from the first phase of qualitative research on programme delivery', *Research report no 821*, London, Department for Work and Pensions.

Novak, T. (1997) 'Hounding delinquents: the introduction of the jobseeker's allowance', *Critical Social Policy*, 17(1): 99–111.

Nozick, R. (1974) *Anarchy, state and utopia*, New York, Basic Books.

Nunn, A. and Tepe-Belfrage, D. (2017) 'Disciplinary social policy and the failing promise of the new middle classes: the Troubled Families programme', *Social Policy and Society*, 16(1): 119–30.

Oakley, M. (2014) *Independent review of the operation of Jobseeker's Allowance sanctions validated by the Jobseekers Act 2013*, London, Department for Work and Pensions.

Oakley, M. (2016) *Closing the gap: creating a framework for tackling the disability employment gap in the UK*, London, The Social Market Foundation.

O'Brien, C. (2013) 'From safety nets and carrots to trampolines and sticks: national use of the EU as both menace and model to help neo-liberalize welfare policy', in D. Schiek (ed) *The EU economic and social model in the global crisis*, Farnham, Ashgate.

OECD (2015) 'Activation policies for more inclusive labour markets', in *OECD employment outlook 2015*, Paris, OECD Publishing, pp 105–66.

Offe, C. (1982) 'Some contradictions of the modern welfare state', *Critical Social Policy*, 2(2): 7–16.

PAC (Public Accounts Committee) (2016) *Troubled families: progress review, thirty-third report of session 2016–17*, HC 711 Public Accounts Committee, London, House of Commons.

PAC (2017) *Benefit sanctions: forty-second report of session 2016–17*, Committee of Public Accounts, 8 February, London, House of Commons.

Palier, B. (ed) (2010) *A long good bye to Bismarck? The politics of welfare reform in continental Europe*, Amsterdam, Amsterdam University Press.

Papadopoulos, T. and Velázquez Leyer R. (eds) (2016a) 'Themed section on assessing the effects of conditional cash transfers in Latin American societies in the early twenty-first century', *Social Policy and Society*, 15(3): 417–512.

Papadopoulos, T. and Velázquez Leyer, R. (2016b) 'Two decades of social investment in Latin America: outcomes, shortcomings and achievements of conditional cash transfers', *Social Policy and Society*, 15(3): 435–49.

Parr, S. (2017) 'Explaining and understanding state intervention into the lives of "troubled" families', *Social Policy and Society*, 16(4): 577–92.

Patrick, R. (2011) 'Disabling or enabling: the extension of work-related conditionality to disabled people', *Social Policy and Society*, 20(3): 309–20.

Patrick, R. (2017) *For whose benefit? The everyday realities of welfare reform*, Bristol, Policy Press.

Patrick, R. and Fenney, D. (2015) 'Disabled people, conditionality and a civic minimum in Britain: reflections from qualitative research', in C. Grover and L. Piggott (eds) *Disabled people, work and welfare*, Bristol, Policy Press, pp 25– 42.

Paz-Fuchs, A. (2008) *Welfare to work: conditional rights in social policy*, Oxford, Oxford University Press.

Peck, J. and Theodore, N. (2000) 'Work first: workfare and the regulation of contingent labour markets', *Cambridge Journal of Economics*, 24(1): 119–38.

Peeters, R. (2013) 'Responsibilisation on government's term: new welfare and the governance of responsibility and solidarity', *Social Policy and Society*, 12(4): 583–95.

Pemberton, S., Fahmy, E., Sutton, E. and Bell, K. (2016) 'Navigating the stigmatised identities of poverty in austere times: resisting and responding to narratives of personal failure', *Critical Social Policy*, 36(1): 2–37.

Pennycook, M. and Whittaker, M. (2012) *Conditions uncertain: assessing the implications of Universal Credit in-work conditionality*, London, Resolution Foundation.

Phoenix, J. (2008) 'ASBOs and working women: a new revolving door?', in P. Squires (ed) *ASBO nation: the criminalisation of nuisance*, Bristol, Policy Press, pp 297–311.

Pierson, C. and Humpage, L. (2016) 'Coming together or drifting apart? Income maintenance in Australia, New Zealand, and the United Kingdom', *Politics and Policy*, 44(2): 261–93.

Pierson, P. (ed) (2001) *The new politics of the welfare state*, Oxford, Oxford University Press.

Plant, R. (1998) 'So you want to be a citizen?', *New Statesman*, 6 February, pp 30–2.

Pollard, T. (2018) *Pathways from poverty: a case for institutional reform*, London, Demos.

Portes, J. (2015) 'A troubling attitude to statistics', *Blog for National Institute for Economic and Social Research*, https://www.niesr.ac.uk/blog/troubling-attitude-statistics#.VzGrnMoUXcu

Portes, J. and Reed, H. (2018) 'The cumulative impact of tax and welfare reforms', *Research report 112*, Manchester, Equalities and Human Rights Commission.

Povey, L. (2017) 'Where welfare and criminal justice meet: applying Wacquant to the experiences of marginalised women in austerity Britain', *Social Policy and Society*, 16(2): 271–81.

Povey, L. (2019) 'Punishment, powerlessness and bounded agency: exploring the role of welfare conditionality with "at risk" women attempting to live "a good life"', in P. Dwyer (ed) *Dealing with welfare conditionality: implementation and effects*, Bristol, Policy Press, pp 41–68.

Powell, A. (2020) 'Work and health programme', *Briefing paper number 7845*, London, House of Commons Library.

Powell, M. (ed) (1999) *New Labour new welfare state? The third way in British social policy*, Bristol, Policy Press.

Pybus, K., Pickett, K.E., Prady, S.L., Lloyd, C. and Wilkinson, R. (2019) 'Discrediting experiences: outcomes of eligibility assessments for claimants with psychiatric compared with non-psychiatric conditions transferring to personal independence payments in England', *BJPsych Open*, 5(2): e19, https://doi.org/10.1192/bjo.2019.3.

Raffass, T. (2017) 'Demanding activation', *Journal of Social Policy*, 46(2): 349–65.

Rahim, N., Graham, J., Kiss, Z. and Davis, M. (2017) 'Understanding how Universal Credit influences employment behaviour, findings from qualitative and experimental research with claimants', *DWP research report 943*, London, Department for Work and Pensions.

Ratzmann, N. (2021) 'Deserving of social support? Street-level bureaucrats' decisions on EU migrants' benefit claims in Germany', *Social Policy and Society*, 20(3): 509–20.

Redman, J. (2020) 'The benefit sanction: a correctional device or a weapon of disgust?', *Sociological Research Online*, 25(1): 84–100.

Rees, A.M. (1995) 'The other T. H. Marshall', *Journal of Social Policy*, 24(3): 341–62.

Reeve, K. (2017) 'Welfare conditionality, benefit sanctions and homelessness in the UK: ending the "something for nothing culture" or punishing the poor?', *Journal of Poverty and Social Justice*, 25(1): 65–78.

Reeves, A. (2017) 'Does sanctioning disabled claimants of unemployment insurance increase labour market inactivity? An analysis of 346 British local authorities between 2009 and 2014', *Journal of Poverty and Social Justice*, 25(2): 129–46.

Reeves, A. and Loopstra, R. (2017) '"Set up to fail?": how welfare conditionality undermines citizenship for vulnerable groups', *Social Policy and Society*, 16(2): 327–88.

References

Ritchie, J., Lewis, J., McNaughton Nicholls, C. and Ormston, R. (eds) (2014) *Qualitative research practice: a guide for social science students and researchers*, 2nd edition, London, SAGE.

Rodger, J.J. (2006) 'Antisocial families and the withholding of welfare support', *Critical Social Policy*, 26(1): 121–43.

Rodger, J. (2008a) *Criminalising social policy: anti-social behaviour and welfare in a de-civilised society*, Cullompton, Willan Publishing.

Rodger, J.J. (2008b) 'The criminalisation of social policy', *Criminal Justice Matters*, 74(1): 18–19.

Roulestone, A. (2015) 'Personal Independence Payments, welfare reform and the shrinking disability category', *Disability and Society*, 30(5): 673–88.

Royston, S. (2012) 'Understanding Universal Credit', *Journal of Poverty and Social Justice*, 20(1): 69–86.

RTF (Respect Task Force) (2006) *Respect action plan*, Respect Task Force, London, Home Office.

Rudd, A. (2019) *The future of the labour market speech*, London, Department for Work and Pensions, https://www.gov.uk/government/speeches/the-future-of-the-labour-market

Saldana, J. (2003) *Longitudinal qualitative research analysing change through time*, Walnut Creek, AltaMira Press.

Salford City Partnership (2015) *DWP benefit conditionality and sanctions in Salford: one year on*, Salford, Salford City Partnership.

Sanders, M., Briscese, G., Gallagher, R., Gyani, A., Hanes, S., Kirkman, E. and Service, O. (2021) 'Behavioural insight and the labour market: evidence from a pilot study and a large stepped-wedge controlled trial', *Journal of Public Policy*, 41(1): 42–65.

Sayer, A. (2017) 'Responding to the Troubled Families Programme', *Social Policy and Society*, 16(1): 155–64.

Schoenberg, N.E. and Ravdal, H. (2000) 'Using vignettes in awareness and attitudinal research', *International Journal of Social Research Methodology*, 3(1): 63–74.

Scottish Government (2021) 'Minimum Income Guarantee Steering Group: background on minimum income guarantee and basic incomes', *Meeting paper*, August 2021, https://www.gov.scot/publications/minimum-income-guarantee-steering-group-background-on-minimum-income-guarantee-and-basic-incomes/

Scullion, L. (2018) 'Sanctuary to sanction: asylum seekers, refugees and welfare conditionality in the UK', *Journal of Social Security Law*, 25(3): 155–69.

Scullion, L. and Curchin, K. (2022) 'Examining veterans' interactions with the UK social security system through a trauma-informed lens', *Journal of Social Policy*, 51(1): 96–113.

Selbourne, D. (1994) *The principle of duty*, London, Sinclair Stevenson.

Serpa, R. (2019) 'Resisting welfare conditionality: constraint, choice and dissent among homeless migrants', in P. Dwyer (ed) *Dealing with welfare conditionality: implementation and effects*, Bristol, Policy Press, pp 69–90.

Shakespeare, T., Watson, N. and Alghaib, O.A. (2017) 'Blaming the victim, all over again: Waddell and Aylward's biopsychosocial (BPS) model of disability', *Critical Social Policy*, 37(1): 22–41.

Shelter Legal (2020) *What is an AST*, London, Shelter, https://england.shelter.org.uk/legal/security_of_tenure/assured_shorthold_tenancies/what_is_an_assured_shorthold_tenancy

Shildrick, T., MacDonald, R., Furlong, A., Roden, J. and Crow, R. (2012) *Are 'cultures of worklessness' passed down the generations?*, York, The Joseph Rowntree Foundation.

Shutes, I. (2011) 'Welfare to work and the responsiveness of employment providers to the needs of refugees', *Journal of Social Policy*, 40(3): 557–74.

Shutes, I. (2016) 'Work related conditionality and access to social benefits for national citizens, EU and non EU citizens', *Journal of Social Policy*, 45(4): 691–708.

Silva, R. (2017) 'Our behavior is easy to predict once you know we're messy and flawed', *The Sunday Times*, 15 October, p 27.

Simpson, M. (2017) 'Renegotiating social citizenship in the age of devolution', *Journal of Law and Society*, 44(4): 646–73.

Simpson, M. (2022) *Social citizenship in an age of welfare regionalism: the state of the social union*, Oxford, Hart Publishing.

SNP (Scottish National Party) (2022) 'Does the SNP oppose the benefit sanctions regime', *Scottish National Party*, https://www.snp.org/policy-area/benefits-social-security/

Southerton, D., McMeekin, A. and Evans, A. (2011) *International review of behaviour change initiatives*, Edinburgh, Scottish Government.

Spotswood, F. (ed) (2016) *Beyond behaviour change: key issues, interdisciplinary approaches and future directions*, Bristol, Policy Press.

Spotswood, F. and Marsh, A. (2016) 'Conclusion: what is the future of behaviour change', in F. Spotswood (ed) *Beyond behaviour change: key issues, interdisciplinary approaches and future directions*, Bristol, Policy Press, pp 283–98.

Squires, P. (2006) 'New Labour and the politics of anti-social behaviour', *Critical Social Policy*, 26(1): 144–68.

SSAC (Social Security Advisory Committee) (2011) *The Jobseeker's Allowance (Mandatory Work Activity Scheme) regulations 2011 (S.I. 2011 No. 688) report by the Social Security Advisory Committee under section 174(1) of the Social Security Administration Act 1992 and statement by the Secretary of State for Work and Pensions in accordance with section 174(2) of that act*, London, Department for Work and Pensions, https://assets.publishing.service.gov.uk/government/uploads/system/uploads/attachment_data/file/229004/9780108510403.pdf

References

SSAC (2019) *Occasional paper 21: the effectiveness of the Claimant Commitment in Universal Credit*, London, Social Security Advisory Committee, https://assets.publishing.service.gov.uk/government/uploads/system/uploads/attachment_data/file/833426/ssac-occasional-paper-21-effectiveness-of-claimant-commitment-in-universal-credit.pdf

Standing, G. (2011) 'Behavioural conditionality: why the nudges must be stopped – an opinion piece', *Journal of Poverty and Social Justice*, 19(1): 27–38.

Stephens, M. (2008) 'The role of the social rented sector', in S. Fitzpatrick and M. Stephens (eds) *The future of social housing*, London, Shelter, pp 27–38.

Stern, P.C. (2000) 'Towards a coherent theory of environmentally significant behaviour', *Journal of Social Issues*, 56(3): 407–24.

Stewart, A.B.R. and Wright, S. (2018) 'Jobseekers', *Final findings, research briefing for the Welfare Conditionality project*, http://www.welfareconditionality.ac.uk/wp-content/uploads/2018/05/40426-Jobseekers-web.pdf

Stewart, M. (2019) 'Preventable harm: creating a mental, health crisis', *Journal of Public Mental Health*, 18(4): 224–30.

Stinson, H. (2019a) *Coping with conditionality? An exploration into the impact of behavioural conditionality in universal credit on 'vulnerable' claimants*, PhD thesis, Department of Social Work and Social Policy, University of York.

Stinson, H. (2019b) 'Supporting people? Universal credit, conditionality and the recalibration of vulnerability', in P. Dwyer (ed) *Dealing with welfare conditionality: implementation and effects*, Bristol, Policy Press, pp 15–40.

Summers, K. and Young, D. (2020) 'Universal simplicity? The alleged simplicity of Universal Credit from administrative and claimant perspectives', *Journal of Poverty and Social Justice*, 28(2): 169–86.

Summers, K., Scullion, L., Baumberg Geiger, B., Robertshaw, D., Edmiston, D., Gibbons, A., Karagiannaki, E., De Vries, R. and Ingold, J. (2021) 'Claimants' experiences of the social security system during the first wave of COVID-19', *Welfare at Distance project report*, https://www.distantwelfare.co.uk/winter-report

Taylor, D., Gray, M. and Stanton, D. (2016) 'New conditionality in Australian social security policy', *Australian Journal of Social Issues*, 51(1): 3–26.

Taylor, N. (2017) 'A job, any job: the UK benefits system and employment services in an age of austerity', *Observatoire de la Société Britannique*, 19: 267–285.

Taylor-Gooby, P. (1998) 'Equality rights and social justice', P. Alcock, A. Erskine and M. May (eds) *The student's companion to social policy*, Oxford, Blackwell, pp 42–8.

Taylor-Gooby, P. (2012) 'Root and branch restructuring to achieve major cuts: the social policy programme of the 2010 UK coalition government', *Social Policy and Administration*, 46(1): 61–82.

Thaler, R.H. and Sunstein, C.R. (2008) *Nudge, improving decisions about health, wealth and happiness*, New Haven, Yale University Press.

Thomson, R. (2007) 'The qualitative longitudinal case history: practical, methodological and ethical reflections', *Social Policy and Society*, 6(4): 571–82.

Titmuss, R.M. (1958) 'The social division of welfare', *Essays on the welfare state*, London, Allen & Unwin; now reprinted in P. Alcock, H. Glennerster, A. Oakley and A. Sinfield (eds) (2001) *Welfare and wellbeing: Richard Titmuss's contribution to social policy*, Bristol, Policy Press, pp 34–55.

Titmuss, R.M. (1970) *The gift relationship: from human blood to social policy*, London, Allen & Unwin.

Tosi, A. (2007) 'Homelessness and the control of public space: criminalising the poor?', *European Journal of Homelessness*, 1: 225–36.

Treolar, P. (2001) 'Compulsion creeps up', *Welfare Rights Bulletin*, 164, October, London, Child Poverty Action Group, http://www.cpag.org.uk/cro/wrb/wrbl64/compulsion.htm

Triandis, H.C. (1989) 'The self and social behaviour in differing cultural contexts', *Psychological Review*, 96(3): 506–20.

TUC (2002) 'New Deal sanctions', *Briefing number 47 TUC Welfare Reform Series*, London, Trades Union Congress.

Turn2us (2021a) *Universal Credit (UC): what activities will I have to do when claiming Universal Credit?*, https://www.turn2us.org.uk/Benefit-guides/Universal-Credit/Claimant-Commitment-Conditionality

Turn2us (2021b) *Single parents: claimant commitment under Universal Credit*, https://www.turn2us.org.uk/Your-Situation/Bringing-up-a-child/Single-parents-and-Universal-Credit

UN (United Nations Statistics Division) (2013) *Principles and recommendations for a vital statistics system, revision 3*, http://unstats.un.org/unsd/demographic/sconcerns/migration/migrmethods.htm#B

UN General Assembly (1966) *International Covenant on Economic, Social and Cultural Rights*, 16 December, United Nations, Treaty Series, vol 993, p 3, https://www.refworld.org/docid/3ae6b36c0.html

van Berkel, R. and Hornemann Møller, I. (eds) (2002) *Active social policies in the EU: inclusion through participation*, Bristol, Policy Press.

van Berkel, R. and van der Aa, P. (2005) 'The marketization of activation services: a modern panacea/some lessons from the Dutch experience', *Journal of European Social Policy*, 15(4): 329–43.

van Berkel, R., de Graaf, W. and Sirovátka, T. (eds) (2011) *The governance of active welfare states in Europe*, Basingstoke, Palgrave Macmillan.

van Oorschot, W., Roosma, F., Meuleman, B. and Reeskens, T. (2017) *The social legitimacy of targeted welfare: attitudes to welfare deservingness*, Cheltenham, Edward Elgar.

Veasey, K. and Parker, J. (2021) 'Welfare conditionality, sanctions and homelessness: meanings made by homeless support workers', *Journal of Humanities and Applied Social Sciences*, https://doi.org/10.1108/JHASS-12-2020-0213

References

Vedung, E. (1998) 'Policy instruments: typologies and theories', in M. Bemelmans-Videc, R.C. Rist and E. Vedung (eds) *Carrots, sticks and sermons: policy instruments and their evaluation*, Abingdon, Routledge, pp 21–58.

Vedung, E. and van der Doelen, F.C.J. (1998) 'The sermon: information programs in the public policy process choice, effects, and evaluation', in M. Bemelmans-Videc, R.C. Rist and E. Vedung (eds) *Carrots, sticks and sermons: policy instruments and their evaluation*, Abingdon, Routledge, pp 103–28.

Watts, B. and Fitzpatrick, S. (2018a) *Welfare conditionality: key ideas*, Oxford, Routledge.

Watts, B. and Fitzpatrick, S. (2018b) *Fixed term tenancies: revealing divergent views on the purpose of social housing*, Edinburgh, I-Sphere Heriot-Watt University.

Watts, B., Fitzpatrick, S., Bramley, G. and Watkins, D. (2014) *Welfare sanctions and conditionality in the UK*, York, JRF.

Watts, B., Fitzpatrick, S. and Johnsen, S. (2018) 'Controlling homeless people? Power, interventionism and legitimacy', *Journal of Social Policy*, 47(2): 235–52.

Weale, A. (1978) 'Paternalism and social policy', *Journal of Social Policy*, 7(2): 157–72.

Webster, D. (2015) *Briefing: the DWP's JSA/ESA sanctions statistics release*, 18 February, Glasgow, University of Glasgow.

Webster, D. (2016) 'Explaining the rise and fall of JSA and ESA sanctions 2010–16', *Briefing, supplement*, 3 October, Glasgow, University of Glasgow.

Webster, D. (2020) *Briefing benefit sanctions statistics, June 2020*, 1 July, Glasgow, University of Glasgow.

Webster, D. (2021) Personal communication to Peter Dwyer, November.

Webster, D. (2022) 'Way to Work scheme: forcing people into jobs they aren't suited for has damaging effects', *The Conversation*, https://theconversation.com/way-to-work-scheme-forcing-people-into-jobs-they-arent-suited-for-has-damaging-effects-175974

Welsh Government (2022) 'Basic Income pilot for care leavers in Wales', *Written Statement*, 16 February, https://gov.wales/written-statement-basic-income-pilot-care-leavers-wales

Welshman, J. (2004) 'The unknown Titmuss', *Journal of Social Policy*, 33(2): 225–47.

Wenham, A. (2017) 'Struggles and silences: young people and the Troubled Families Programme', *Social Policy and Society*, 16(1): 143–54.

Wenham, A., Czarnecki, S. and Mackinder, S. (2015) *Local evaluation of the Troubled Families Programme: final report*, York, Department of Social Policy and Social Work, University of York.

Weston, K. (2012) 'Debating conditionality for disability benefits recipients and welfare reform: research evidence from Pathways to Work', *Local Economy*, 27(5–6): 514–28.

White, S. (2000) 'Review article: social rights and social contract – political theory and the new welfare politics', *British Journal of Political Science* 30(3): 507–32.

White, S. (2003) *The civic minimum*, Oxford, Oxford University Press.

Whiteford, M. (2008) 'Street homelessness and the architecture of citizenship', *People, Place and Policy Online*, 2(2): 88–100.

Whitworth, A. (2016) 'Neoliberal paternalism and paradoxical subjects: confusion and contradiction in UK activation policy', *Critical Social Policy*, 36(3): 412–31.

Whitworth, A. and Griggs, J. (2013) 'Lone parents and welfare-to-work conditionality: necessary, just, effective?', *Ethics and Social Welfare*, 7(2): 124–40.

Wilding, M.A., Jones, K., Martin, P. and Scullion, L. (2019) *Housing works: assessing the impact of housing association employment support*, report by the Sustainable Housing and Urban Studies Unit, University of Salford.

Williams, E. (2021) 'Punitive welfare reform and claimant mental health: the impact of benefit sanctions on anxiety and depression', *Social Policy and Administration*, 55(1): 157–72.

Wincott, D. (2003) 'Beyond social regulation? New instruments and/or a new social policy agenda at Lisbon', *Social Policy and Administration*, 81(3): 533–53.

WPC (Work and Pensions Committee) (2013) *Can the Work Programme work for all user groups? First report of session 2013–14*, HC 162 House of Commons, Work and Pensions Committee, London, The Stationery Office.

WPC (2014) *Employment and Support Allowance and Work Capability Assessments, first report of session 2014–15*, HC 302 House of Commons, Work and Pensions Committee, London, The Stationery Office.

WPC (2015) *Benefit sanctions beyond the Oakley review*, 5th report of session 2014–15, HC 814, London, House of Commons, Work and Pensions Committee, London, The Stationery Office.

WPC (2016) *In work progression in Universal Credit*, 10th report of session 2015–16, HC 549 House of Commons, Work and Pensions Committee, London, The Stationery Office.

Wright, S. (2003) 'The street level implementation of unemployment policy', in J. Millar (ed) *Understanding social security: issues for policy and practice*, Bristol, Policy Press, pp 235–53.

Wright, S. (2011a) 'Relinquishing rights? The impact of activation on citizenship for lone parents in the UK', in S. Betzelt and S. Bothfeld (eds) *Activation and labour market reforms in Europe: challenges to social citizenship*, Basingstoke, Palgrave, pp 59–78.

Wright, S. (2011b) 'Steering with sticks, rowing for rewards: the new governance of activation in the UK', in R. van Berkel, W. de Graaf and T. Sirovatka (eds) *The governance of active welfare states in Europe*, Basingstoke, Palgrave, pp 85–109.

Wright, S. (2012) 'Welfare to work, agency and personal responsibility', *Journal of Social Policy*, 41(2): 309–28.

Wright, S. (2016) 'Conceptualising the active welfare subject: welfare reform in discourse, policy and lived experience', *Policy and Politics*, 44(2): 235–52.

Wright, S. (2022) *Gender and welfare conditionality: lived experience, street-level practice and welfare reform*, Bristol, Policy Press.

Wright, S. and Dwyer, P. (2022) 'In-work Universal Credit: claimant experiences of conditionality mismatches and counterproductive benefit sanctions', *Journal of Social Policy*, 51(1): 20–38.

Wright, S., Kopač, A. and Slater, G. (2004) 'Activation within paradigmatic change: activation, social policies and citizenship within the context of welfare reform in Slovenia and the UK', *European Societies*, 6(4): 511–34.

Wright, S., Dwyer, P., McNeill, J. and Stewart, A.B.R. (2016) 'First wave findings Universal Credit', *Research report*, http://www.welfareconditionality.ac.uk/wp-content/uploads/2016/05/WelCond-findings-Universal-Credit-May16.pdf

Wright, S., Dwyer, P.J., Jones, K., McNeill, J.M., Scullion, L. and Stewart, A.B.R. (2018a) 'Final findings: Universal Credit', *Research briefing for the Welfare Conditionality project*, http://www.welfareconditionality.ac.uk/wp-content/uploads/2018/05/40414-Universal-Credit-web.pdf

Wright, S., Stewart, A.B.R. and Dwyer, P. (2018b) 'Final findings: social security in Scotland', *Research briefing for the Welfare Conditionality project*, http://www.welfareconditionality.ac.uk/wp-content/uploads/2018/09/40677-Scottish-final2.pdf

Wright, S, Fletcher, D. and Stewart, A.B.R (2020) 'Punitive benefit sanctions, welfare, conditionality, and the social abuse of unemployed people in Britain: transforming claimants into offenders?', *Social Policy and Administration*, 54(2): 278–94.

Wu, C.F., Cancian, M. and Wallace, G. (2014) 'The effect of welfare sanctions on TANF exits and employment', *Children and Youth Services Review*, 36(C): 1–14.

Young, M. and Lemos, G. (1997) *The communities we have lost and can regain*, London, Lemos and Crane.

Index

References to figures appear in *italic* type;
those in **bold** type refer to tables. References to
endnotes show both the page number and the note number (115n2).

A

Acceptable Behaviour Contracts (ABCs) 96, 100, 101, 115n2
agency, conceptualisation of individual 54–5
Ajzen, I. 49
alternative payment arrangements (APAs) 29
Anti-social Behaviour, Crime and Policing Act 2014 37, 47n5
antisocial behaviour (ASB)
  compound conditionality 109–13
  devolution and policy 45
  effectiveness and impacts of welfare conditionality in tackling 46, 64–6, 94–115, 158
  evictions for 33, 100, 101, 103, 105, 109–10, 111
  family intervention policies 102–8
  Housing Act 1996 definition 47n4
  local responsibility 37
  management 35–40
  in people with complex/multiple needs 95–108, 130
  punishing victims of 100–1, 102–3, 104–5
antisocial behaviour orders (ASBOs) 33, 35, 37, 96, 115n1
  effectiveness for behavioural change 96–7, 98, 99, 103, 111–12
austerity 41–2, 46
Australia 13

B

Barr, B. 62, 84
Bedroom Tax 42, 110, 121–2
behaviour change
  effectiveness of welfare conditionality for 60–6, 67, 155–60
  models 59–60
  motivations for 114
  significance of discretion 55–7, 66–7
  theories 48–51
  tools 57–60
  understanding behaviour and agency of welfare recipients 51–60
  welfare conditionality and negative 125–35
    counterproductive compliance 125–8
    disengagement from social security system 72–4, 125, 128–35, 158

'behavioural conditionality' 6
behavioural economics 50–1, 58–9
behavioural science 51, 59, 67
Bemelmans-Videc, M. 57–8
Benefit Cap 43
benefit sanctions
  annual number 2001–21 *117*
  community service an alternative to 146–7
  compound conditionality and application of 110, 111–13
  counterproductive compliance to avoid 125–8, 136, 158
  devolution and 44
  effectiveness for behavioural change 60–1
  expansion to lone parents and disabled people 22–3, 27
  financial costs of implementing 117–18
  'great sanctioning drive' 1, 116–20
  impact of 60–1, 72–6, 120–5, 130, 135–6
  inappropriate application 81, 111, 120, 122–3, 124, 149
  for insufficient job applications 121, 127
  leading to poverty and destitution 72–4, 120–2, 124, 133
  for missed appointments due to requirement to be at paid work 134, 135, 136
  move into work despite repeat 74–6
  moving people further away from paid work 64, 72–4, 92, 120–2, 124, 129–30
  reflection on perceived positive effect 90, 91
  reintroduced after COVID-19 pandemic 118–19
  a tool to enhance 'in-work progression' within paid labour market 68, 87–92
  Universal Credit and enhanced regime 1, 26–7, 32, 63–4, 68
  WSUs not understanding 130–1
Beveridge, W. 7–8, 10, 143
Big Society 41

C

Cameron, D. 24, 41, 41–2
Canada 13
charity support 73, 80–1, 100–1, 101, 105, 112–13

202

child age thresholds for work-related requirements 118, 149
Child and Adolescent Mental Health Services (CAMHS) 107, 108
Child Benefit 42–3
child welfare benefits in US 13
childcare responsibilities, welfare conditionality for people with 82–6
see also lone parents
children, conditionality for benefits for mothers and young 23–4
choice architecture 50, 67
Claimant Commitments 28, 44, 76, 118, 143
Clarke, J. 22, 42
Clasen, J. 5, 6
classic economic theory 49, 150–1
Clegg, D. 5, 6
community service 146–7
compound conditionality 94, 109–13
'conditional' citizenship 7
'conditionality earnings threshold' 27
Conservative governments (1979–1997) 20–1, 33
Conservative governments (2015 onwards)
family intervention projects 40
firm commitment to welfare conditionality 156–7
social housing policy 34–5
welfare reform 43, 118, 156–7
Conservative/Liberal Democrat Coalition government (2010–2015)
austerity 41–2
Big Society 41
management of antisocial behaviour 36–7
poverty rhetoric 52
social housing reform 34, 42
'Strategy for Social Justice' policy 36–7
Troubled Families Programme 39–40, 65
Universal Credit 24–7
welfare reform 24–7, 40–3
welfare spending reductions 42
Work Programme (WP) 31–2
contractualism 5, 8, 9–10, 138–9
WSUs' views on 142–4, 151
Corden, A. 165
Council Tax Reduction Scheme 43
counterproductive compliance 125–8, 136, 158
COVID-19 pandemic 118–19, 160
Crime and Disorder Act 1998 33, 35, 38
crime, survival 112, 129–30
Curchin, K. 6, 7, 13, 51, 67, 78, 125, 135, 140, 153

D

Deacon, A. 1, 4, 5, 8, 10, 12, 13, 24, 52, 138, 139, 140
decommodification 11
Deeming, C. 13, 51, 66
'deserving' and 'undeserving' welfare claimants 4–5, 15
devolution 43–4, 156
Disability Living Allowance 43
disabled people
effectiveness of welfare conditionality to move people into work 62, 82–4
ethical debates on welfare conditionality for 151–3
extension of welfare conditionality to 12, 22, 61–2
Personal Independence Payment 43
removal of 'limited capability for work' payment 118
Work Capability Assessments 23, 24, 29, 62, 70
views on 152–3
discretionary powers of street-level bureaucrats 31, 32, 38, 76
need for empathetic use 81–2, 92, 128, 159
significance 55–7, 66–7
disengagement from social security system 72–4, 125, 128–35, 158
Djuve, A.B. 53, 57, 82
Duncan Smith, I. 1, 24, 25, 123
Dwyer, P. 1, 4, 5, 6, 7, 10, 11, 12, 13, 15, 17, 22, 23, 24, 26, 27, 33, 40, 52, 56, 61, 62, 64, 65, 68, 70, 84, 87, 91, 93, 120, 125, 135, 139, 142, 148, 151, 153, 154, 155, 158, 160

E

'earned' citizenship 7
easements 29, 31, 38, 149, 159
eligibility for welfare support 3–5, 5–6, 7, 10–11, 15
behavioural requirements to retain 138, 141
as distinct from entitlement to welfare 56
increasingly stringent criteria for 43, 57
Ellison, N. 13, 91
Employment and Support Allowance (ESA) 23, 62, 151
'new style' 32, 47n2
sanctions 61, 62, 116
Support Group 23, 102, 153
Work Programme for recipients of 32, 62, 117
Work Related Activity Group (WRAG) 23, 62, 83–4, 118
employment, moving from welfare into *see* work, moving from welfare into paid
employment training 76, 77, 78–9, 82, 91
entitlement to welfare 6, 7–8
challenging notion of 8, 9, 10, 20

as distinct from eligibility for welfare 56
international attitudes to 13, 14
unconditional 137, 141, 147–8, 149
Esping-Andersen, G. 7, 11, 12, 13, 142
ethical debates on welfare
    conditionality 137–54, 159
  adversaries of welfare
    conditionality 141–2
  advocates of welfare
    conditionality 137–41
  contractualism approach 138–9, 142–4, 151
  disabled people 151–3
  lone parents 148–51
  mutualism approach 140–1, 145–7
  paternalism approach 139–40, 144–5
  unconditional entitlement approach 137, 141, 147–8, 149
  WSUs' views on questions of
    principle 142–8, 153–4
ethnic difference and disadvantage 86–7
Etzioni, A. 9, 138, 146
European Union 12
ex-offenders 38–9, 64, 96–7, 111–13, 129–30
expectancy-value theory 49

F

Fair Start Scotland Scheme 44
family intervention projects 39–40, 159
  differential impact 102–8
  Families with Multiple Problems
    programme 40
  Troubled Families Programme 39–40, 65
financial crisis 2008 41–2, 46
Fishbein, M. 49
Fitzpatrick, S. 1, 5, 6, 29, 32, 33, 34, 35, 45, 56, 65, 95, 96, 114, 138, 148
fixed-term tenancies 34, 35, 65
Flint, J. 6, 7, 15, 33, 36, 37, 39, 64, 65, 95, 100, 102, 104, 114, 125, 136

G

gender and conditionality 54, 86
'gendered moral rationalities' 54, 151
Global South 14
Goroff, N.N. 95, 155

H

Hardship Payments 29, 118
homeless people
  help from support organisations 80–1, 100–1, 101–2
  intervention strategies 37–8
  welfare conditionality and 64–5
housing
  devolution and policy for 45
  evictions for antisocial behaviour 33, 100, 101, 103, 105, 109–10, 111
  family intervention projects and help with 105
  rent arrears 72–3, 110, 111, 112, 121, 122
  see also social housing
Housing Act 1996 33, 47n4
Housing and Planning Act 2016 34–5
housing benefit (HB)
  reductions 42, 43, 132
  Spare Room Subsidy 42, 110, 121–2
  withdrawal 36, 85, 112
human right, entitlement to a basic welfare state as 137, 141, 147–8, 149
Hunter, C. 33, 34, 39

I

in-work conditionality 26–7, 40, 63–4, 133
  and employment progression 68, 87–92
  and giving up on 'in-work' benefits 133–5
  for those earning below the 'conditionality earnings threshold' 27
In-Work Progression Commission report 91–2
Incapacity Benefit (IB) 22, 23, 151
Income Management Policy 13
Income Support (IS) 22, 23
'instrumental behaviourism' 10–11, 155
international application of welfare conditionality 12–15, 155–6
International Covenant on Economic, Social and Cultural Rights 11
interpersonal behaviour theory 49–50
Ireland 13

J

Jobcentre Plus
  changing primary role of 125–6
  criticism of support received from 74–5, 76–8, 112–13, 158–9
  positive experience with 104
Jobseeker's Act 1995 21
Jobseeker's Agreement 21
Jobseeker's Allowance (JSA) 1, 22, 23, 62
  'new style' 32
  sanctions 61, 116
Jobseeker's Allowance (Mandatory Work Activity Scheme) Regulations (2011) 24–5
Johnsen, S. 6, 23, 37, 38, 62, 64, 65, 66, 95, 96, 109, 129, 149
Jones, K. 6, 68, 87, 91, 125

K

Kavli, H.C. 53, 57, 82

L

Larkin, P.M. 95
Le Grand, J. 53, 54
Levy, J.J. 14

Index

Lipsky, M. 44, 55–6, 80, 159
Lister, R. 4, 7, 22, 54–5
loans, discretionary 29
Local Housing Allowance 42
Localism Act 2011 34
lone parents
   child age thresholds for work-related requirements 118, 149
   effectiveness of welfare conditionality to move people into work 62–3, 82–6
   ethical debates on welfare conditionality for 148–51
   expansion of benefit sanctions to 22–3, 27
   'gendered moral rationalities' 54, 151
   marginalisation of parenting role 149–50
low-paid workers, welfare conditionality for *see* in-work conditionality

M

Marshall, T.H. 4, 7, 8, 10, 52, 139, 143
McNeill, J. 6, 7, 33, 34, 37, 38–9, 114
Mead, L.M. 1, 4, 5, 8, 9, 10, 20, 52, 53, 123, 133, 138, 139–40, 144, 155
migrants
   difference and disadvantage 86–7
   understanding of benefit receipt and sanctions 131
Millar, J. 12, 22, 28, 62, 68, 165
mothers, conditionality for benefits for young children and 23–4
Murray, C. 4, 8, 9, 20, 53
mutualism 140–1
   WSUs' views on 145–7

N

neoliberalism 46, 51, 95, 140
New Communitarianism 9–10, 52, 140, 146
New Deals 22, 31
   New Deal for Young People 22, 27
New Labour governments (1997–2010)
   advance of welfare conditionality in social security policy 21–4, 45, 46
   family intervention projects 39
   managing antisocial behaviour 33–4, 35–6, 39
   New Deals 22, 27, 31
   'Respect Action Plan' 36, 39
New Right thinkers 4, 8, 10, 20, 41, 52, 148, 155
New Zealand 13
Newman, J. 42
Northern Ireland 43
nudge economics 50–1, 58–9, 140

O

Oakley, M. 61, 62, 84, 131
Organisation for Economic Co-operation and Development (OECD) 12

P

parenting role, marginalisation of 149–50
paternalism 139–40
   WSUs' views on 144–5
Pawson, H. 6, 32, 33, 35
'Pay to Stay' plans 35
Personal Independence Payment 43, 113
Plant, R. 9–10
poverty
   cognitive load of welfare conditionality on people in 67
   individualist and behavioural approaches to 24, 40, 52–4
   Lister's typology to understand actions of those living in 54–5
   as a result of benefit sanctions 72–4, 120–2, 124, 133
   structural causes of unemployment and 52, 53, 54, 141, 159–60
prisoners, ex- 38–9, 64, 96–7, 111–13, 129–30
prostitution 96, 130

Q

qualitative longitudinal research (QLR) 162–5

R

repeat work–welfare recycling trajectories 70, 71, 84–6, 87–91, 123, 157
'Respect Action Plan' 36, 39
rights and responsibilities, reciprocal 5, 8, 9–10, 138–9, 156

S

Scotland 43, 44, 45, 156
Scullion, L. 6, 7, 87, 125, 135, 153
secure tenancies 33, 34, 35
Selbourne, D. 9, 138, 147
selectivism 4
social citizenship, welfare conditionality and reconfiguration of 7–12, 14–15, 139, 141, 160
social housing 32–5, 46
   Bedroom Tax 42, 110, 121–2
   managing tenants' behaviour 33–4
   'Pay to Stay' plans 35
   tenancies 33, 34–5, 65
   see also housing
social insurance principle 4–5, 8, 143
Social Security Act 1989 21
Social Security (Scotland) Act 2018 44
social security system 20–32
   devolution and 43–4
   mandatory support for claimants 27–32
   Universal Credit 24–7
   welfare reforms since 2010 40–5

Stewart, A.B.R. 136
stick–carrot–sermon typology 58–9, 66, 155
'Strategy for Social Justice' policy 36–7
street-level bureaucrats (SLBs)
  'clerks' or 'carers' 57
  discretionary powers 31, 32, 38, 55–7, 66–7, 76
    need for empathetic use of 81–2, 92, 128, 159
  see also Work Coaches
substance addiction
  limitations of welfare conditionality in cases of 97–9, 130
  support to overcome 80–1
Sunstein, C.R. 50–1, 59, 140, 155
Sure Start Maternity Grant and Welfare Food Scheme 24
Sweden 14

T

tax credits 25, 43, 64
tenancies
  fixed-term 34, 35, 65
  introductory 33
  secure 33, 34, 35
Thaler, R.H. 50–1, 59, 140, 155
Thomson, R. 69
Titmuss, R.M. 8, 18n4, 52, 54, 155
training, employment 76, 77, 78–9, 82, 91
Treolar, P. 2, 22, 156
Triandis, H.C. 49–50
Troubled Families Programme (TFP) 39–40, 65

U

'underclass', welfare-dependent 9, 20, 53
United States 12–13
Universal Credit (UC) 24–7, 45–6
  alternative payment arrangements (APAs) 29
  Claimant Commitments 28, 44, 76, 118, 143
  conditionality groups 28–9, **30–1**
  disengaging from 131–5
  easements 29, 31, 38, 149, 159
  enhanced regime of benefit sanctions 1, 26–7, 32, 63–4, 68
  family benefits reform 43
  homeless claimants 38
  loans 29
  mandatory support for claimants 27–32
  Way to Work campaign 156–7
  White Paper 2010 25
  in-work conditionality 26–7, 40, 63–4, 133
  and employment progression 63, 87–92
Universal Jobmatch 93n3, 121, 126, 127
universalism 4, 137, 141, 147–8

V

voluntary work 73, 101, 104, 145–6
vulnerable people, conditional welfare interventions and 37–40

W

Wales 43, 44, 45, 156
Watts, B. 1, 5, 6, 32, 33, 34, 35, 38, 56, 60, 64, 65, 114, 133, 138, 142, 147, 148, 156
Way to Work campaign 156–7
Webster, D. 1, 11, 116, 117, 119, 157
welfare chauvinism 86–7
welfare conditionality 1–2
  and addressing antisocial behaviour 95–108
  compound conditionality 109–13
  defining 5–7
  in early 20th century 20
  effectiveness for changing behaviour 60–6, 67, 157–60
  ethical debate 137–54
  impact on work/welfare trajectories 72–82
  international application 12–15, 155–6
  political consensus on 156
  questions of principle and priority 3–5, 142–8
  and reconfiguration of social citizenship 7–12, 14–15, 139, 141, 160
  'thin' and 'thick' forms of activation 14
  unintended outcomes 125–35
  and welfare reform since 2010 40–5
Welfare Conditionality: Sanctions, Support and Behaviour Change project (WelCond) 2–3
  core aims 161
  ethical considerations and data handling/analysis 166–8
  qualitative approach 16, 161–6
welfare contractualism 5, 8, 9–10, 138–9
  WSUs' views on 142–4, 151
welfare dependency 8–9, 10, 20, 42, 53, 138
  broadening definition of dysfunctional 27, 64
Welfare Reform Act 2007 23, 36
Welfare Reform Act 2012 25
Welfare Reform and Work Act 2016 118
welfare reform since 2010 24–7, 40–5, 118, 156–7
Work and Health Programme (WHP) 44–5
Work and Pensions Committee (WPC) 27, 32, 61
Work Capability Assessments (WCA) 23, 24, 29, 62, 70
  disabled people's views on 152–3

Index

Work Coaches 24, 38, 45, 63
  failure to adequately address issues of difference 86, 149
  support for benefit claimants 28–31, 74–5, 76–82, 86, 91, 112–13, 126, 128, 158–9
  viewed as prioritising compliance and sanctions 74–5, 78–9, 124, 125–6, 126, 133, 149, 158
  see also street-level bureaucrats (SLBs)
'work first' welfare regimes 14, 21, 27, 78, 82, 86, 91, 156, 158
  limitations for lone parents 84–6
work-focused interviews (WFIs) 23, **30–1**, 104
  sanctions for failure to attend 26, 61, 124, 135, 136
work, moving from welfare into paid 68–93, 157–8
  dealing with difference 82–7, 157–8
  impact of welfare conditionality on work/welfare trajectories 72–82
    repeat sanctions and destitution 72–4
    transition into work despite repeat sanctions 74–6
  pathways into and out of work 69–72, 70
    negative employment trajectories 71
    positive employment trajectories 70–1
    repeat work–welfare recycling trajectories 71
    stasis trajectories 69–70
  support in finding work
    enabling successful moves into work 78–80, 128
    from Work Coaches 28–31, 74–5, 76–82, 86, 90, 112–13, 126, 128, 158–9
  in-work conditionality and promotion of employment progression 87–92
Work Programme (WP) 31–2, 38, 117
  experiences of 73, 79–80, 112
  replaced by Work and Health Programme 44–5
  welfare conditionality and sanctions 61, 62
Work Related Activity Group (WRAG) 23, 62
  contesting allocation to 83–4
  removal of 'limited capability for work' payment 118
work searches, compulsory
  child age thresholds 118, 149
  counterproductive compliance 78–9, 125–8, 136, 158
  exemption from 102
  as a full-time occupation 77, 126
  lone parents 84–6, 118, 149
  prioritising of 76–82, 121, 123–4
  Way to Work campaign 156–7
  in-work employment 'progression' and 87–9, 133
Wright, S. 1, 7, 10, 12, 13, 27, 28, 29, 40, 44, 50, 53, 54, 55, 56, 62, 64, 68, 78, 86, 87, 92, 93, 120, 125, 135, 136, 142, 148, 158